A defence of witchcraft belief

Manchester University Press

A defence of witchcraft belief

A sixteenth-century response to Reginald Scot's *Discoverie of Witchcraft*

Edited by

Eric Pudney

MANCHESTER UNIVERSITY PRESS

Introduction, critical apparatus, etc.
© Eric Pudney 2021

The right of Eric Pudney to be identified as the editor of this work has been asserted by him in accordance with the Copyright, Designs and Patents Act 1988.

Published by Manchester University Press
Oxford Road, Manchester M13 9PL

www.manchesteruniversitypress.co.uk

British Library Cataloguing-in-Publication Data
A catalogue record for this book is available from the British Library

ISBN 978 1 5261 4776 9 hardback
ISBN 978 1 5261 7445 1 paperback

First published 2021
Paperback published 2023

The publisher has no responsibility for the persistence or accuracy of URLs for any external or third-party internet websites referred to in this book, and does not guarantee that any content on such websites is, or will remain, accurate or appropriate.

Typeset by
Servis Filmsetting Ltd, Stockport, Cheshire

Contents

List of figures and tables	*page* vi
Acknowledgements	vii
A note on abbreviations and references	viii
Introduction	1
About this edition	1
Witchcraft in late sixteenth-century England	2
The manuscript and its provenance	6
Date	8
Authorship	13
The significance of the treatise	22
Relationship to the *Discoverie*	43
Sources	60
Notes on the text	64
The treatise	67
Bibliography	212
Index	219

List of figures and tables

Figures

1 Humfrey Wanley's catalogue entry for Harley MS 2302 (detail). © The British Library Board, Add MS 45707, fol. 213r.   7
2 Harley MS 2302, fol. 57r. © The British Library Board.   9
3 Harley MS 2302, fol. 97v (detail). © The British Library Board.   11
4 Lambeth Palace Library MS 2009, fol. 34: hand of William Redman. Reproduced by permission of Lambeth Palace Library.   20
5 Lambeth Palace Library MS 2004, fol. 8: hand of John Coldwell. Reproduced by permission of Lambeth Palace Library.   21
6 British Library Add MS 12506, fol. 271r: hand of Tobie Matthew. © The British Library Board.   21
7 SP12/176/1: hand of Richard Rogers. Reproduced by permission of The National Archives.   22
8 British Library Harley MS 2302, fol. 66r. © The British Library Board.   25
9 British Library Harley MS 2302, fol. 79v. © The British Library Board.   27
10 British Library Harley MS 2302, fol. 65r. © The British Library Board.   32
11 British Library Harley MS 2302, fol. 105v. © The British Library Board.   49

Tables

1 Examples of verbal similarities between the *Discoverie* and the treatise.   44
2 Reasons in the treatise and corresponding sections in the *Discoverie*.   47

Acknowledgements

Any project of this nature will necessarily incur a multitude of debts, and a list of all the people who have supported it would be very long indeed. My greatest debt, however, is certainly to my colleagues at the English department of mid-Sweden University, which is where the project found a home and funding during my employment as a postdoctoral researcher there, and where the work was completed. I am extremely grateful to all members of the higher seminar, but especially to Professor Terry Walker, who shares my love of the early modern world and its manuscripts, and to Dr Martin Shaw, whose kindness and support made it possible for me to balance teaching and research during this time. Without my time at MiUn, this book might never have been completed.

The idea and inspiration for the project grew out of previous research conducted at Lund University, and I am grateful to all of my former colleagues there for their support during the earliest stages, and for their many insightful and encouraging comments, both in seminars and informally. In particular I am grateful to Professor Cian Duffy, both for inviting me to present the project at seminars and for his constructive criticism, and to Professor Emerita Marianne Thormählen, whose steadfast support and encouragement – both during this project and before it – have been so vital to me as a junior researcher.

I owe a particular debt to Dr Victor Wahlström of Lund for his generosity in providing assistance with the Latin passages in the treatise. I am also indebted to all of the peer reviewers for their kind and helpful comments, and to my editor Meredith Carroll at MUP, whose expert advice has helped to make the edition much more reader-friendly.

Finally, and as always, I'm grateful to my family: to my parents and parents-in-law for many things, not least the practical help and babysitting, and to my wife, Charlotte, and our children, Jake and Gabriel, for being there and providing many welcome distractions from the sixteenth century.

A note on abbreviations and references

The following abbreviations have been used:

ODNB – Oxford Dictionary of National Biography
OED – Oxford English Dictionary
SP – State Paper

References to Reginald Scot's *Discoverie of Witchcraft* are to the Brinsley Nicholson edition, but in the introduction, page references to the original 1584 edition have also been provided in square brackets for the benefit of readers who prefer it. All references to excerpts from Scot in the main text are to book and chapter.

All English printed books published before 1700 were consulted in electronic editions from the Early English Books Online database.

Introduction

About this edition

This edition is of a late sixteenth-century treatise on witchcraft that forms part of Harley MS 2302 in the British Library's manuscript collection. The anonymous treatise is almost completely unknown to modern scholarship, and what survives of it is incomplete, missing the first few pages and ending abruptly in mid-sentence. But despite these unpromising characteristics, it is deserving of much greater scholarly attention than it has yet received.

The treatise is a defence of witchcraft belief, in the form of a numbered list of 'reasons', and was evidently written by a highly educated person – almost certainly a clergyman, in view of its content and the attitude of its author. It is, therefore, effectively a new primary source on learned witchcraft belief, which dates to the period when Elizabethan witchcraft persecution was at its most intense. It is also a highly unusual one. Unlike virtually all other sources of information on this subject, it is very explicit in discussing the theological underpinnings of witchcraft belief, and outlining precisely why such belief is, in the author's view, required of all Christians. Part of the treatise's value is that it was not intended for publication, but as a private communication within a particular scribal network: it was written for the benefit of a friend. This explains the candour and openness of the treatise, and allows its author to deal with sensitive topics in much greater depth than is usual.

In addition to this, as I have discovered, the treatise is a response to a pre-publication draft of a much more famous work: Reginald Scot's *Discoverie of Witchcraft* (1584). It is evident from the text that it was written by a personal friend of Scot's, and is a kind of early modern peer-review, written by an author who clearly considers himself to be on good terms with Scot, but also superior to him in authority, status, and knowledge. The author tends to disagree, at times quite strongly, with most of what Scot says, and sometimes corrects his views sharply, but without ever becoming hostile or condemnatory (as many published reactions to Scot did). In the process, the treatise reveals in great detail why Scot's views would come to be seen as controversial, and explicitly warns Scot of the reaction he could expect (and did in fact receive). It also sheds considerable light on the composition of the *Discoverie*, by revealing in broad outline the content of an early draft version of that book.

The treatise should therefore be of great interest to scholars of early modern witchcraft as an unusual and original work of demonology in its own right, for the light it casts on the genesis of Scot's *Discoverie*, and as the most extensive extant piece of evidence of contemporary reaction to that work. The remainder of this introduction begins with a brief overview of witchcraft prosecution and the debate around witchcraft in Elizabethan England, before turning to the manuscript and its provenance and presenting detailed arguments as to the date and authorship of the treatise. It then goes on to consider the significance of the work in relation to other early modern English writing on demonology, and the place of witchcraft within Elizabethan intellectual and religious culture. The treatise's relationship to Scot's *Discoverie* is then discussed in more detail, and the implications of the anonymous author's work for scholarship on Scot are considered. The final section of the introduction briefly considers what conclusions can be drawn about the sources used in the composition of the treatise.

Witchcraft in late sixteenth-century England

Witchcraft persecution, as a historical phenomenon, has arguably received a disproportionate amount of scholarly attention in relation to its significance within its own time. The first secular law against witchcraft in early modern England was passed in the reign of Henry VIII in 1542. This law, the wording of which suggests a very dubious attitude towards the idea of effective magic, was apparently hardly ever used and was soon afterwards repealed during the brief reign of Henry's son Edward in 1547.[1]

Witchcraft was criminalised in England in 1563 for the second time, in all probability as a reaction to a Catholic plot against Queen Elizabeth a few years previously rather than because of popular demand for action against

---

1 The law, 33 Henry VIII c. 8, refers to people 'gyving faithe & credit to suche fantasticall practises' as making magical images and other items; quoted in Marion Gibson (ed.), *Witchcraft and Society in England and America, 1550–1750* (Ithaca, NY: Cornell University Press, 2006), p. 2.

witches.² The legislation of 1563 was used more frequently than the previous witchcraft law, but witchcraft remained a relatively peripheral issue in England, and prosecutions for it were both rare and unevenly distributed geographically; Essex, for example, appears to have been troubled with witchcraft accusations much more than other parts of the South.³ When prosecutions for witchcraft did take place, they tended to be isolated cases where the alleged witch – often, but not always, an older woman – had long been suspected of the crime and had made enemies in the local community. Most recorded prosecutions nevertheless ended in an acquittal, and the total number of executions for witchcraft in England (estimated at anything between 500 and 1000 over a period of roughly 120 years) was low by European standards.⁴ One major exception to this pattern took place during the civil war period, when the self-styled 'witchfinder' Matthew Hopkins and his associate John Sterne orchestrated a major witch-hunt (in the sense of a sustained, active search for witches), which led to around 100 executions.⁵ An earlier, albeit much less extensive, example of an English witch-hunt took place in St Osyth in 1582, and its significance in relation to the present edition is discussed in the 'Relationship to the *Discoverie*' section below.

However, the phenomenon of witchcraft persecution is, to a considerable extent, distinct from, although connected to, the debate about witchcraft that took place in Europe during the early modern period. While people making accusations of witchcraft were overwhelmingly motivated by fear of the supposed harm caused by it – often called *maleficium* in learned works on the subject – writers on witchcraft were frequently more concerned with the belief that witches were in league with the devil, and were therefore a particularly egregious type of heretic. It is no coincidence that the most intense period of European witchcraft persecution took place during the Reformation, a time when religious belief was the subject of vigorous dispute, and indeed warfare, throughout Europe. From at least the fifteenth century, when early works such as Johannes Nider's *Formicarius* (1435–37, printed 1475) were produced, until the end

---

2 Norman Jones, 'Defining Superstitions: Treasonous Catholics and the Act against Witchcraft of 1563', in *State, Sovereigns and Society in Early Modern England*, edited by Charles Carlton (New York: St. Martin's Press, 1998), pp. 187–202.
3 James Sharpe, *Instruments of Darkness: Witchcraft in England, 1550–1750* (London: Hamish Hamilton, 1996), p. 110.
4 Brian P. Levack, *The Witch-hunt in Early Modern Europe*, 4th ed. (London: Routledge, 2016, first edition published in 1987), p. 21.
5 This episode is the subject of Malcolm Gaskill's book *Witchfinders* (London: John Murray, 2005).

of the seventeenth century, the reality and precise nature of witchcraft was the subject of considerable debate throughout Europe – although a variety of opinions on the matter continue to be expressed right up to the present day.

The publication of printed books on witchcraft in early modern England began at around the same time as the re-criminalisation of it in 1563. The first few works include an allegorical poem by John Hall condemning the use of magic, the confession of a 'necromancer' called Francis Coxe, a wide variety of pamphlets recording early witchcraft trials and interrogations, and two translations of works by the Protestant theologians Lambert Daneau and Andreas Hyperius.[6] The works of Hall and Coxe are evidently linked to the 1563 legislation and are propagandistic in nature; Hall's poem is a warning to anyone involved in magical activity that such activity was, from that point on, liable to be punished. Coxe's text, as he explains in his epistle to the reader, was written as a warning to others after his own transgression and punishment. The works of Hyperius and Daneau, meanwhile, are theoretical works on witchcraft, but as translations they have little to say about local conditions in England.

The first major, original work on witchcraft to be written in English was Reginald Scot's *Discoverie of Witchcraft* (1584). Scot's book – which denies outright the possibility of witchcraft understood as a pact between witch and devil – has received a great deal of scholarly attention from its first publication onwards. Itself indebted to Johannes Weyer's *De Praestigiis Daemonum* (Basel, 1568), it influenced virtually all later sceptical writers on witchcraft, as well as several who were, on the face of it, less sceptical. It received a considerable amount of hostile comment during the period in which witchcraft was a crime, before increasingly being seen as a courageous, humane and prescient book by later authors. By the twentieth century, Scot and his book were lauded by early historians of witchcraft such as Wallace Notestein.[7] But during its own time, the *Discoverie* was controversial. One early response to it in print, Henry Holland's *Treatise*

---

6 John Hall, *A Poesie in Forme of a Vision* (London, 1563); Francis Coxe, *A Short Treatise Declaringe the Detestable Wickednesse of Magicall Sciences* (London, 1561); Lambert Daneau, *A Dialogue of Witches* (London, 1575); Andreas Hyperius, *Two Common Places Taken out of Andreas Hyperius, a Learned Diuine*, translated by R. V. (London, 1581). The most recent and comprehensive study of the pamphlet sources on witchcraft is Charlotte-Rose Millar's *Witchcraft, the Devil, and Emotions in Early Modern England* (London: Routledge, 2017), and Marion Gibson's *Reading Witchcraft* (London: Routledge, 1999) is also valuable.
7 Wallace Notestein, *A History of Witchcraft in England, 1558–1718* (Washington, DC: American Historical Association, 1911), pp. 57–72.

against Witchcraft (London, 1590), called for it to be burned.[8] No less a personage than King James VI of Scotland, later to be James I of England as well, condemned Scot as a 'Sadducee', implying that his work denied the existence of spirits.[9] Many other critical comments followed, supplemented by a smaller number of sympathetic references to Scot, including from the author and playwright Thomas Nashe.[10]

However, while many works refer to Scot and the *Discoverie*, they often do so obliquely – sometimes without naming it, or Scot, at all. The most extensive published reactions to Scot in early modern England were also the first – George Gifford's *Discourse of the subtill Practises of Deuilles by Witches and Sorcerers* (1587), soon followed by Holland's *Treatise* (1590). Gifford is obviously responding to Scot in parts of his book, but never mentions him or the *Discoverie*, while Holland provides references to the *Discoverie* in the margin of his book, but without naming Scot; instead Holland refers vaguely to 'some [people]', or to 'adversaries'.[11] Later writers on witchcraft typically say even less about Scot, usually merely dismissing his opinions as impious before moving on to set out their own case for the reality of witchcraft. An interesting example in this regard is Richard Bernard who, despite distancing himself from Scot's views in his preface, also cites the *Discoverie* as an authority on fraudulent cases of witchcraft.[12] Scot's influence on subsequent English writers on witchcraft may therefore have been greater than would at first appear from the widespread condemnation of his views.[13]

---

8 Henry Holland, *A Treatise against Witchcraft* (London, 1590), sig. F3v. This comment might have contributed towards the later legend that the *Discoverie* was ordered to be burned by King James I – a tradition documented by Philip Almond, 'King James I and the Burning of Reginald Scot's *The Discoverie of Witchcraft*: The Invention of a Tradition', *Notes and Queries* 56:2 (2009), 209–13.
9 James VI and I, *Daemonologie* (Edinburgh, 1597), p. 2. The Sadducees were members of a Jewish sect, referred to with hostility in the New Testament, who did not believe in the existence of spirits or the immortality of the human soul.
10 A fuller account of contemporary reactions to Scot can be found in Simon F. Davies, 'The Reception of Reginald Scot's *Discovery of Witchcraft*: Witchcraft, Magic, and Radical Religion', *Journal of the History of Ideas* 74:3 (July 2013), 381–401.
11 George Gifford, *A Discourse of the subtill Practises of Deuilles by Witches and Sorcerers* (London, 1587). For some examples of responses to specific arguments put forward by Scot, see sigs A2r, C1r, C3v, C4r. Holland's *Treatise* provides references to the *Discoverie* throughout the first two chapters.
12 Richard Bernard, *A Guide to Grand-Jury Men* (London, 1627), p. 33.
13 See also Davies, 'The Reception of Reginald Scot's *Discovery of Witchcraft*', p. 384.

The present volume is an edition of the only extant text that responds directly and at length to Scot, addressing him as 'you' throughout. It is, in content, scope, purpose, and tone, unlike any published text on witchcraft from early modern England (including Scot's). The only published references to it that I have found are a footnote in Wallace Notestein's *History of Witchcraft in England from 1558 to 1718* (published in 1911) and an endnote in Glyn Parry's recent biography of John Dee. Notestein had not read it and merely notes its existence, information he credits to 'Professor [George Lincoln] Burr', the historian, librarian of Cornell University, and discoverer of Cornelius Loos' manuscript treatise on witchcraft.[14] Parry refers to the treatise, again in a brief endnote, as evidence of contemporary disagreement with Scot.[15] The treatise is also mentioned, at slightly greater length, in an unpublished PhD thesis by Simon F. Davies.[16] Insofar as I can tell, I am at the time of writing the only living person to have read what survives of the treatise in its entirety – a task which was necessary in order to understand the precise nature of it. The conclusions that I have reached from reading the treatise, and the evidence supporting those conclusions, is outlined in the following sections. Some of this reasoning is, inevitably, speculative, and I hope that others will now also read the treatise and reach their own conclusions about it.

The manuscript and its provenance

Harley MS 2302 comprises two different works on different paper and in different hands. According to the British Library's catalogue entry, these 'treatises' are:

> A Replication in further Meintenaunce of Free Will, to an Answeare of a Protestant Devyne to the Treatis in that behalf first made by a Romish Catholicke Priest; by one ... Burne, another Popish Priest. [...] Next follows, [...] A Treatise imperfect at both ends, written in Answer to some

---

14 Notestein, *A History of Witchcraft in England, 1558–1718*, footnote to p. 69. Burr published relatively little during his career, although his notes, held in the library at Princeton, are extensive; unfortunately I have not been able to consult them. The Loos MS is an unpublished tract, *De Vera et Falsa Magia*, written (like Scot's) in opposition to witchcraft persecution. Unlike Scot, Loos was imprisoned for writing it.
15 Glyn Parry, *The Arch-Conjuror of England* (New Haven: Yale University Press, 2011), p. 312, note 11.
16 Simon F. Davies, *Witchcraft and the Book Trade in Early Modern England* (unpublished PhD thesis, University of Sussex, 2012), p. 153.

Introduction

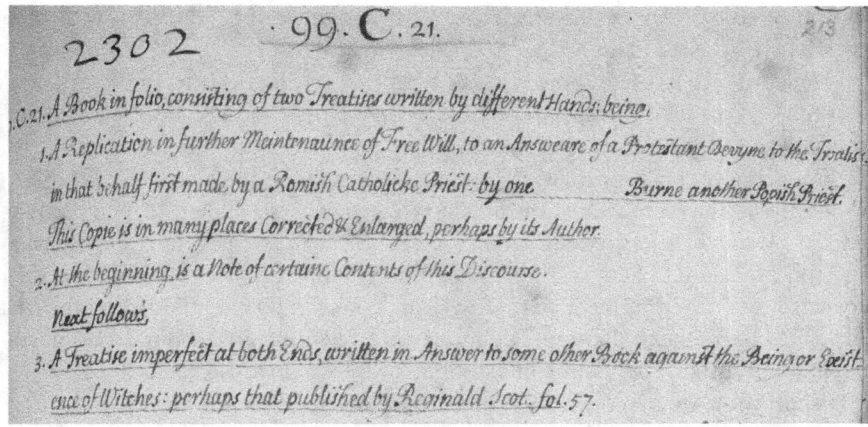

Figure 1 Humfrey Wanley's catalogue entry for Harley MS 2302 (detail).

other Book against the Being or Existence of Witches: perhaps that published by Reginald Scot.[17]

The British Library's manuscript catalogue dates back to the nineteenth century, so the entry does not reflect great familiarity with the manuscript on the part of present-day scholars. In fact, the catalogue for the Harley manuscripts, as the orthography above suggests, dates back to before the establishment of the British Museum in 1753. The entry quoted above has simply been copied from the manuscript catalogue of the Harley family librarian, Humfrey Wanley (1672–1726); see figure 1 above. The entire Harley collection was bought by the newly established British Museum in 1753.

The provenance of the manuscript is not possible to trace before it was bought by the Harley family, but the purchase itself is at least well-recorded. According to the study of the sources of the Harley collection conducted by Cyril and Ruth Wright, MS 2302 was part of a bundle of manuscripts bought from the bookseller Nathaniel Noel.[18] Noel's diary also survives, again in the British Library's collection, and records the transaction.[19] While Noel's diary does not specifically identify the manuscript, merely recording its sale as part of a package of manuscripts, the date of purchase

---

17 *Catalogue of the Harleian Manuscripts*, vol. 2 (British Library: Department of MSS), p. 646.
18 Cyril E. Wright and Ruth C. Wright, *The Diary of Humfrey Wanley*, 2 vols (London: The Bibliographical Society, 1966), p. 196.
19 London, British Library, Egerton MS 3777.

was entered by Wanley into the front of the manuscript, establishing that it was part of the 'parcel of MSS' recorded by Noel.

The contents of the manuscript, as Wanley's catalogue entry indicates, are mixed. The present book is an edition of the last item in the catalogue entry, the treatise on witchcraft. This comprises 49 sheets numbered from 57 to 105, written on both sides, with significant damage to the edges of the paper, especially to the recto side of the first surviving sheet (see figure 2). The treatise was, as Wanley suspected and as I can now confirm, written in response to a version of Reginald Scot's *Discoverie of Witchcraft*. It is written in a straightforward and (for the most part) easily legible secretary hand, although it is obviously not a scribal copy. The numerous deletions, insertions and corrections suggest that the document is a first, and probably also final, draft.

In addition to the author's hand, there are a small number of marginal annotations made by a different hand, in what appears to be pencil.[20] These notes appear on folios 79r, 79v, 81r, 84r, and 84v; they have not been reproduced in this edition since they are evidently not authorial. Many are illegible, but some of the notes suggest that the annotator was a Catholic who objected to some of the author's reasoning on religious grounds. Taken together with the fact that this document was bound together with a defence of free will written by a Catholic priest, these annotations suggest that the manuscript was owned by a Catholic with an interest in theological issues at some point prior to its acquisition by Noel.

Date

The two scholars who have previously commented in print on the date of the treatise take different views on the subject. Wallace Notestein, writing in 1911 without having read the treatise, was repeating the opinion of the witchcraft scholar and manuscript expert George Lincoln Burr when he described it as 'contemporary or nearly so' with Scot's *Discoverie*, citing the 'handwriting'.[21] More recently, Simon Davies takes the view that the treatise dates from 'the first half of the seventeenth century', again on the

---

20 Pencil marks seem to be very unusual in early manuscripts. The date of the annotations is unknowable, although they presumably predate Harley's purchase of the MS. The earliest recorded description of a 'recognizable ancestor of today's pencil' dates back to 1565. Little is known about the early manufacture of pencils, but a large deposit of graphite was discovered near Keswick during the sixteenth century and this was being mined with help from German experts by the late 1560s: Henry Petroski, *The Pencil* (New York: Alfred A. Knopf, 1990), pp. 36, 46.

21 Notestein, *A History of Witchcraft in England, 1558–1718*, footnote to p. 69.

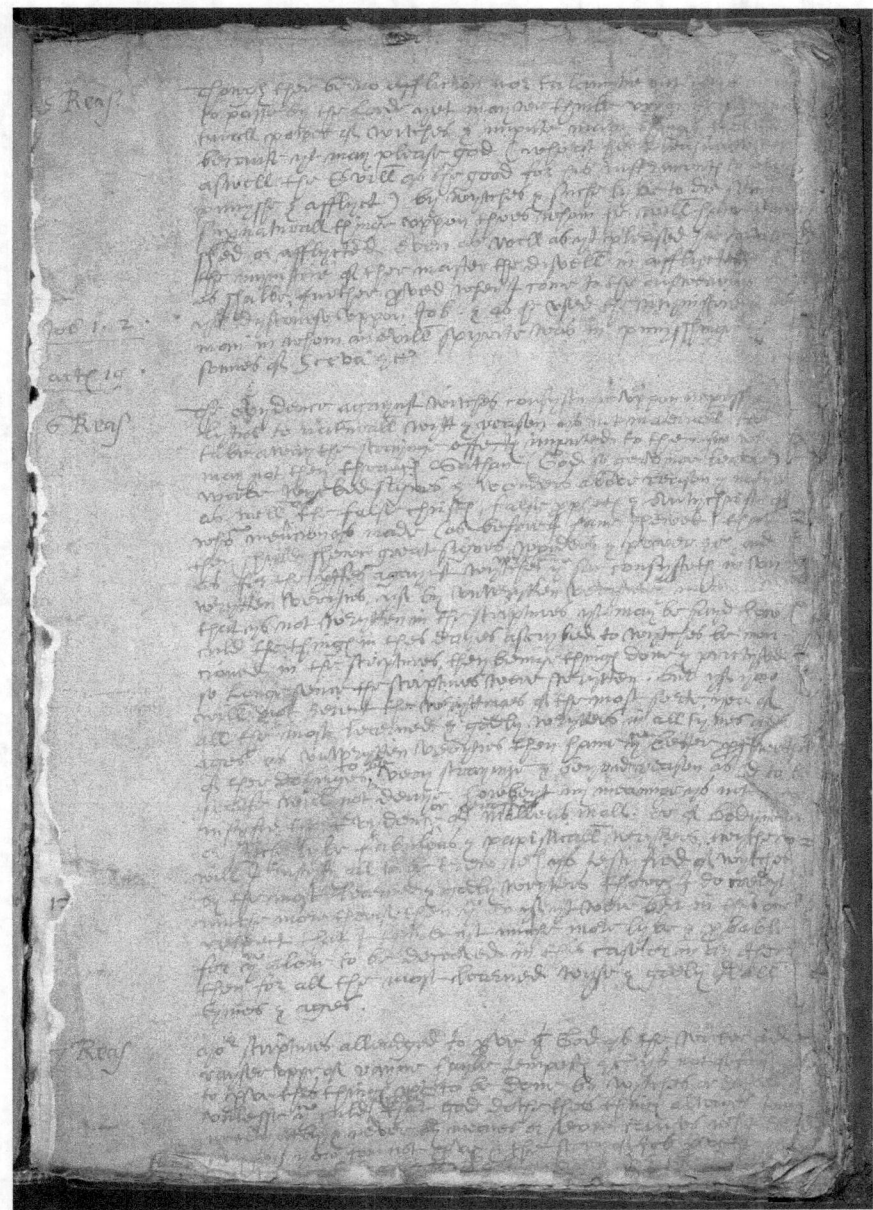

Figure 2 Harley MS 2302, fol. 57r.

basis of the hand.²² The treatise is written in a fairly typical example of the kind of secretary hand in use throughout the sixteenth century and well into the seventeenth, which does not seem to provide solid grounds for a precise date within the period. But in any case, establishing the date of the treatise does not require study of the hand or the paper; it can be done on the basis of strong internal evidence.

While the author of the treatise did not make a note of the date anywhere in it, there are a number of specific references to contemporary and, it is implied, recent events which provide evidence for a date not before the early 1580s. These references are as follows:

1. On folio 68r, in arguing for the reality of miracles, the author asks 'what can we think of the wonderful preservation of Rochelle from famine or yielding by the strange and extraordinary coming and departing of the fishes reported in the late French histories but that it was a mighty good miracle?' La Rochelle was besieged in 1572–73 during the French wars of religion. The earliest of the 'French histories' available in print to deal with the story of the supposedly miraculous appearance of large numbers of fish in the harbour of the besieged port was *The fourth parte of Commentaries of the ciuill warres in Fraunce* (London, 1576), translated by Thomas Tymme.
2. On the same page, the author writes that 'I for my part think our earthquakes, especially the first of them, to be a great miracle of God to advise us of his wrath and to call us to repentance'. This must be a reference to the Dover straits earthquake of 6 April 1580 and the aftershock which followed it on 1 May. Earthquakes are a rare occurrence in England, and this one caused two fatalities and was the inspiration for a number of books published at the time, most of which – like the author – regarded them as a sign of God's wrath.²³
3. On folio 97, the author refers to 'Elks', and states that 'he remaineth a pri{soner}'. This is a reference to Thomas Elks (or Elkes), who was arraigned in the court of King's Bench on 28 November 1580, as noted recently by a number of historians and as recorded in Holinshed's *Chronicles*.²⁴ Given that the author refers to Elks as being imprisoned

---

22 Davies, *Witchcraft and the Book Trade in Early Modern England*, p. 153.
23 Reactions to the earthquake are described in Alexandra Walsham, *Providence in Early Modern England* (Oxford: Oxford University Press, 2001), pp. 130–5.
24 On Elks see Peter Elmer, *Witchcraft, Witch-Hunting, and Politics in Early Modern England* (Oxford: Oxford University Press, 2016), pp. 25–30; Parry, *The Arch-Conjuror of England*, pp. 136–7, 213; Pierre Kapitaniak (ed.), *La Sorcellerie Démystifiée* (Grenoble: Jérôme Millon, 2015), pp. 36–40; Raphael Holinshed, *Chronicles*, vol. 6 (1587), pp. 1314–15.

at the time of writing, the treatise must date from after this time. According to the *Discoverie*, he remained imprisoned until at least 1583; Scot's book reproduces a letter dated 8 March 1582 (i.e. 1583), which, Scot claims, was sent to him by 'T. E. Maister of art'. I have not found any evidence of Elks' release.

Taken together, these references provide solid grounds for dating the treatise, and the third of them alone is sufficient to establish the earliest possible date of composition as very late 1580. In fact, this is the earliest possible date, not only for the treatise, but for the document to which it responds, on the assumption that this was also written after Thomas Elks' arrest. Since there must have been some gap between the writing of the draft and the writing of the treatise, it seems unlikely that the treatise could have been written any earlier than 1581.

That the treatise was written in response to a draft of the *Discoverie*, and not the printed version, is also clear from internal evidence. On folio 97v (see figure 3), the author issues a kind of plea for Scot to reconsider part of his argument. The following quotation is the entire 101st reason, with the spelling and punctuation modernised and conjectural readings provided in curly brackets for words that are obscured or partially obscured by tight binding:

> I am sorry to see you so much leaning to your own opinion in this place as to pronounce so hard a sentence generally of all the writers of this matter, sith many of these writers are most learned and godly men and have written

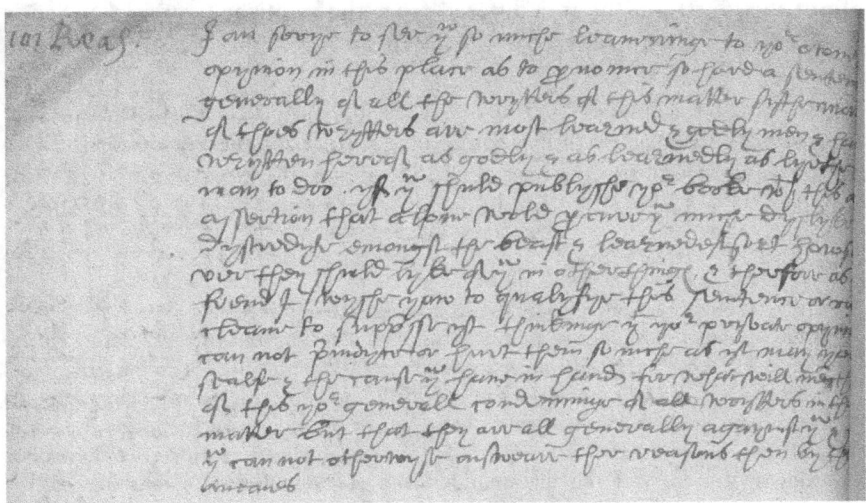

Figure 3 Harley MS 2302, fol. 97v (detail).

hereof as godly and as learnedly as lieth {in} man to do. If you should publish your book with this assertion, that alone would procure you much dislike and discredit amongst the best and learnedest sort, howsoever they should like of you in other things. And therefore as y{our} friend I wish you to qualify this sentence or rath{er} clean to suppress it, thinking that your private opinion cannot prejudice or hurt them so much as it may you{r}self and the cause you have in hand. For what will men thi{nk} of this, your general condemning of all writers in this matter, but that they are all generally against you and that you cannot otherwise answer their reasons than by th{ese} means?

From this warning it can be concluded that the author was a personal friend of Scot's – or conceivably a relative, if the word 'friend' is used in another sense (now obsolete, at least in Scot's native Kent).[25] Furthermore, it clearly implies that the *Discoverie* was not yet 'published', since publication is referred to as a hypothetical possibility, and the response as a whole would make little sense if it were too late to make changes to the text.[26] It also seems clear that Scot's intention to publish his book was known to his friend, who refers to 'the cause you have in hand'.

It follows from the reasoning above that the treatise's response is not to the published version of Scot's *Discoverie*, but to a pre-publication draft version (albeit a draft that must have been very similar to large parts of the final version). A proper reading of the treatise must therefore take not two but three texts into account. Firstly, there is the treatise itself. Secondly, there is the published version of the *Discoverie*. Thirdly, and most problematically, there is the now-lost draft version of the *Discoverie* to which the treatise responds. The question of what can be concluded about this draft and how it differed from the published version of Scot's *Discoverie* will be considered in the 'Relationship to the *Discoverie*' section below.

The internal evidence therefore allows the date of composition of the treatise to be placed within a range of dates: from the very end of 1580 at the earliest, to some point in 1584, when the *Discoverie* was published, at the latest. It is, perhaps, just about possible that the author

---

25 OED: 'A close relation, a kinsman or kinswoman.'
26 At least since Harold Love's study of *Scribal Publication in Seventeenth-Century England* (Oxford: Oxford University Press, 1993), 'publication' is no longer equated with the printing of a book. It is now widely known that large-scale circulation of manuscripts persisted well beyond the advent of printing in early modern England, and that this could also be considered a form of publication. However, the author evidently regards Scot's circulation of his draft as falling short of 'publishing' – in the sense of making it public – while being aware of his intention to either have it printed or at least circulate it much more widely.

of the treatise, unaware that the book had been published, wrote (or continued to write, having begun earlier) after the publication of the *Discoverie* in 1584. But given the apparent friendship between the author and Scot, this seems unlikely. In addition, a careful comparison of the published version of the *Discoverie* and the treatise provides a few scattered hints that Scot may have changed his draft in response to the criticism provided in the treatise (see the 'Relationship to the *Discoverie*' section below).

Authorship

There are some hints within the text of the treatise, and within the printed *Discoverie*, at the possible identity of the author, but no conclusive evidence. Before considering specific candidates, however, some general claims about the author's background and position in early modern England can be advanced with some degree of confidence on the basis of the content of the treatise.

Firstly, there can be little doubt that the author was highly educated and had almost certainly studied at University. While a sixteenth-century grammar school education would have provided the 'small Latin and less Greek' that Ben Jonson credited Shakespeare with, some of the learning on display in the treatise goes beyond what would typically be learned in such an environment. The author displays a familiarity with a wide range of theological writings, most of which are quoted in Latin, and is familiar with terms used in the formal logical argumentation that was primarily used in a University setting.[27] If the author's position as a University student and/or graduate is granted, it also follows that the author was male.[28] For this reason, I have used male pronouns to refer to him.

---

27 In the universities, logic formed a major part of the curriculum: 'Cambridge's statutes, laid down in 1570, specified the study of rhetoric for the first year of the BA; logic for years two and three, and philosophy for the fourth.' Helen M. Jewell, *Education in Early Modern England* (Basingstoke: Macmillan, 1998), p. 62. Some logic may have been taught at grammar school level; Jewell (p. 101) refers, for example, to the recommendations of William Kempe, author of *The Education of Children in Learning* (London, 1588). However, Kempe only recommends the teaching of 'the precepts concerning the divers sorts of arguments in the first part of Logike [i.e. part one of Aristotle's *Organon*]' as a preparation for the study of rhetoric (sig. C2v).
28 James Daybell points out that secretary hand was much more frequently used by male letter-writers, while women were frequently taught an italic hand; *The Material Letter in Early Modern England: Manuscript Letters and the Culture and Practices of Letter-Writing, 1512–1635* (Basingstoke: Palgrave Macmillan, 2012), p. 89.

A second and related point is that it seems all but certain that the author was a clergyman. It is unlikely that the author was a medical doctor or a lawyer – the other occupations requiring university-level study – judging by the way these professions are referred to in the treatise. The author states, for example, that 'Your 6 reason I leave to physicians' (fol. 80r, reason 71), which implies that he is not himself a physician. Elsewhere, he writes that 'Where the law of God hath appointed death or other punishment to any sin or sinner (as to witches it hath done), there we are not to regard what the law of man sayeth to the contrary' (fol. 63r, reason 25). This sentiment seems unlikely in a lawyer, but more appropriate in a clergyman – especially a puritan clergyman. There are also some mildly disparaging remarks made about 'philosophers', who are said to be unable to solve various problems (fols 62r, 68r, 68v), and whose opinions are not considered to be as important as those of theologians: 'As for philosophers they are seldom well coupled with good divines, and in matter handled in the scriptures (as this is) we are not to regard what they say' (fol. 75v, reason 58). While the author is comfortable discussing non-religious sources as well, referring for example to Aristotle, Cicero, and Ovid among others, it is always scripture, and the interpretation of it by learned authors, to which he grants ultimate authority.

The author also claims to have had some experience of dealing with witches, and explicitly connects this experience to his occupation, writing that 'by reason of the calling and authority I have, I have had to do in the examination of many of them' (fol. 79v, reason 71 – see figure 9). This tantalisingly vague claim is consistent with a position in the Church or in the civil judicial system, although the connotations of 'calling' suggest the former, and there was in fact considerable overlap between the two. The clergy were often involved in the criminal justice system in various ways; bishops were asked, for example, to prepare reports on the justices of the peace within their dioceses and to present recusants at assize court trials.[29] Senior clergy often held positions as justices of the peace, and several are listed as such in the Elizabethan assize records for Kent. Furthermore, witchcraft and related offences continued to be tried in Church, as well as secular, courts, after the passage of the 1563 act against witchcraft.[30] Clergymen are

---

29 J. S. Cockburn, *A History of English Assizes* (Cambridge: Cambridge University Press, 1972), pp. 158–9, 191–2, 209, 214.

30 Studies of the role of Church courts in prosecuting cases of witchcraft include Philip Tyler, 'The Church Courts at York and Witchcraft Prosecutions 1567–1640', *Northern History*, 4:1 (1969), 84–110; Peter Rushton, 'Women, Witchcraft, and Slander in Early Modern England: Cases from the Church Courts of Durham, 1560–1675', *Northern History* 18:1 (1982), 116–32; Malcolm Gaskill, 'Witches and

known to have played a role in interrogating suspected witches on several occasions; Henry Goodcole, the 'visitor' or 'ordinary' of Newgate prison, was instrumental in, as he put it, 'extorting' a confession from Elizabeth Sawyer before her execution for murder by witchcraft in 1621, as described in his pamphlet account of her trial and confession.[31] Another clergyman author on witchcraft, Richard Bernard, claims in his preface to have been involved in investigating a case of witchcraft.[32]

Based on the assumption that the author of the treatise was a clergyman, it is possible to identify some potential candidates based on his connection to Reginald Scot. Scot appears to have been well-connected within the local Kentish elite, in particular through his cousin Sir Thomas Scot. As readers familiar with the *Discoverie* will be aware, all of the dedicatees of that book were substantial people in Kent, none of whom lived further than 30 miles from Scot. Scot printed three epistles with the *Discoverie*: the first and longest is to Sir Roger Manwood, who served as Lord Chief Baron of the Exchequer from 1578–92, and the second is to Scot's kinsman Sir Thomas Scot, who was a major local landowner. The third is addressed 'To the right worshipfull his loving friends, Maister Doctor Coldwell Deane of Rochester, and Maister Doctor Readman Archdeacon of Canturburie, &c.'[33] These two clerics both match the profile already established by the internal evidence of the treatise.

The exact version of the letter printed in the *Discoverie* must have been composed for the published version of the *Discoverie* rather than being an exact copy of a private letter sent previously to either man, since it addresses both Redman and Coldwell directly, at different times, by their titles ('Good Maister Deane' and 'O Maister Archdeacon'). It also makes reference to a third cleric, Tobias Matthew, who was dean of Durham from 3 September 1583 and later became Archbishop of York.[34] It was not unknown in the early modern period for authors to send virtually identical dedicatory epistles to more than one recipient; the humanist Roger

---

Witchcraft Prosecutions, 1560–1660', in *Early Modern Kent, 1540–1640*, edited by Michael Zell (Woodbridge: Boydell & Brewer, 2000); and Karen Jones and Michael Zell, '"The Divels Speciall Instruments": Women and Witchcraft before the "Great Witch Hunt"', *Social History* 30:1 (2005), 45–63.

31 Henry Goodcole, *The Wonderfull Discouerie of Elizabeth Sawyer, a Witch* (London, 1621), sig. B4r.
32 Bernard, *A Guide to Grand-Jury Men*, sigs A3v–A4r.
33 Reginald Scot, *The Discoverie of Witchcraft*, edited by Brinsley Nicholson (London: Elliot Stock, 1886), p. xvi [n.p.].
34 Kapitaniak (ed.), *La Sorcellerie Démystifiée*, p. 33. For a recent biography of Matthew, see Rosamund Oates, *Moderate Radical: Tobie Matthew and the English Reformation* (Oxford: Oxford University Press, 2018).

Ascham is known to have sent gifts with near-identical epistles to three different potential patrons.[35] The version of the epistle in the printed book is therefore probably a combination of epistles that Scot actually sent to two or more correspondents with a draft version of the book as a gift; the circulation of manuscripts in this way is a well-known feature of literate early modern society.[36]

The dedication to Coldwell and Redman differs substantially from the dedications to Thomas Scot and Manwood. The epistles to the latter pair follow convention in lavishing praise upon both men, but there is also a sense of familiarity about them. The third epistle, however, adopts quite a different tone. It begins as follows:

> Having found out two such civill Magistrates, as for direction of judgement, and for ordering matters concerning justice in this common wealth (in my poore opinion) are verie singular persons, who (I hope) will accept of my good will, and examine my booke by their experience, as unto whom the matter therin conteined dooth greatlie apperteine: I have now againe considered of two other points: namelie, divinitie and philosophie, whereupon the groundworke of my booke is laid. Wherein although I know them to be verie sufficientlie informed, yet dooth not the judgement and censure of those causes so properlie apperteine to them as unto you, whose fame therein hath gotten preeminence above all others that I know of your callings: and in that respect I am bold to joine you with them, being all good neighbours togither in this commonwealth, and loving friends unto me. I doo not present this unto you, bicause it is meet for you; but for that you are meet for it (I meane) to judge upon it, to defend it, and if need be to correct it; knowing that you have learned of that grave counseller Cato, not to shame or discountenance any bodie.[37]

Scot's primary purpose is to influence those 'civill Magistrates' responsible for applying the law to accused witches and who are experienced in these matters. However, he is also interested in hearing the opinions of those more qualified to judge the theoretical basis for his book: 'divinitie and philosophie'. He seems to ask for feedback, expressing a readiness to be corrected if need be, in a deferential manner. Scot's epistle to Redman

---

35 J. R. Henderson, 'On Reading the Rhetoric of the Renaissance Letter', in *Renaissance-Rhetorik*, edited by Heinrich F. Plett (Berlin: de Gruyter, 1993), pp. 143–62 (p. 152).

36 Mark Bland, *A Guide to Early Printed Books and Manuscripts* (Chichester: Wiley-Blackwell, 2010), pp. 97–8. The treatise fits the typical features of Bland's third category of manuscript, 'documents that were intended to circulate through personal and scribal networks', including the use of a slightly larger script than is typical in private documents and the fact that it is written on single folio sheets.

37 Scot, *The Discoverie of Witchcraft*, p. xvi [n.p.].

and Coldwell in the published *Discoverie* is signed with a right-aligned signature; as Cathy Shrank has pointed out, this detail probably indicates that Scot felt himself to be addressing people who are his social superiors.[38] Scot's attitude towards these dedicatees is consistent with the nature of the response in the treatise, which adopts a tone of superiority in terms of knowledge and authority on matters of religious doctrine, and certainly does not hesitate to 'correct' Scot's draft.

Scot's letters to Manwood and Scot seem confident of their recipients' agreement, but he is more hesitant in the third epistle. He moderates, and perhaps misrepresents, the views expressed in the *Discoverie* when he writes that, 'My question is not (as manie fondlie suppose) whether there be witches or naie: but whether they can doo such miraculous works as are imputed unto them.'[39] This is accurate in a strictly literal sense, but it is also an incongruous sentiment in the best-known sceptical work on witchcraft in the English language. Scot presumably did this because he thought that clergymen were less likely to be open to such views. Later in the epistle, Scot attacks the tendency of people to seek magical aid when they suspect themselves to be bewitched – a criticism of 'white witchcraft' which was repeated by many clerical writers on witchcraft during the period.[40] Again, this is a sentiment calculated to appeal to the clergy, but it is not very indicative of the contents of the rest of the *Discoverie*.

There is one further hint in Scot's printed epistle which suggests the possibility that a recipient of a similar letter might have been the author of the treatise. Scot writes, towards the end of the epistle, that he has 'beene bold to deliver unto the world, and to you, those simple notes, reasons, and arguments, which I have devised or collected out of other authors'.[41] Even accounting for the false modesty required in an early modern dedicatory epistle, this seems an inadequate, and simply inaccurate, description of the finished version of the *Discoverie*, which is not a collection of simple notes and reasons, but a huge work, divided into 16 books and supplemented by a further treatise on the nature of spirits. But the reference to 'reasons' – the same word used by the author for his numbered section headings – could

---

38 Cathy Shrank, '"These fewe scribbled rules": Representing Scribal Intimacy in Early Modern Print', *Huntington Library Quarterly* 67:2 (June 2004), 295–314 (p. 306). However, Daybell argues that opinions varied on this point (p. 91).
39 Scot, *The Discoverie of Witchcraft*, p. xvii [n.p.].
40 The most notable critics of white witchcraft in this period were the puritan clergymen George Gifford and William Perkins, although the physician Edward Poeton also wrote an attack on it in the 1630s, *The Winnowing of White Witchcraft*, recently published in a modern edition by Simon F. Davies (Tempe, AZ: ACMRS, 2018).
41 Scot, *The Discoverie of Witchcraft*, pp. xviii–xix [sigs B1r–B1v].

sensibly refer to the draft version of the *Discoverie* to which the treatise responds.

There is independent evidence that Scot was on good enough terms with John Coldwell to be able to ask for, and receive, his assistance in this respect. Nicholas Gyer, the author of a book on bloodletting, dedicated this work to Reginald Scot. In the dedicatory epistle, Gyer writes that

> I have thought your worship a meet person to dedicate this booke unto ... for that, thorow you whe[n] the same was first penned it passed the view and apportatio[n] of that right worshipfull and wise man M. *Doctor Coldwel*, a piller in this our age of that noble profession. I assure you I thought my selfe happy to haue my little Latine examined by the direction of his iudegement to whose worthy and famous faculty, the matters therein me[n]tioned were most properly appertaining.[42]

Apparently, Scot was able to call on Coldwell for help in reviewing a scholarly work prior to its publication, on this occasion at least, and must have regarded him as someone whose opinion was worth asking. Since Coldwell was willing to look at Gyer's book as a favour to Scot, he would presumably have been happy to look at and comment on Scot's own book. Coldwell had been operating as a medical practitioner in Kent from 1564, well before his appointment as dean of Rochester in that county, so he would have had plenty of time to make Scot's acquaintance by the time the *Discoverie* was written. However, the author's apparent lack of interest in and knowledge of medical arguments seems inconsistent with Coldwell's reputation for expertise as a physician.[43]

The author's claim to occupy a position which required frequent contact with witches, meanwhile, is consistent with Redman's position as a Justice of the Peace for Kent. His name (and position as Archdeacon of Canterbury) is listed among the JPs in documents relating to the Kent assizes in 1580–81 – along with those of Sir Roger Manwood and Thomas Scot – although his actual attendance is not indicated in any of the three assizes in this period, and his position was probably an honorary one.[44] Two other fairly senior clerics are also regularly listed as JPs in the Kent assizes from the later 1570s and early 1580s: Thomas Goodwin (or Godwin), Dean of Canterbury, and Richard Rogers, Suffragan Bishop of Dover. Scot spent a good deal of time in Dover in 1583, the year before the publication of the *Discoverie*. He played a key role in the improvements to Dover harbour

---

42 Nicholas Gyer, *The English Phlebotomy* (London, 1592), sig. A5r.
43 ODNB, 'John Coldwell'.
44 J. S. Cockburn (ed.), *Calendar of Assize Records: Kent, Elizabeth I* (London: HMSO, 1979), pp. 171–82.

that were carried out in that year – one of the major engineering projects of the Elizabethan period.⁴⁵ Scot seems likely to have come into contact with Rogers during this period; Rogers certainly worked together with his kinsman Thomas Scot later in the decade as part of a commission to disarm Catholic recusants in the county.⁴⁶

Another possible author, this one from well outside Scot's immediate vicinity in Kent, is Tobias Matthew. As mentioned above, he is named in Scot's epistle to Redman and Coldwell, suggesting that he too formed part of Scot's circle of acquaintance and correspondence.⁴⁷ Two of Matthew's sons, Tobie and John, eventually converted to Catholicism, to their father's great distress. If the elder Matthew had written the treatise and it had ended up in the possession of one of his sons, this might account for the annotations made in the treatise and the fact that it was at some point bound together with writings by a Catholic priest (as noted above). However, there is a strong piece of internal evidence against the likelihood of Matthew's authorship. At one point in the treatise, the author mentions 'a woman of Kennington which came to my examination' (fol. 75r, reason 54). The reference to Kennington must be to the village that is now a suburb in the north of Ashford in Kent. Given that a woman from Kent would be very unlikely to come to the examination of the dean of Durham, this detail would suggest that the author was, like Scot, based in Kent.

A consideration supporting the possible authorship of either Rogers or Matthew is the treatise's evident disapproval of the *Discoverie* (if not of its author). This suggests that its author's name could have been deliberately omitted from the printed version of the dedicatory epistle, where it might otherwise have appeared alongside those of Redman and Coldwell. Many of the views expressed in the treatise are consistent with the moderate puritanism of both Rogers and Matthew (see the 'Significance' section below). Coldwell and Redman, on the other hand, appear to have been much less 'precise', in the language of the period. Both men were able to secure the patronage of three successive archbishops of Canterbury as different in their outlooks as Parker, Grindal, and Whitgift; Redman is described in his ODNB entry as a 'loyal and moderate churchman' who 'avoided conflict' throughout his long and successful career.

Since all of the people discussed here as potential authors of the treatise were relatively senior clergymen, samples of their handwriting have been

---

45 Pierre Kapitaniak, 'From Grindal to Whitgift: The Political Commitment of Reginald Scot', *Études Épistémè* 29 (2016), http://episteme.revues.org/1263, para. 4.
46 J. J. N. McGurk, 'Lieutenancy and Catholic Recusants in Elizabethan Kent', *Recusant History* 12:2 (1973), 157–70 (p. 159).
47 Kapitaniak (ed.), *La Sorcellerie Démystifiée*, p. 33.

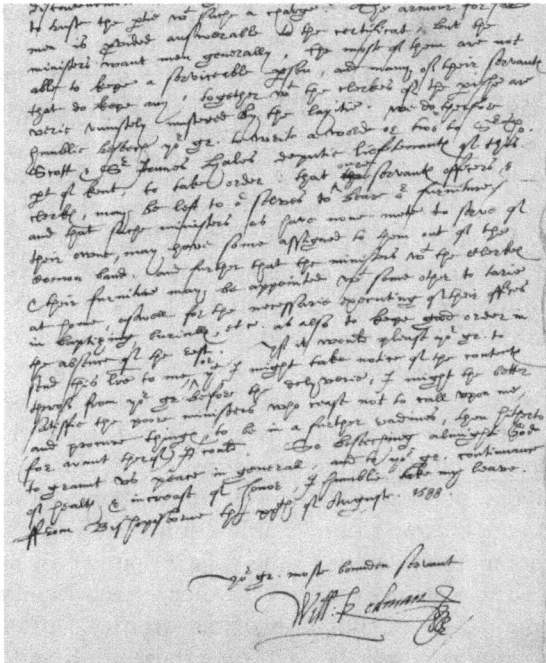

Figure 4 Lambeth Palace Library MS 2009, fol. 34: hand of William Redman.

preserved in various archives, allowing for comparison with the hand of the treatise author (see figures 4–7). This type of evidence should be treated with caution; James Daybell points out that people used multiple hands for different purposes, and that handwriting could change over time.[48] Nevertheless, even taking this into account, it seems safe to conclude that William Redman is unlikely to have been the author of the treatise – his letter-writing hand is very different from the hand in which the treatise is written (see figure 4). Thomas Goodwin's hand – not reproduced in this edition – is also very unlike that of the treatise's author.[49] The closest hand to that of the treatise author is, to my mind, that of Richard Rogers (see figure 7). The sample of his handwriting reproduced here is from a letter to his patron, Lord Burghley, and is much neater and more stylish than the hand in the treatise – but this is to be expected in a letter to such an important person, and the forms of Rogers' letters are nevertheless similar to those of the treatise's author. Readers can

---

48 Daybell, *The Material Letter in Early Modern England*, pp. 89–90.
49 Goodwin's hand can be seen in SP 12/190/6.

Introduction

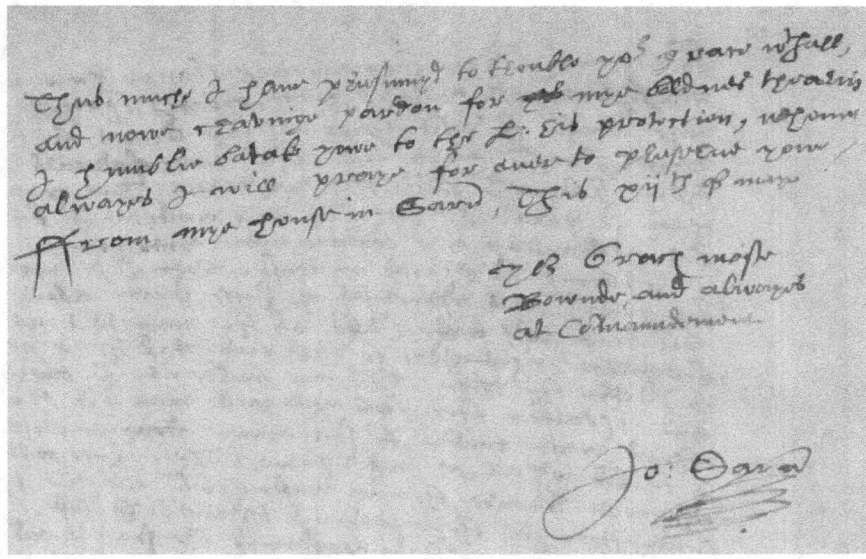

Figure 5 Lambeth Palace Library MS 2004, fol. 8: hand of John Coldwell.

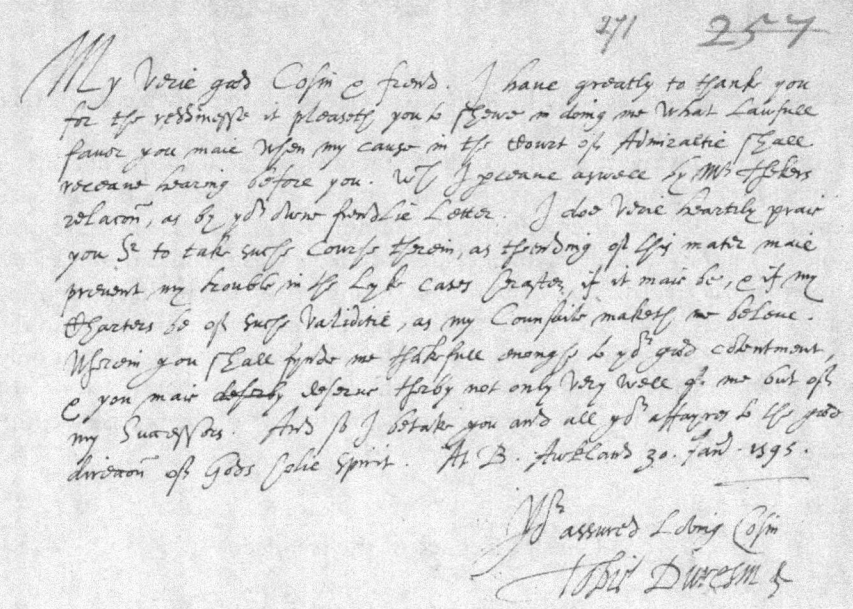

Figure 6 British Library Add MS 12506, fol. 271r: hand of Tobie Matthew.

Figure 7 SP12/176/1: hand of Richard Rogers.

of course examine the samples themselves and reach their own conclusions, or suspend judgement on this point.

Ultimately, while it would be disingenuous not to acknowledge that I suspect Richard Rogers to have been the author of the treatise, the evidence remains inconclusive. But whoever the author was – and it is of course possible that none of the clergymen discussed above was the author – it seems clear that the treatise was written by a person of some standing within the Church. The theological perspective of the author as a clergyman – and the many differences between his views and those of other clergy who not only wrote but actually published works on the subject of witchcraft – is one of the main points of interest of the treatise, irrespective of the precise identity of its author.

The significance of the treatise

The treatise is strikingly different from any other English book on witchcraft from the early modern period. As noted above, this is partly a matter of its personal nature; not intended for publication, it is familiar in tone, addresses itself directly to another author, and is in many respects more candid and less obviously 'rhetorical' than a printed text would normally be. But the content of the treatise is also highly unusual for a witchcraft text. It goes into much greater detail than is usual on the scriptural authority behind witchcraft, advancing analogical arguments on the basis of passages from the Bible unrelated to the question of witchcraft to build a solid basis of theological reasoning for its positions. It also advances alternative explanations for some of the claims advanced in the sceptical arguments it seeks to rebut – arguing, for instance, that the mental confusion that accused witches allegedly display arises not from a natural illness, melancholy, but from a tortured conscience (reason 42). The author also presents a fairly convincing argument, based on his understanding of the extreme corruption of human nature after the fall, and in particular the malice engendered by the sin of envy, to counter the sceptical case that the devil's bargain is so disadvantageous that no-one would ever agree to it (reason 45). A range of scriptural and historical examples are offered in support of the author's pessimistic analysis of human nature and psychology. These and many other arguments in the work are not familiar from printed books on witchcraft from the period, which tend to be quite formulaic.

The personal nature of the document allows its author to allude to his own experience of witchcraft rather than discussing the phenomenon in purely theoretical terms; as noted above, he claims to have had extensive experience of dealing with witches. The author's allusions to his personal experience are interesting in that they flatly reject several aspects of the sceptical depiction of the typical witch. Scot's book presents the typical witch as 'doting, scolds, mad, divelish; and not much differing from them that are thought to be possessed with spirits' (1.3, p. 7). These claims were often followed by later authors; whether this was based on personal experience of witchcraft or simply on Scot's influence is unclear.[50] The major historian of English witchcraft in the 1970s, Keith Thomas, tended to assume that Scot's image of the witch was basically accurate, while some

---

50 To take two examples, John Gaule, in his *Select Cases of Conscience Touching Witches and Witchcrafts* (London, 1646), criticises those who see a witch in 'every old woman with a wrinkled face, a furr'd brow, a hairy lip, a gobber tooth, a squint eye, a squeaking voyce, or a scolding tongue' (pp. 4–5). Samuel Harsnett's *Declaration of Egregious Popish Impostures* (London, 1603) describes the stereotype of a witch as 'an olde weather-beaten Croane, hauing her chinne, & her knees meeting for age, walking like a bow leaning on a shaft, hollow eyed, vntoothed, furrowed on her face, hauing her lips trembling with the palsie, going mumbling in the streetes' (p. 136).

later scholars have questioned this.[51] The author comes down firmly against Scot's view, writing that:

> whereas you would annihilate their confessions which either are extorted or wilfully made in respect they are diseased both in body and mind, it will never be granted you that all or the most sort of witches are in this sort diseased, but are in mind and body to the outward appearance (beyond which we cannot judge) as sound and as sensible as other women are which be not of their sort. And not one amongst a thousand of them shall you meet withal which willingly will confess anything of their secret practices but will deny them with more vehement oaths and protestations than any other sort of malefactors use to make in their defence, whereof I myself have had very great experience. (fol. 66r, reason 36 – see figure 8)

Scot's role in defining what Marion Gibson has called the 'narrational stereotype' of the witch may well have influenced later texts, but it clearly does not reflect the author's experience in the dealings he has had with accused witches.[52]

The author also makes clear, in the passage quoted above, that witches were not, in his experience, typically willing to confess. Partly because he was motivated by a concern to respond to Bodin and other authors who claimed that witches freely confessed their crimes, Scot spent a good deal of time trying to show that witches often made false confessions. But this issue was probably less relevant to the actual prosecution of witchcraft cases in England, where judicial torture was illegal and witches were therefore less likely to confess. The treatise suggests that questions over witches' confessions within the English context might well have been largely irrelevant to actual criminal proceedings – although the St Osyth witch trials (see also the 'Relationship to the *Discoverie*' section below), during which confessions were obtained by coercive means, were a significant exception that was still recent at the time Scot and his interlocutor were writing. This, and the many other pamphlet accounts of witchcraft that reported confessions made by accused witches may not have been representative of most cases; it is possible that a confession helped to make witchcraft trials more newsworthy.

---

51 Keith Thomas, *Religion and the Decline of Magic* (London: Penguin, 1991), pp. 620–8; Malcolm Gaskill, 'Witchcraft in Early Modern Kent: Stereotypes and the Background to Accusations', in *New Perspectives on Witchcraft, Magic, and Demonology*, vol. 3, edited by Brian Levack (New York: Routledge, 2001), pp. 173–203; Marion Gibson, 'Understanding Witchcraft? Accusers' Stories in Print in Early Modern England', in *Languages of Witchcraft*, edited by Stuart Clark (Basingstoke: Macmillian, 2001), pp. 41–54.
52 Gibson, 'Understanding Witchcraft?', p. 46.

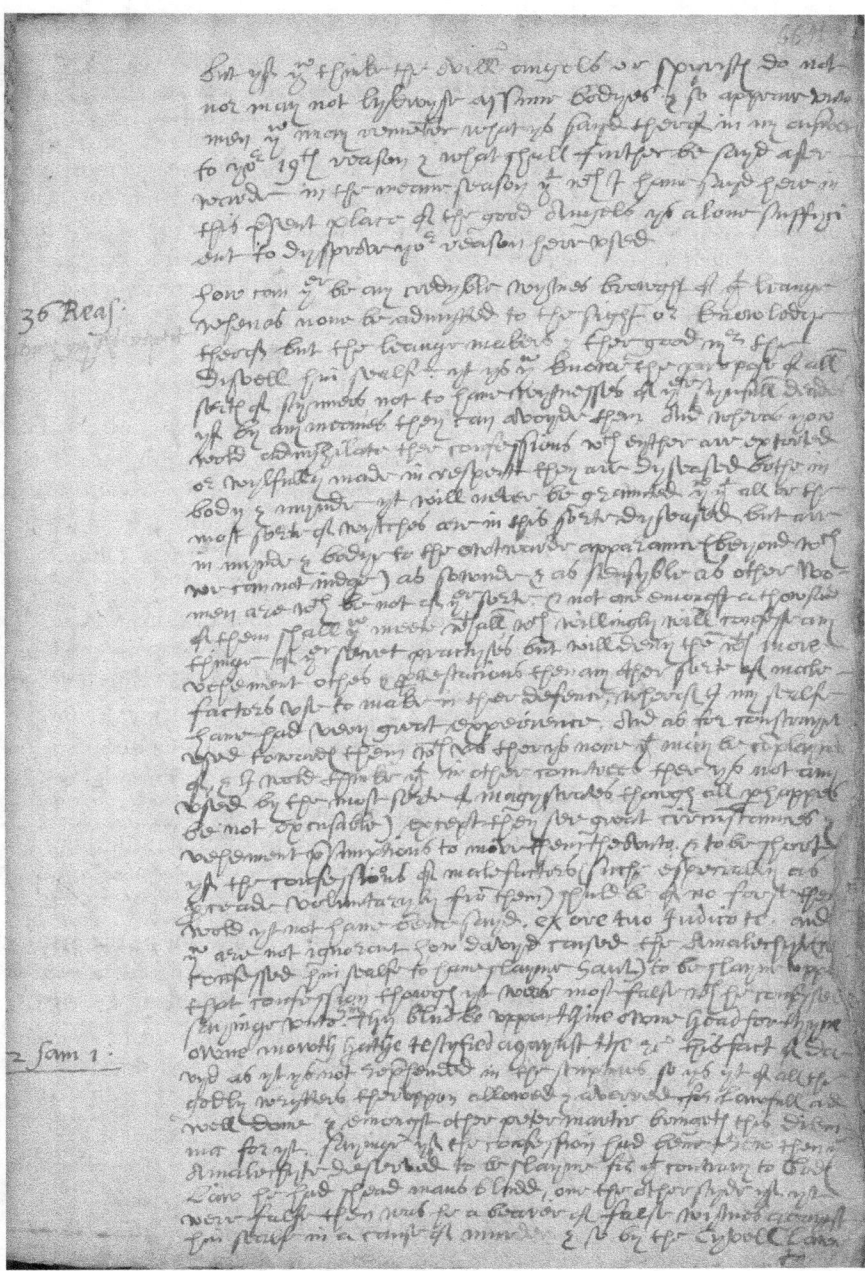

Figure 8 British Library Harley MS 2302, fol. 66r.

The author's experience also lends some support to a hypothesis put forward by the historian of witchcraft Christina Larner, that witches tended to be 'disturbers of the social order'.[53] The author likewise suggests that witches are usually people who are difficult to get along with:

> never did I find more subtle, crafty, and crabbed queans than the most of them were. And where you said before they do not defend any impiety, but do after good admonition repent, I did never yet meet with any of them which did not from time to time continue in their old trade, how well so ever they were admonished to the contrary, or what fair promises so ever they made of amendment when they stood in danger of punishment. (fol. 79v, reason 71 – see figure 9)

In addition to characterising witches as 'crabbed' – producing and thriving on acrimony – the author suggests that they tend to recidivate after a first offence. This might be taken to refer to the activities of 'cunning' or 'wise' men and women, who made a living by offering magical services in return for payment; such people were not always clearly distinguished from malevolent witches – especially in the view of clerical authors on witchcraft. It might also indicate that supposed witches benefited in some ways from the fear generated by their reputation, and with few other options within the early modern labour market, were thereby forced to 'continue in their old trade', as some historians have suggested.[54] But it could also simply mean that 'witches' who had made numerous enemies within their local communities continued to have fractious relationships with their neighbours after complaints were made against them, perhaps resorting to cursing, which could easily bring suspicions of witchcraft upon them again.

The author's use of the derogatory term 'quean' raises the question of his attitude towards women. The role of gender in witchcraft accusations and theory have long been a central part of the historiography of witchcraft. One school of thought, perhaps more common in discussions of the history of witchcraft outside of academia, has regarded witch-hunting as motivated primarily by hatred and fear of women.[55] This hypothesis is hampered by an inability to account for why witchcraft persecution should have taken place at the particular time that it did; there is little to suggest that levels of misogyny were much higher in the late 1500s and early to mid-1600s than in the years preceding or following. But this view remains at least superficially convincing in the light of the misogynistic statements sometimes made

---

53 Christina Larner, *Witchcraft and Religion* (Oxford: Blackwell, 1984), p. 87.
54 Thomas, *Religion and the Decline of Magic*, p. 674.
55 For an account and critique of this tradition from a feminist perspective, see Diane Purkiss, *The Witch in History* (London: Routledge, 1996), pp. 7–26, and Christina Larner, 'Was Witch-hunting Woman-hunting?', in her *Witchcraft and Religion*.

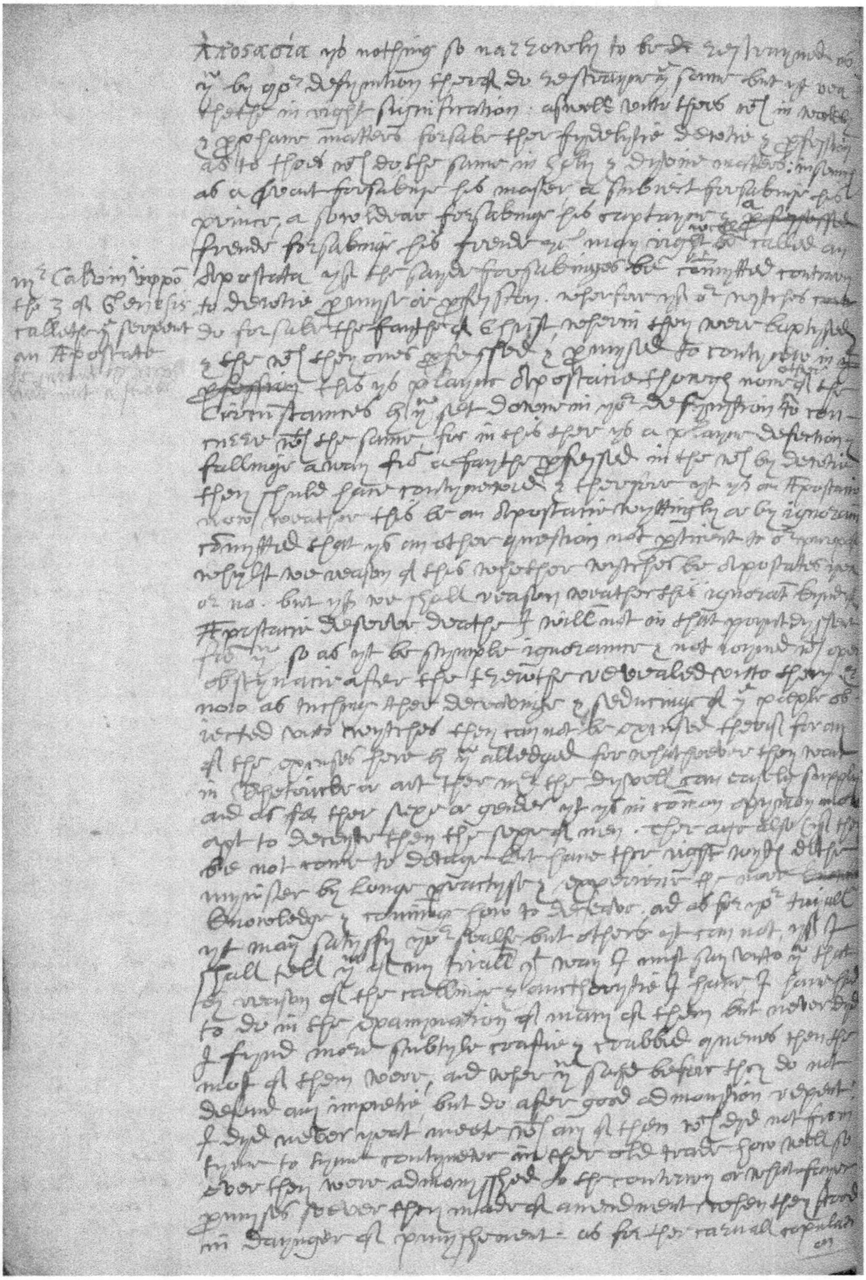

Figure 9 British Library Harley MS 2302, fol. 79v.

in books on witchcraft, especially the *Malleus Maleficarum*, despite its inadequacies as an explanation.

The present treatise has an ambiguous attitude towards the question of gender. On the one hand, it is conventional in adopting the usual explanation for the much greater numbers of women to be accused of witchcraft; as the author sees it, women are 'by nature the weakest vessels' and are therefore 'more apt to be entrapped' by the devil (fol. 62v, reason 23). The author is also guided, as ever, by the example of scripture, and in particular the story of the witch of Endor, who represents perhaps the closest approximation of an early modern witch in the Bible. At the same time, in some respect the treatise grants more agency to women than Scot, describing accused witches – in contrast to Scot's view of them as mentally incompetent – as being 'as sound and as sensible as other women are which be not of their sort' (fol. 66r, reason 36). The author has little sympathy for women accused of witchcraft, who are not only 'wicked women', as the author writes, they are also 'so notoriously known to be for the most part' (fol. 74r, reason 51). However, the author does not express such contempt for women who are not witches, and refers to the existence of praiseworthy women who can be described as 'honest and sober' (fol. 69v, reason 44), as 'godly' (fol. 93v, reason 87), or as 'wise' (fol. 74r, reason 51). While the author's views on gender are clearly those of a sixteenth-century man, it would be a distortion to claim that the treatise is primarily characterised by fear or hatred of women. By the standards of the time, the author's general attitude to women is if anything unusually positive.

Furthermore, it seems clear that the author sees nothing distinctively feminine about witchcraft. The devil's ministers can be both male and female, and Simon Magus, the enchanter who makes a brief appearance in Acts 8, is as relevant as the witch of Endor to the central question of what is and is not possible for the agents of the devil. Witchcraft is often compared to other forms of idolatry and heresy; it is not so much an exceptional crime (as it was sometimes called by other authors) as a particular expression of an unfortunate but universal human tendency towards corruption and diabolism. Stuart Clark has noted that 'the literature of witchcraft conspicuously lacks any sustained concern for the gender issue', and in this respect the treatise is fairly typical.[56] The fact that most witches are female is, for the author, a contingent fact to be explained rather than a defining feature of witchcraft. In other respects, however, the treatise takes positions that are more surprising.

---

56 Stuart Clark, *Thinking with Demons* (Oxford: Oxford University Press, 1997), p. 116.

One such position is that the treatise entirely rejects the claim that 'miracles have ceased', which might have been thought to be an uncontroversial view among English Protestants. Until quite recently, the idea that early modern Protestants believed that miracles ceased to happen shortly after the time of the apostles has largely been taken for granted; Keith Thomas commented merely that the idea 'took some time to establish itself', while D. P. Walker described it confidently as a 'doctrine firmly held'.[57] More recent work has raised serious questions about this claim.[58] But the author of the treatise not only rejects the 'doctrine' of the cessation of miracles, he disputes the very existence of any such doctrine:

> I say for true and godly miracles that although we are not now to require or look for any for the confirmation of our faith because the miracles already done and mentioned in the scriptures are sufficient, yet is there nothing that I know in divinity to persuade us that God hath so utterly determined to cease from all such miracles that he will never show any after Christ's time and the time of his Apostles, for if we will not discredit the histories of all times and ages, we cannot (as I said in another place before) deny but that God hath showed some miracles in all ages both immediately and by means. (fols 67v–68r, reason 44)

The important distinction made here is between expecting miracles and merely accepting that they are possible in principle. On the one hand, the treatise plays down the significance of miracles, countering Scot's claim that only Christ was able to perform miracles by pointing to numerous examples of others who did so and arguing that miracles are a weak ground for Christian belief. At the same time, the author disputes the claim that miracles no longer happen. While expecting miracles is unacceptable in that it shows both presumption and a lack of faith, going to the other extreme and actually denying the possibility of miracles would be, in effect, to limit the power of God. The unacceptability of doing this is at the heart of the argument in favour of witchcraft belief that the treatise presents.

The arguments advanced in the treatise are largely negative, in the sense that they respond to and reject arguments against the reality of witchcraft, but in doing so the treatise makes the grounds for witchcraft belief much clearer than those printed texts from the period which lay out a positive case for the existence of witches, which tend to be rather cursory and often rely on assertion rather than extended argument. Most authors on

---

57 Thomas, *Religion and the Decline of Magic*, p. 147; D. P. Walker, *Unclean Spirits* (Philadelphia, PA: University of Pennsylvania Press, 1981), p. 5.
58 See, for example, Jane Shaw's *Miracles in Enlightenment England* (New Haven: Yale University Press, 2006), which includes a section on the Reformation.

witchcraft who responded to scepticism simply condemned it and then moved swiftly on; while authors on other subjects were often much more sympathetic to scepticism in general and Scot in particular, they were generally equally brief.[59] Holland's *Treatise* and Gifford's *Discourse* contain the most extensive printed responses to Scot, but even in these books there is a lack of willingness to engage. George Gifford, evidently writing in response to Scot's reading of the book of Job (which suggests that God rather than the devil inflicted Job's suffering), retorts that 'the holie ghost doth so manifestlie teach that the diuell did this, that to denie it is flat impietie, and the vaine and friuolous cauils to prooue the contrarie not woorth the answering'.[60] The hostility evinced by Gifford, as he points out himself, makes his response briefer and less illuminating. The author of the present work, by contrast, presents a detailed response in reason 65 (fol. 77r). While written in a more generous spirit, this response, in outlining the scriptural justifications for the author's position, is at the same time much more convincing than Gifford in demonstrating Scot's argument to be both vain and frivolous.

The comprehensive nature of the work provides detailed evidence of the thinking of a theologically trained Elizabethan in relation to one of the most controversial aspects of sceptical arguments against witchcraft – the denial that spirits and humans could interact at all. Present-day historians have recognised this issue as central in the witchcraft debate, but despite its importance it is an issue on which many early modern authors say very little.[61] In his work on witchcraft, *Daemonologie* (1597), King James VI of Scotland (later also James I of England) singled out Scot for criticism, writing that he 'is not ashamed in publike print to deny, that ther can be such a thing as Witch-craft: and so mainteines the old error of the Sadducees, in denying of spirits.'[62] But while James was shocked enough to make what must have been a very serious allegation, this is all he really had to say about the matter. Henry Holland dealt with the question almost as briefly as James, merely stating that the devil can transform himself into various shapes, citing 2 Corinthians 11:14.[63] Gifford, at slightly greater

---

59 Davies, 'The Reception of Reginald Scot's *Discovery of Witchcraft*', pp. 386–7.
60 Gifford, *A Discourse of the subtill Practises of Deuilles by Witches and Sorcerers*, sig. D2v.
61 See, in particular, Walter Stephens, *Demon Lovers* (Chicago, IL: University of Chicago Press, 2001) and Stuart Clark, *Thinking with Demons* (Oxford: Oxford University Press, 1997).
62 James VI of Scotland and I of England, *Daemonologie* (Edinburgh, 1597), p. 2.
63 Holland, *A Treatise against Witchcraft*, sig. F1r.

length, employs similar reasoning in discussing the ability of the devil to take on corporeal form, referring to Exodus 7 and Acts 19 instead.[64]

The nature of spirits is frequently at issue in the treatise, which provides the only explicit statement in an early modern English work on witchcraft about precisely why the idea that spiritual beings cannot make bargains with corporeal beings was so troubling. The author highlights an enormous theological problem with this view: if this were the case, how could God have made a covenant with Abraham in Genesis 17:2 (fol. 65r, reason 32 – see figure 10)? God, after all, was a spiritual being, and, according to some authorities, the only purely spiritual being. While Holland and Gifford both present scripturally plausible counter-arguments to Scot's view, the treatise's author shows it to be completely incompatible with a literal belief in one of the most important stories of the Hebrew Bible. This is a much more fundamental refutation of Scot's anti-pact position, from the perspective of an early modern Christian – but even raising the possibility that the covenant with God might be thought to be impossible may have been too uncomfortable an idea for Holland or Gifford to address in print; the treatise, here and elsewhere, is much less guarded.

The parallel between God's bargain and the devil's bargain is not the only point on which the treatise recognises a connection between the infernal and the holy. Refusing to accept the devil's capacity to cause direct harm implies, in the author's view, a refusal to accept the possibility of God's grace. A blanket denial of anything operating beyond the limitations imposed by nature rules out the very possibility of religion, as the treatise author argues in reason 28:

> Neither can any of us by [natural] power believe in God or think so much as a good thought. For flesh and blood (that is to say natural wit, power, strength, and knowledge) did not reveal unto Peter or cause him to believe and confess Christ to be the son of the everliving God but as Christ sayeth, it was his heavenly father which revealed this to Peter {and} wrought this faith and confession in him ... If therefore our natural power were not enlarged (and that by an extraordinary power of God working in us by his holy spirit a further faith, knowledge, holiness, and sanctification than we have naturally in us) we were in a most desperate and damnable estate and condition[.] (fols 64r–64v)

The author's view of human nature, which follows the views of both Augustine and Calvin, is that it is so corrupt that constant supernatural intervention is required in order to maintain any sort of goodness, which

---

64 Gifford, *A Discourse of the subtill Practises of Deuilles by Witches and Sorcerers*, sigs C1r–C1v.

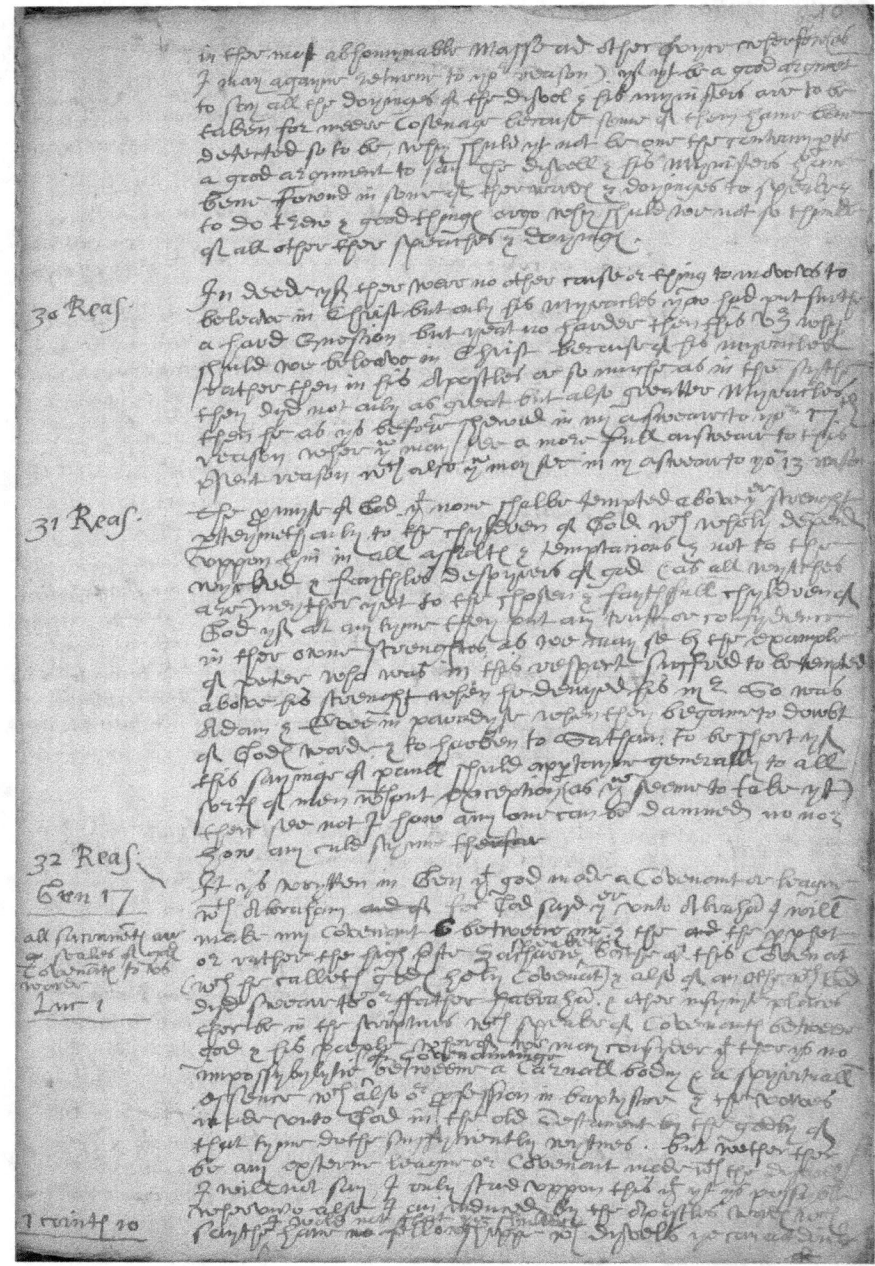

Figure 10 British Library Harley MS 2302, fol. 65r.

necessitates a belief in spiritual forces that are always at work in the world. Any argument attempting to do away with the idea of the devil's supernatural activity on earth will also necessarily threaten the supernatural grace of God. Walter Stephens has convincingly argued that religious anxiety was the major impetus behind elite witchcraft belief, and the close link between God and the devil is made especially clear and explicit in this treatise.[65]

Arguments against the possibility of interaction between spiritual and corporeal beings are unacceptable for their theological implications, but also because they are part of a broader sceptical tendency which threatens to undermine the literal truth of the Bible. It is in response to this tendency that the treatise makes clear that, for example, the serpent in Genesis was indeed a serpent; that the word 'spirit' is not typically used in a metaphorical sense in the Bible; that references to demonic possession in the scriptures are precisely that and should not be understood to refer to madness or natural illnesses; and that the words in the Bible translated into English as 'witch' refer to witches and not to poisoners or tricksters. The author always insists on the literal truth of the scriptures, while acknowledging that this literal truth may coexist with an allegorical or 'mystical' meaning. In taking this position the author follows the examples set by Calvin and by one of the leading English Calvinist theologians of the period, the anti-Catholic propagandist William Whitaker.[66]

One of the most noteworthy aspects of the argument advanced in the treatise is that its rejection of scepticism about witchcraft is reliant on a specifically Christian form of philosophical scepticism.[67] Again and again, the author argues not so much for the reality of witchcraft and the crimes alleged to be committed by witches, but for a suspension of final judgement about these matters and a refusal to rule out anything absolutely, on the scripturally solid ground that with God, all things are possible (fol. 81v, reason 76). The limitations of human knowledge are emphasised repeatedly, to demonstrate that Scot's own investigations into witchcraft cannot be as conclusive as he claims (fol. 79v, reason 71), that the emperor Nero's judgement was likewise fallible (fol. 97r, reason 98), and that we should

---

65 Stephens, *Demon Lovers*, esp. pp. 365–6.
66 Richard A. Muller, *Post-Reformation Reformed Dogmatics*, vol. 2 (Grand Rapids: Baker, 2003), pp. 471–3.
67 On the use of philosophical scepticism to support belief in witchcraft, see Walter Stephens, 'The Sceptical Tradition', in *The Oxford Handbook of Witchcraft in Early Modern Europe and Colonial America*, edited by Brian Levack (Oxford: Oxford University Press, 2013), and Eric Pudney, *Scepticism and Belief in Witchcraft Drama, 1538–1681* (Lund: Lund University Press, 2019), pp. 10–39.

simply reserve judgement in matters unnecessary to our salvation on which the Bible is silent or unclear. Instead of assuming that empirical investigation can lead to certainty, as Scot does, the author embraces probabilistic reasoning based on the balance of learned opinion, which, as he notes, is firmly in favour of the reality of witchcraft and the intervention of demons in the physical world (fols 57r, 94v, 102r). However, he tends to advance this argument not to reach firm conclusions, but to suggest what ought to be provisionally believed in the absence of certainty – a certainty which can only ever be provided by the Bible itself. In these respects, the author again presents a characteristically Reformed attitude towards human and scriptural authority.

The author does express doubts about specific aspects of witchcraft belief – in particular, those aspects associated with the Catholic demonology of Bodin and the *Malleus Maleficarum*. He is unwilling to believe that witches engage in sexual relationships with demons, writing that 'for carnal copulation with devils I think thereof as you do' (fols 79v–80r, reason 71), but even in this instance he scrupulously refuses to trust too much in his own judgement, adding that many great authorities, including St Augustine, have believed this to be true. Similarly, in the very lengthy response to reason 76, the author begins by stating that he agrees with Scot that a story about a witch transforming a young man into an ass is untrue, before disputing in detail every argument that Scot advances in support of this opinion. The ambiguity of the author's view is partly informed by his sceptical willingness to consider possible unknown factors that might contradict Scot's reasoning.

The author is also doubtful of the existence of a formal pact between witches and the devil, taking the position that 'whether there be any extern league or covenant made with the devil I will not say, I only stand upon this: that it is possible' (fol. 65r, reason 32). Here, his view is distinct from that of later Calvinist demonologists, such as William Perkins, whose brand of covenant theology laid great stress on the pact supposedly made between devil and witch, although it also seems to anticipate Perkins' distinction between explicit and implicit demonic bargains.[68] But as the author points out, there is no particular reason to rule out the possibility of witchcraft as *maleficium* or magic even if the idea of a demonic pact is ruled out. He is thereby able to defend a minimal witchcraft belief by refusing to defend

---

68 Perkins, in his *Discourse of the Damned Art of Witchcraft So Farre Forth as It Is Reuealed in the Scriptures* (Cambridge, 1610), describes the pact in his chapter heading as 'the Ground of all the practises of witchcraft' (p. 41), and explicitly distinguishes between 'expresse' and 'secret' pacts; cf. the distinction between the devil's 'league' and his 'secret and subtle suggestions' in reason 46 of the treatise below.

particular aspects of a more elaborate version of it. A recurring argumentative tactic is to show that, even if his opponent's reasoning holds, nothing follows from it. This leads the author, ultimately, to take a view similar to the somewhat extreme position later adopted by the civil lawyer John Selden: that witches deserve to be executed even if they have no power and their confessions are false.[69]

The treatise's discussion, unlike most published English works on witchcraft from this period, also touches on what Walter Stephens has described as 'the oldest and most important' text for the development of the idea of witches' flight, the canon *Episcopi*.[70] This passage became part of the canon law that was the basis for the Church court system from the middle ages on, and it provided a challenge for European witchcraft writers because it denied the possibility of one of their central tenets – the idea that witches flew to nocturnal gatherings called sabbats. The idea of the sabbat is not found in Elizabethan witchcraft pamphlets, although Millar has recently argued that witches' assemblies did become a significant feature of English witchcraft lore in the seventeenth century.[71] Nevertheless, the canon *Episcopi* is a text of fundamental importance, and its interpretation by a relatively disinterested theologian is therefore significant. In the context of the English witchcraft tradition, the author is freed from the need to defend the reality of witches' flight and the sabbat, writing that:

> If no general council had condemned the matters here mentioned as parcel of their league yet I think all wise men would never have believed them as things truly done. But what is this to prove the vanity of witches' confessions and of men's credulity in all other parts and practices of witches, which are more probable and apparent and with the which there concur very great and vehement presumptions? Yet this by the way, you have to note that the council here by you alleged doth not impute these confessions of the witches to the force of any melancholy humour as you do, but to the illusions and vain visions whereby they are of Satan seduced and deceived, being made to believe and profess those things; vz. their riding by night with Diana &c there mentioned. Neither doth that council hold and excuse these women for simple and innocent persons as you do but contrariwise pronounces them to be wicked women, such as are turned backward after Satan, also that they are subverted and holden captive of him, and having left their creator do seek the helps and

---

69 John Selden, *Table Talk* (London, 1689), p. 59. Selden regards the use of harmful magic as attempted murder, even if the magic is ineffective, while the treatise author sees false testimony – including false confessions – as deserving death on scriptural grounds (fols 66r–66v, reason 36).
70 Stephens, *Demon Lovers*, p. 127.
71 Millar, *Witchcraft, the Devil, and Emotions in Early Modern England*, pp. 155–6.

succours of the devil, and are therefore to be by all means dishonested and cast out of the Church by excommunication, that so the Church may be delivered of such pestilence or poison. (fol. 78r, reason 67)

The author is comfortable dismissing the idea of night-flying witches, since these are largely irrelevant in an English context, and points to the lack of connection between this belief and the more mundane, and (at least to him) more plausible, claims of *maleficium* typically found in witches' confessions in England. Rather than stressing the impossibility of flight, which was the key issue to be resolved in the canon *Episcopi* for those witchcraft theorists discussed by Stephens, the author can emphasise the same canon's condemnation of the women who claimed to be capable of it. While present-day historians have (in many respects, rightly) seen discontinuity between the canon *Episcopi* and later witchcraft belief, the author primarily sees that which has *not* changed: the canonist's condemnation of heresy.

As noted above, the treatise provides an original, and uniquely detailed, discussion of the theological underpinnings of witchcraft belief (rather than a discussion of witches or witchcraft itself) from the perspective of an Elizabethan churchman. Clergymen produced a number of texts on witchcraft in early modern England; certainly more than members of any other occupation, although medical doctors and lawyers also sometimes took an interest in the subject. However, the positions taken by the clergy towards witchcraft varied considerably. I would not want to propose a simplistic equation of witchcraft belief with puritanism throughout the early modern period; many Reformed Protestants throughout Europe provide counter-examples, and Protestant attitudes towards witchcraft were complex and ambiguous.[72] Nevertheless, in the late Elizabethan and early Jacobean context, the clerical author whose arguments were most hostile to the prosecution of witchcraft was the vigorously anti-puritan archbishop of York, Samuel Harsnett, while clerics with puritan sympathies – in particular, the famed theologian William Perkins – tended to support belief in witches.[73]

---

72 Pudney, *Scepticism and Belief in Witchcraft Drama, 1538–1681*, pp. 55–7.
73 On Harsnett's opposition to puritanism see Patrick Collinson, *Richard Bancroft and Elizabethan Anti-Puritanism*, pp. 157–64 and Marion Gibson, *Possession, Puritanism and Print: Darrell, Harsnett, Shakespeare and the Elizabethan Exorcism Controversy* (London: Pickering & Chatto, 2006). It should be added that Perkins was a moderate and basically conformist clergyman, and by no means a radical or separatist puritan: Leif Dixon, 'William Perkins, "Atheisme," and the Crises of England's Long Reformation', *Journal of British Studies* 50:4 (October 2011), 790–812; p. 810. His

In terms of his position on the spectrum of Elizabethan religious belief, the author of this treatise displays some signs of puritan sympathies. His uncompromising assertion of the view that human law be ignored where it conflicts with scripture and his frequently dismissive attitude to philosophy have already been noted.[74] At one point, the author discusses in passing the meaning of the verb 'prophesy', writing that:

> the learned interpreters of this place of Paul take by the gift of prophecy in this place not to be meant the gift of foreshowing things to come but rather the gift of teaching, exhorting, and comforting, whereof the same apostle speaketh in another place, saying he which doth prophesy speaketh edification, exhortation, and consolation. And again: 'ye may all prophesy one by one that all may learn and all receive consolation'. (fol. 93r, reason 87)

The term 'prophesy', and the author's understanding of it, had special significance at this point in Elizabeth's reign. The puritan movement of the 1570s had encouraged conferences of clergy – called 'prophesyings' or 'exercises', for the godly and educational purposes outlined by the author above. Prophesyings are known to have taken place in Kent from 1572 – in some cases there are records identifying attendees – and continued to take place there well into the 1580s, often with the quiet encouragement of sympathetic ecclesiastical officials, and in spite of the Queen's demand that they be suppressed.[75] The author's seemingly enthusiastic attitude towards this type of prophesying therefore suggests a degree of sympathy with puritan demands for further reformation in the Church.

The author's puritan leanings also make themselves known through his verbal habits. He occasionally uses variations on a phrase associated with puritans, in particular with the early English Protestant and Bible translator William Tyndale. In appealing to 'the whole course of the [biblical] text', he echoes Tyndale, and throughout the treatise he lays a similarly great

---

career, which was still in its infancy in the 1580s, reflects the turn away from political activism and towards 'weighty moral analysis' taken by most puritans following Whitgift's appointment as archbishop and the movement's failure to secure reforms in the liturgy and Church government; see Diarmaid MacCulloch, *Reformation: Europe's House Divided* (London: Penguin, 2004), pp. 389–91.

74 The attitude of a more conformist thinker can be seen in Richard Hooker, *Of the Laws of Ecclesiastical Polity*, vol. 1 (London: J. M. Dent, 1969), who of course accepts the priority of scripture over human law in principle, but does so in the course of a defence of human law and the use of reason or philosophy; pp. 264–76, 310–19.

75 Peter Clark, 'The Prophesying Movement in Kentish Towns during the 1570s', *Archaeologia Cantiana* 93 (1977), 81–90 (p. 82); Patrick Collinson, *The Elizabethan Puritan Movement* (Oxford: Oxford University Press, 1967), p. 212.

stress on the literal sense of the words of the Bible.[76] Another hint of puritanism can be found in his attitude to women, which is at times unusually favourable in an early modern author, as noted above. This attitude might reflect the fact that puritanism, as has often been noted, derived much of its energy from women, who were often able to exercise influence, and even leadership, within the movement.[77] There are also faint traces of the levelling, anti-elitist Calvinist ethic that would later become strongly associated with opposition to the early Stuart monarchs, for example when the author writes that 'God bestoweth many times more wisdom, more learning, more strength {&c} upon the reprobate than he doth upon his children' (fol. 93v, reason 87). More than any of this, though, the author's frequent insistence on the authority of scripture above all else seems indicative of his ideological orientation.

On the other hand, the author is far from being the rigid, dogmatic caricature of a 'precisian' that was already starting to become widespread at this time.[78] His moderation is perhaps most evident in some of his remarks about Catholicism. He is undoubtedly a Protestant, condemning the Catholic mass and displaying typical English hostility to the papacy itself, apparently identifying the antichrist of Revelation with the pope (fol. 57v, reason 7). Nonetheless, he is also relatively mild in his disapproval of Catholicism and Catholics (as distinct from the institution of the papacy), writing at one point that 'our papists do not utterly forsake Christ though they seek salvation by other things as well as by him' (fol. 76r, reason 59). He is also familiar with Roman canon law – the study of which had been ended in the reign of Henry VIII, but which continued to remain in force, largely because no adequate replacement existed.[79] Many 'forward Protestants' strongly disapproved of the Elizabethan Church's continued use of the Church court system, which relied on canon law, so the author's tacit acceptance of this body of doctrine is also a sign of moderation, as is his respect for patristic writings.[80]

---

76 Collinson, *The Elizabethan Puritan Movement*, p. 27.
77 See, for some examples, Collinson, *The Elizabethan Puritan Movement*, pp. 93, 379–80. Again, the author's attitude differs from that of the more conservative Richard Hooker, who criticises puritanism on the ground that it seeks to attract 'them whose judgements are commonly weakest by reason of their sex' (*Of the Laws of Ecclesiastical Polity*, vol. 1, p. 103).
78 Collinson, *Richard Bancroft and Elizabethan Anti-Puritanism*, p. 29.
79 MacCulloch, *Reformation*, p. 408; Collinson, *The Elizabethan Puritan Movement*, pp. 38–9.
80 R. H. Helmholz, *Roman Canon Law in Reformation England* (Cambridge: Cambridge University Press, 1990), pp. 52–3; MacCulloch, *Reformation*, p. 594.

If the author's perspective is that of a mainstream churchman with some puritan sympathies – more moderate, perhaps, than that of many other authors on witchcraft – then the treatise occupies a religious middle ground. In addition, it presents the opinion of a clergyman who wrote on the subject not because he held such strong views that he felt moved to do so, or because he was personally implicated in a particularly controversial case (as was the case, it seems, with writers like Bernard, Gifford, and Goodcole), but as a favour to a friend.[81] Most authors on witchcraft have an axe to grind, while the author of the treatise presents an interesting and unusual perspective precisely because he seems *not* to have any particular interest in witchcraft, notwithstanding his involvement in witchcraft cases by reason of his position.

The views most frequently and loudly expressed in writing on this topic tended to be partisan views, often arguing for change in the form of more aggressive witchcraft persecution, which may not have been representative of more widely held opinions among the Elizabethan elite. The Elizabethan authorities did little to encourage witch-hunting, and actively discouraged the activities of exorcists like Darrell. At the same time, however, they also did little to discourage more mundane witchcraft prosecutions. This 'moderate' position did not call out for more trials and executions, but it also defended against critics like Scot the legitimacy of the regime and its laws. Such a view did not need to be expressed in printed polemics, as it represented an infrequently challenged status quo, but the present treatise represents one very thorough exposition and defence of it. The strongly authoritarian streak that Ethan Shagan finds in the language of moderation, so frequently used by those in positions of power in early modern England, is certainly discernible in the present work.[82]

However, while the treatise's objections to the draft of the *Discoverie* may have been widely shared within the Church, they were not universally held. If a draft version of the *Discoverie* was sent to several different clergymen, as has been suggested above, their responses to his draft might also have prompted him to name some, but not all, of these correspondents in the published epistles. If the author of the treatise was Richard Rogers or Tobias Matthew, he may have appreciated Scot's discretion in removing his name from the heading of the epistle, since he probably would not have wished to be associated with opinions which he clearly did not agree with.

---

81 See Bernard, *A Guide to Grand-Jury Men*, sigs A3v–A4r; Goodcole, *The Wonderfull Discouerie of Elizabeth Sawyer*, sigs A3r–A3v; on Gifford see Alan Macfarlane, 'A Tudor Anthropologist: George Gifford's *Discourse* and *Dialogue*', in *The Damned Art*, edited by Sidney Anglo (London: Routledge & Kegan Paul, 1977), pp. 140–55.

82 Ethan Shagan, *The Rule of Moderation: Violence, Religion and the Politics of Restraint in Early Modern England* (Cambridge: Cambridge University Press, 2011).

Whether Scot received detailed feedback from other correspondents cannot now be known, but it seems likely that he would at least have sought their consent before publicly associating a book on such a controversial topic with them. Coldwell, in any event, does not seem to have been troubled by the dedication; as noted above, Scot remained on good enough terms with him to be able to call on him at a later date for his scholarly expertise. (Whether Scot's friendship with the author of the present treatise survived their obvious disagreement is open to conjecture.) While the author of the treatise clearly disapproves of Scot's reasoning, then, not all clergymen would necessarily have done so.

Given that the opinions of the clergy diverged on this point, it is worth considering what this might say about the place of witchcraft belief and the theological position underlying it in the England of the early to mid-1580s. There might seem to be a tension between the nature of Scot's theological position and the recent contention of Glyn Parry and Peter Elmer that the *Discoverie* might have formed part of the anti-puritan campaign launched by John Whitgift following his ordination as Archbishop of Canterbury in 1583.[83] It would seem, at first sight, peculiar for a 'conformist', as Parry describes Scot, to get away with being connected to such unorthodox views.[84] But in fact, it was the more militant Protestants who demanded greater 'discipline' in the Church and its government, while 'conformists' were in practice willing to tolerate greater diversity of private belief as long as people conformed to the practices of the English Church and did not question the legitimacy of its episcopal hierarchy.[85] The Queen herself, as has often been pointed out, cared little about what people privately believed as long as her authority was not challenged. On her accession to the throne, all of her closest advisers, as well as her first Archbishop of Canterbury, Matthew Parker, were not former exiles but Protestants who had put their private beliefs aside and conformed during the reign of her Catholic half-sister, Mary.[86]

Scot's use of arguments resembling the beliefs of the Family of Love – a spiritualist sect which had radical beliefs, but whose members

---

[83] Elmer, *Witchcraft, Witch-Hunting, and Politics in Early Modern England*, p. 18; Parry, *The Arch-Conjuror of England*, p. 208.

[84] Parry, *The Arch-Conjuror of England*, p. 208. Elmer writes of Scot that his 'explicit disavowal of religious heterodoxy and opposition to radical puritanism in *The Discoverie* suggests a man fearful of religious extremism' (p. 23).

[85] On the puritan demands for disipline and the (real or perceived) threat that this presented to the established Church, see Collinson, *Richard Bancroft and Elizabethan Anti-Puritanism* (Cambridge: Cambridge University Press, 2013), pp. 7–12.

[86] MacCulloch, *Reformation*, p. 290.

were prepared to practise outward conformity to any Church – would therefore have been more troubling to 'puritan' Protestants than to the conformist elements in the Church.[87] It might be fruitful to distinguish between Familist 'radicals' and puritan 'extremists': the puritans had few objections to the doctrine of the established Church; their principal complaints were about the form of the liturgy and the structures of Church government (hence the demands for 'discipline'). They therefore aspired to bring about ecclesiastical changes to which the Queen, and the more conservative among her counsellors, objected. The Family of Love, on the other hand, held radical beliefs which diverged greatly from Church doctrine, but these beliefs were no barrier to outward conformity (or to pursuing conventional, and often successful, careers). It was rumoured that Elizabeth herself had Familist sympathies, but probably only because a number of her personal bodyguard, the yeomen of the guard, who were discovered to be Familists in the 1580s, did not suffer any serious consequences as a result.[88] The powerful anti-puritan courtier Christopher Hatton was captain of the yeomen of the guard, and played a part in ending a puritan parliamentary attempt to legislate against the Family, circumstances suggestive of a 'conformist' faction, tacitly tolerant of well-behaved religious radicalism, squaring up to a puritan grouping that wanted to take active steps to impose doctrinal uniformity on the population at large.[89]

Puritan clergymen were the most likely people to write on the subject of witchcraft. Many of the best-known English authors – Henry Holland, George Gifford, William Perkins, Richard Bernard, Thomas Cooper – could be described as puritans to a greater or lesser degree: Gifford was

---

87 On the similarities between Scot's arguments and some of the views of the Family of Love, see David Wootton, 'Reginald Scot / Abraham Fleming / The Family of Love', in *Languages of Witchcraft*, edited by Stuart Clark (Basingstoke: Macmillan, 2001), pp. 119–38.

88 The instructive case of one of the yeomen, Robert Seale, is described in Christopher W. Marsh, *The Family of Love in English Society, 1550–1630* (Cambridge: Cambridge University Press, 1994), pp. 164–5.

89 Marsh, *The Family of Love in English Society, 1550-1630*, pp. 132–3; Christopher Carter, 'The Family of Love and Its Enemies', *The Sixteenth Century Journal* 37:3 (2006), 651–72. In the early 1580s at least, Sir Thomas Scot was a very active part of this puritan group, pressing questions in parliament such as the execution of Mary Queen of Scots and calling for tougher measures to be taken against Catholics. But his position changed during the Whitgift era: see Collinson, *The Elizabethan Puritan Movement*, pp. 257–9; Elmer, *Witchcraft, Witch-Hunting, and Politics in Early Modern England*, p. 25; Kapitaniak, 'From Grindal to Whitgift', 26–7.

even deprived of his position as minister for his refusal to subscribe to Whitgift's articles in 1584.[90] For these authors, belief in witchcraft (although not necessarily in encouraging witchcraft prosecutions, as Gifford's and Bernard's texts indicate) was an important part of their faith. It had to be, since it was given such clear support by the scriptural authority which was at the heart of the Protestant Reformation, and which the more rigorous (or rigid) English Protestants insisted on interpreting literally as far as possible. At the particular historical moment in which the treatise was written, the author's objections to Scot's radically (or carelessly) unscriptural arguments were almost certainly grounded in a similar outlook. More flexible (or unscrupulous) clergymen – like the careerists Redman and Coldwell – were more likely to be willing to turn a blind eye to some of the ideas in the *Discoverie*.

The author of the treatise does not condemn Scot, but he clearly distances himself from the troubling arguments that Scot advances. It is remarkable that, throughout the text, what is at stake has little or nothing to do with the execution of women for witchcraft – a subject the author seems rather uninterested in for its own sake. His text reveals what the real issues behind witchcraft were, at least for part of the educated elite, in a uniquely clear light. What is important are the beliefs and commitments underlying, as the author sees it, all genuine Christian faith. These beliefs do not necessitate the reality of witchcraft or of any particular aspect of witchcraft lore. But the author unambiguously rules out an absolute *disbelief* in witchcraft. Whether a given person felt the need to take a stand on witchcraft belief or not depended to a great extent on how much importance they attached to such private beliefs, and whether they thought that alternative views should be quietly tolerated or loudly denounced, and perhaps also suppressed. Many educated people, perhaps especially among the clergy, probably saw the issue of prosecuting actual witches as trivial by comparison.

The historiography of witchcraft has tended to be based primarily on readings of two groups of printed sources: the pamphlet literature dealing with individual cases of witchcraft on the one hand, and polemical works debating the existence and nature of witchcraft more generally on the other. The former have been highly valued as providing the only available insight, beyond the bare bones of legal records, into how people perceived and discussed the issue of witchcraft in practice. The latter group of sources have usually been understood to represent the views of a small but influential 'elite' – as distinct from the more 'popular' ideas represented

---

90 Collinson, *The Elizabethan Puritan Movement*, p. 265.

in pamphlets.[91] There are legitimate questions about how representative these printed sources are. In the case of pamphlet literature, it is often acknowledged that only a small minority of witchcraft cases were dealt with in pamphlets, and these cases may well have been unusually 'sensational', and perhaps unrepresentative, cases. But such questions are less frequently asked about the polemical works debating witchcraft, which risks leaving the impression that such works do indeed accurately represent the full range of educated opinion on the matter.

But the treatise demonstrates that educated opinion on the question of witchcraft was capable of much greater nuance and breadth than the printed polemics allow for. Its author was capable of going beyond the usual assertions about what witches could and could not do and the nature of their relationship with the devil, instead suspending judgement on most such matters in favour of a positive case for the doctrinal necessity of a minimal witchcraft belief. The author's case rests on ideas about, among other things, scriptural interpretation, human nature, conscience, and the correct understanding of the place of miracles and the supernatural in Christian belief. The treatise suggests the potential for, and perhaps the actual existence of, a sixteenth-century debate about witchcraft which was broader, more nuanced, and less formulaic than the surviving printed sources would suggest. A wider range of thought than what appeared in print was evidently possible for educated and theologically inclined English people.

Relationship to the *Discoverie*

Nobody who has read both books in their entirety could reasonably doubt that the treatise is a response to a draft version of Scot's *Discoverie of Witchcraft*. Side-by-side comparison of the two texts reveals countless verbal parallels, as the author frequently reproduces Scot's wording precisely in responding to his arguments, as well as addressing Scot as 'you'. In addition, specific references made in Scot's work, for example to particular authors or passages from the Bible, are countered by different interpretations of the same texts in the treatise. The text of the treatise itself is presented together with extracts from the corresponding sections of the printed *Discoverie* so that readers can compare the texts in detail for themselves. For the purposes of this introduction, table 1 below shows a few excerpts

---

91 This view is something of a simplification, as there was certainly crossover between pamphlets and learned works on witchcraft, as Millar points out (p. 16).

Table 1 Examples of verbal similarities between the *Discoverie* and the treatise.

Discoverie	Treatise
But if all the divels in hell were dead, and all the witches in England burnt or hanged; I warrant you <u>we should not faile to have raine, haile and tempests</u>. (bk 1, ch 1, p. 3)	It is to be confessed that <u>we should not fail to have rain, hail, and tempests</u> though there were neither devil nor witch (fol. 58r)
if all the old women in the world were witches; and all the priests, conjurers: we should not have <u>a drop of raine, nor a blast of wind the more or the lesse</u> for them (bk 1, ch 1, p. 3)	neither witch nor devil hath any power to do these or other thing imputed unto them but of God, and therefore no marvel though it lie not in them at their pleasure to send <u>a drop of rain more or less</u> &c (fol. 58r)
The Imperiall lawe (saith <u>Brentius</u>) condemneth them to death that trouble and infect the aire: but I affirme (saith he) that it is neither in the power of witch not divell so to doo, but in God onelie. Though (besides Bodin, and all the popish writers in generall) it please <u>Danaeus, Hyperius, Hemingius</u>, Erastus, &c. to conclude otherwise ... <u>S. Augustine</u> saith ... We must not thinke that these visible things are at the commandement of the angels that fell, but are obedient to the onelie God. (bk 1, ch 1, p. 3)	you say that <u>Danaeus, Hyperius and Hemmingius</u> do otherwise conclude of the power of witches than <u>Brentius</u> doth who attributeth all to the power of God ... as for the authority of <u>Brentius</u> and <u>St August</u> how alleged they are not as I think gainsaid by any writer (fols 58r–58v)
If Christ had knowne them, he would not have pretermitted to <u>invaie</u> against their presumption, in taking upon them his office: as, to heale and cure diseases; and to worke such miraculous and supernaturall things, as whereby he himselfe was speciallie <u>knowne, beleeved, and published</u> to be God (bk 1, ch 5, p. 11)	Touching Christ's not speaking or <u>inveighing</u> particularly against the particular actions imputed to witches ... there be many and sundry ways besides whereby Christ was thus <u>known, believed and published</u> (fols. 59v–60r)
For alas! What an unapt instrument is a <u>toothles, old</u>, impotent, and unweldie woman to flie in the aier? Truelie, the divell <u>little needs such instruments to bring his purposes to passe</u>. (bk 1, ch 6, p. 13)	As you say <u>the devil needeth not such instruments to bring his purpose to pass</u> as our <u>old and toothless</u> women are, so I may say God needeth not any man, woman or other creature to bring his purposes to pass, and yet we know that God, in infinite of his actions and purposes, useth the help and means of sundry his creatures (fol. 62v)

from Scot's arguments in the published version of the *Discoverie* next to the responses found in the treatise. Specific words, phrases or names that appear in both texts have been underlined.

Even these few examples should suffice to show that the treatise must be a response to Scot. In fact, the responses to Scot are so close to his words that there are even places where it is possible to identify what seem to be compositor's errors in the published *Discoverie*. In the printed version, Scot writes of witches that 'If anie man advisedlie marke their words, actions, cogitations, and gestures, he shall perceive that melancholie abounding in their head, and occupieng their braine, hath deprived or rather depraved their judgements'.[92] This passage receives a response in the treatise using almost exactly the same nouns as Scot: 'the countenances, gestures, words, and actions of our witches when they come before authority to be examined' (fol. 73v, reason 51). Instead of writing 'cogitations', however, the author uses the word 'countenances', and this word makes much more sense in context. 'Cogitations' – thoughts – by their nature cannot be 'marked' or observed, but 'countenances' obviously can be. Similarly, where the printed *Discoverie* claims that 'The art alwaies presupposeth the power', the response to the corresponding passage in Scot's draft uses a slightly different word: 'the act doth not evermore presuppose such a power as that the doers of the act should always be able to show how and by what means they do it' (fol. 62r, reason 20).[93] Again, 'act' makes more sense here than 'art', suggesting that the author was better able to read Scot's handwriting and understand his meaning than the compositor responsible for typesetting the *Discoverie*.

While it is of course very difficult to make claims about a text that is now lost, some conclusions can be drawn about the nature of the lost draft of Scot's *Discoverie* on the basis of the treatise's responses. Perhaps the most important point is that the structure of the draft version of the *Discoverie* must have been significantly different from that of the printed version. This is evident from the structure of the treatise, which is a direct, point-by-point response to the draft. As has been pointed out by Wanley, Notestein, and Davies, the treatise consists of a numbered list of 'reasons'. However, what none of these scholars mentioned is that the choice of this structure is not made by the author of the treatise. This becomes evident in several passages of the treatise, where the author uses formulations like the following: 'The strangeness of the imagination here spoken of is taken away sufficiently in my answer to your 21 and 22 reasons' (fol. 63r, reason 24); '… as is before showed in my answer to your 17th reason, where you may see a more full

---

92 Scot, 3.9, p. 41 [52].
93 Scot, 1.6, p. 10 [13].

answer to this present reason, which also you may see in my answer to your 13 reason' (fol. 65r, reason 30); 'you may remember what is said thereof in my answer to your 19th reason' (fol. 66r, reason 35). (A simple text search reveals that there are 14 such formulations – 'my answer to your [reason]' – in the treatise.) These repeated references to 'your' reasons must surely indicate that the format of the treatise reflects the format of Scot's draft version of the *Discoverie*. This is, of course, quite unlike the printed version, which is divided into 16 books, some of which have more than 40 chapters, plus a further book, Scot's *Discourse upon divels and spirits*, appended to the main work.

These circumstances suggest that the scope of the *Discoverie* was originally much more modest than is the case in the printed version. Having carefully compared the published *Discoverie* with the treatise, I have compiled a table showing which sections of the treatise correspond with which chapters in Scot's book (table 2 below). This overview reveals significant gaps in the draft version of the *Discoverie* compared to the published version. While the draft appears to have presented content (for the most part) in the same order as the published version, there are whole sections of the printed book that appear not to have been included in the draft. It seems likely that at least some of these sections were added after the draft was sent to its anonymous respondent, although some material may have appeared later in the draft version, since the treatise in its current state ends abruptly in the middle of reason 108.

Since the treatise is incomplete, missing both beginning and end, it is possible that some sections missing from the surviving pages and appearing in the published *Discoverie* were discussed in pages of the treatise that are now lost. It seems that the order of some sections of the draft was altered in the published version of the *Discoverie*. The very last reason in the treatise – reason 108 – responds to an argument that can now be found in Scot's published *Discoverie* in book 7, chapter 4 (see figure 11). This point arises *after* material responding to arguments now found in the final book of the published *Discoverie*. It is therefore not possible to say with any degree of certainty that material not dealt with in the treatise was also not included in the draft which its author read.

Nonetheless, it does seem from the table below that only a few of the extant reasons in Scot's draft – 84, 91, and 108 – were moved out of their original order prior to publication. This represents very light editing on Scot's, or his editor's, part – understandably, given the practical difficulties involved at a time when everything had to be written by hand, and paper was expensive. The very close verbal resemblances between the treatise and the published *Discoverie* also suggest that Scot did not make very major changes to the original draft. Rather than changing what

Table 2 Reasons in the treatise and corresponding sections in the *Discoverie*.

Reason(s)	Corresponding book/ chapter in *Discoverie*	Topics or phrases allowing identification of the treatise with the *Discoverie*
5, 6	epistle to the readers	Use of phrases 'affliction nor calamity' (5), 'unwritten verities' (6) in both the treatise and the *Discoverie*
7–16	book 1, chapters 1 and 2	Discusses the nature of miracles, who can perform them, and the supposed power of witches
17–29	1.5–7	The nature of the devil, and whether and how witches can have power to do impossible things
30	2.10	Belief in Christ on the basis of his miracles
31	2.12	Discussion of 1 Cor. 10:13
32–4	3.4	The possibility or otherwise of demonic pacts
35–70	3.6–16, 3.18	Pacts between spiritual and corporeal creatures, witches' confessions and other legal issues, and melancholy. Several specific examples, authorities, and stories are present in both texts
71	3.18–19, 4.10–12	The author responds to a series of 8 offences of which witches are accused. These 8 separate points are spread out across a number of different chapters in the published *Discoverie*
72–3	5.1	Transformation into animal form; Deuteronomy 32:24
74–80	5.3–8	More on animal transformation and the story of the Knight of Rhodes, witches' flight and Christ's temptation in the gospels, the book of Job and Calvin's interpretation of it
81	5.9, 6.4	Moses' view of witchcraft and Hebrew words for 'witch'
82–3	6.1–2	Simon Magus, Biblical prohibition of witchcraft
84	13.21	Discussion of 'Jannes & Jambres' and Moses

Table 2 Continued

Reason(s)	Corresponding book/chapter in *Discoverie*	Topics or phrases allowing identification of the treatise with the *Discoverie*
85	7.11–13	The story of the Witch of Endor in 1 Samuel 28
86–8	7.15, 8.1–3	Cessation of miracles, prophecy, and oracles
89	unknown	A similar argument to those above, concerning prophecies made by witches and devils
90	9.7	Exorcism
91	12.15	Psalm 58
92–6	12.2–4	Extent of witches'/the devil's power
97	12.15	Refers to answer 91 and to a rhetorical question asked by Scot in 12.15
98–100	15.32, 15.42	The views of Nero, Agrippa, Gallus, and Thomas Elkes on magic
101	unknown (perhaps 2.10?)	Responds to a general rejection of virtually all previous writers on witchcraft
102–7	17.12–14, 17.16, 17.29–30	The nature of spirits, literal vs. non-literal interpretation of scripture, the serpent in the Garden of Eden
108	7.4	The story of Doubting Thomas and Christ's resurrection in Luke 24.36–39

he had already written, it seems, he preferred to supplement it with more material. This supposition is also consistent with the somewhat repetitive nature of the published *Discoverie*; Scot frequently makes an argument briefly before providing an extended version of the same argument later in the book.

This tentative hypothesis – that some of the material not covered in the treatise was added to the *Discoverie* after the draft version was written – is supported by the circumstance that much of the material in books 1 and 2 on which the treatise is silent relates to events that were fairly recent at the time of the *Discoverie*'s publication. Much of book 1 of the *Discoverie* is dealt with in a very thorough fashion in the treatise. However, as table 2 above shows, there is a gap in the treatise's coverage stretching from the end of chapter 2 until chapter 5. In the published

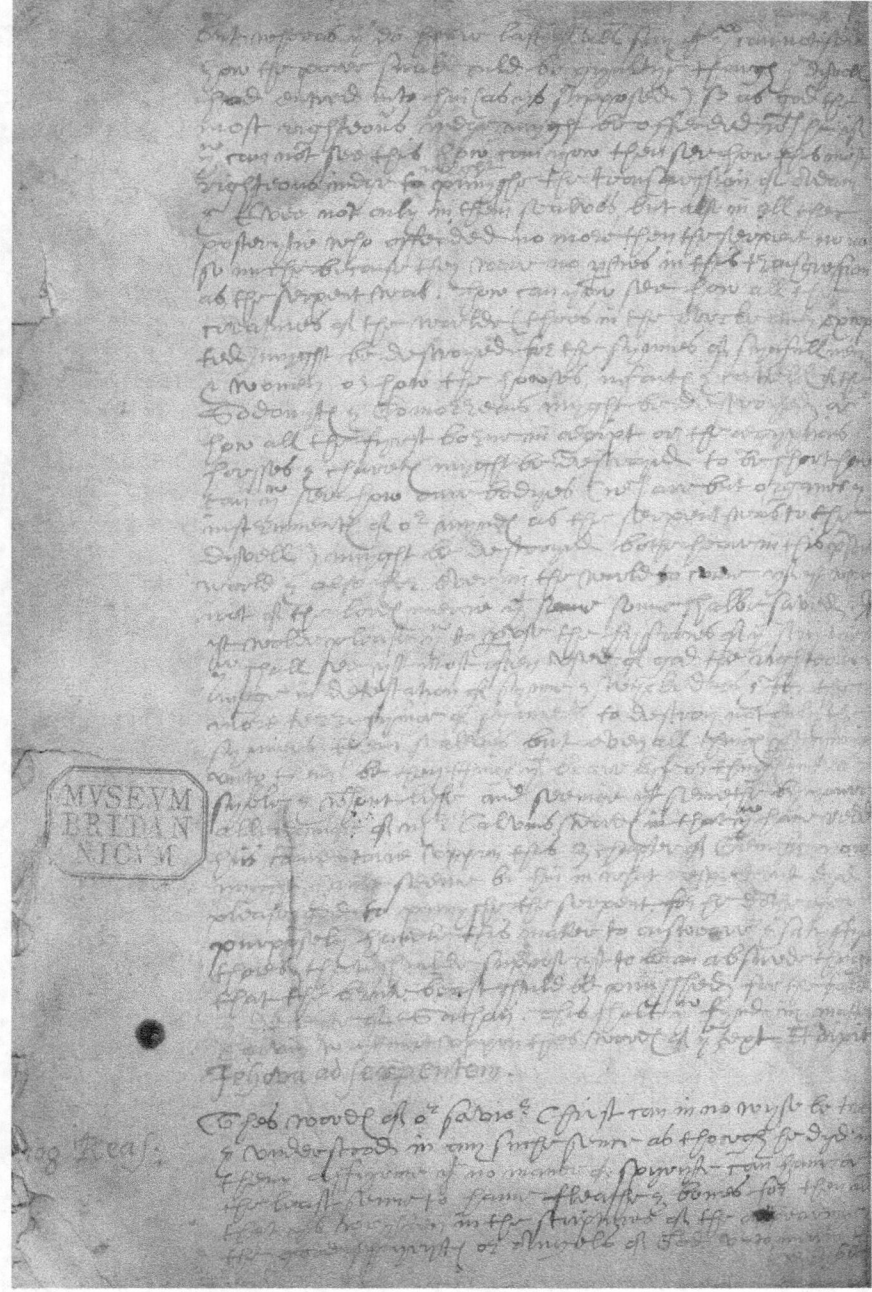

Figure 11 British Library Harley MS 2302, fol. 105v.

Discoverie, Scot tells the story of Margaret Simons at the end of chapter 2, helpfully providing a date:

> At the assises holden at Rochester, Anno 1581, one Margaret Simons, the wife of John Simons, of Brenchlie in Kent, was araigned for witchcraft, at the instigation and complaint of divers fond and malicious persons; and speciallie by the meanes of one John Ferrall vicar of that parish[.][94]

While many of Scot's stories in the *Discoverie* do receive a direct response in the treatise, this is not one of them, and it is one of relatively few local stories to be given a specific date – recent at the time of the *Discoverie*'s publication. The 1581 Rochester Assizes took place on 3 July, and records of the trial to which Scot refers have survived, showing that Margaret Simons was found not guilty of the murder of Agnes Champe by witchcraft.[95] There is no indication anywhere in the treatise that the author has read Scot's telling of this story. In view of how comprehensive his response is in general, it seems that this story was either not in the draft which he read, or that it originally appeared later in the draft (so that the response to it has now been lost) and was moved forward in the printed *Discoverie*.

Other parts of the printed *Discoverie* which are missing from the treatise also have interesting connections to recent events in England. In chapter 8 of book 1, which does not receive a response in the treatise, Scot writes dismissively of 'a foolish pamphlet dedicated to the lord *Darcy* by W. W. 1582.'[96] The bulk of book 2 (and again, the treatise is silent on all of this material) is devoted to an extended attack on Jean Bodin, Scot's main antagonist in the *Discoverie*. Bodin is mentioned in the treatise, and was evidently also mentioned in the draft to which it responds, but much less frequently than in the published *Discoverie*. Given the rather brief treatment of Bodin in the treatise, it may be that Scot expanded his discussion of Bodin in the version of the *Discoverie* that eventually went to print.

Scot's interest in responding to Bodin's book could have gained urgency after the latter's visit to England in 1581–82 as part of the Duke of Alençon's entourage. As historians of witchcraft have often suggested, this visit may well have inspired a well-known episode of witch-hunting in Essex. The 'foolish pamphlet' referred to above explains that:

> there is a man of great cunning and knowledge come over lately unto our Queenes Majestie, which hath advertised her what a companie and number

---

94 Scot, 1.2, p. 4 [5].
95 Cockburn (ed.), *Calendar of Assize Records*, p. 184. Another woman, Agnes Maye, was also found not guilty of witchcraft at the same assizes (p. 185).
96 Scot, 1.8, p. 13 [17].

of Witches be within Englande: whereupon I and other of her Justices have received Commission for the apprehe[n]ding of as many as are within these limits, and they which doe confesse the truth of their doeings, they shall have much favour: but the other they shall be burnt and hanged.[97]

This, as several scholars have argued, seems certain to be a reference to Bodin, whose 'great cunning' was certainly well-known and celebrated at this time, and who is explicitly cited in the margin of W. W.'s dedicatory epistle.[98] Scot's evident hostility to W. W. and his 'foolish' book is motivated by the 'crueltie' of witch-hunting, and the St Osyth witchcraft trials are notable for the fact that the presiding judge, Brian D'Arcy, promised the first of the witches to be accused, Ursula Kemp, that she would be treated favourably if she confessed, in accordance with interrogation methods recommended by Bodin.[99] Despite this promise, she was hanged along with several other women convicted of witchcraft in 1582. Bodin's second visit to England, and the possibility that it may have led directly to his recommendations being put into practice in this manner, may have provided Scot with an immediate motivation to expand his book, and in particular to add lengthy sections devoted to rejecting Catholic demonology in general and Bodin's *Démonomanie* in particular.

Other sections of the *Discoverie* to which the treatise does not respond also contain elements of some of Scot's more complex arguments against witchcraft. The first three chapters of book 3 and the entirety of book 4 are omitted, sections which deal with specific aspects of demonology in greater detail – witches' flight, the 'homage' paid by witches to the devil, including the notorious anal kiss and other lurid stories such as the penis-stealing witches mentioned in the *Malleus Maleficarum*. These kinds of stories are not present in Elizabethan pamphlets, but they are dealt with at length in a number of important witchcraft texts by Catholic authors (a circumstance Scot constantly uses to attack witchcraft belief). There seems also to be no response to most of books 6 and 7, which deal with the precise signification of Hebrew words and rely heavily on Johannes Weyer's *De Praestigiis*

---

97 W. W., *A true and iust recorde, of the information, examination and confession of all the witches, taken at S. Oses in the countie of Essex* (London, 1582), sig. B6v.
98 Elmer, *Witchcraft, Witch-Hunting, and Politics in Early Modern England*, p. 28; Kapitaniak, 'From Grindal to Whitgift', 5.
99 W. W., *A true and iust recorde*, sig. A7v; Jean Bodin, *On the Demon-Mania of Witches*, translated by Randy A. Scott (Toronto: Centre for Reformation and Renaissance Studies, 1995), p. 176. If all else fails, Bodin recommends arresting the witches' 'young daughters' in order to persuade them to incriminate their mothers (p. 177).

Daemonum.¹⁰⁰ Here it seems likely that the material was expanded from brief remarks to a more thorough argument, since the treatise does respond to the parts of these arguments found in the opening chapter of book 6 and some of the later chapters of book 7 (see table 2 above).

One noteworthy aspect of the printed *Discoverie* that is not referred to in the treatise is Scot's interpretation of the biblical story of the witch of Endor in 1 Samuel 28, who appears to raises the spirit of Samuel in order to predict the future for King Saul. Scot explains this event by claiming that the witch of Endor used ventriloquism to trick Saul. In the *Discoverie*, this claim is made rather briefly and backed up with reference to a more recent example of similar trickery in Westwell in Kent. The absence of any reference to ventriloquism in the treatise is notable in view of the lengthy responses the author provides to Scot's other comments on the witch of Endor, especially in reason 85. In this section of the treatise, the author responds to arguments found in chapters 11, 12, and 13 of book 7 of the printed *Discoverie*. At the end of chapter 13, Scot provides a cross-reference to his ventriloquism argument, which appears in the opening chapters of the same book. The fact that this argument is presented separately from the rest of the discussion, together with the fact that the author does not respond or refer to Scot's ventriloquism argument at any point in the treatise, suggests that Scot developed these ideas (relying, again, on Weyer) at a later date, but inserted them into the *Discoverie* at the start of book 7 rather than after his earlier thoughts on the subject.

The treatise also provides a faint hint that all or part of book 13, the section in which Scot deals with the subject of natural magic, might originally have formed a separate book in much the same way that the *Discourse upon divels and spirits* does in the printed version. While the contents of book 13 do not receive a direct response in the treatise, the author is clearly aware of some of them. Pointing out that Scot denies miraculous power to witches, but grants it to natural phenomena, the author writes that 'you confess a true transubstantiating of wood into stones by the quality of certain waters here in England, and that coral of herbs in the sea become stones being taken thence' (fol. 57v, reason 8). Later, he returns to this point, saying 'I dare affirm that all the philosophers in the world were never able to render any reason for the natural effects of those herbs and stones and bodies of men which you in your treatise of magic natural have mentioned' (fol. 68v, reason 44). The use of the word 'treatise' here seems to imply that the section of the *Discoverie* on natural magic – now forming the first part

---

100 Kaptianiak (ed.), *La Sorcellerie Démystifiée*, p. 215, footnote 2, and several subsequent notes to books 6 and 7.

of book 13 – was originally a distinct work, perhaps appended to the draft as book 17 was eventually appended to the final version of the *Discoverie*.

In the end, theories about whether specific parts of the *Discoverie* were or were not included in the draft version can only be speculative. Nevertheless, it is apparent from a careful reading of both the treatise and the printed *Discoverie* that the original format of the lost draft of the *Discoverie* became unsuited to the expanding text, suggesting that Scot had originally planned a much shorter work than the one he eventually completed. In the early part of the treatise, the reasons to which the author responds correspond to very short passages of text. As can be seen from table 2 above, reasons 17 to 29 cover just three short chapters; pages 11 to 15 in the printed *Discoverie*. Reason 17 responds to what is now the first paragraph of book 1, chapter 5; reason 18 responds to the following paragraph and the opening of the first paragraph of chapter 6; reasons 19 to 29 respond to the remainder of chapters 6 and 7 almost line by line. The individual reasons frequently deal with arguments that do not, in the printed book, form a whole paragraph. This suggests that much of the early part of Scot's draft was composed of short arguments, sometimes little more than bullet points, rather than an extended argumentative text.

However, later in the treatise it becomes clear that the author is responding to quite lengthy pieces of text. Reason 85, referred to above, is a response to a series of arguments about the interpretation of the story of the witch of Endor. These arguments are presented in book 7 of the published *Discoverie*, where they have been broken up into three chapters: 11 to 13 (pp. 143–50). Having gone from arguments composed of a sarcastic sentence or two to discussions of complex exegetical and theological matters, it would eventually have become obvious to Scot that a list of numbered reasons would no longer be adequate as a structure for his work. The awkwardness of a format in which some sections consisted of a sentence or two, while others took up several pages, necessitated the reorganisation of the draft from numbered reasons into books and chapters.

At some point after the draft version was composed, Scot (or his editor, Abraham Fleming) must therefore have taken the early parts of his work and combined reasons to form chapters, and then organised the chapters into books; Scot's translator Pierre Kapitaniak has recently argued that the structure of the printed *Discoverie* was inspired by Johannes Weyer's book *De Praestigiis Daemonum* (along with much else).[101] Some of the later reasons could instead form entire chapters by themselves – reasons 86, 87, and 88, for example, seem to correspond very closely to chapters 1, 2, and

---

101 Kaptianiak (ed.), *La Sorcellerie Démystifiée*, p. 17.

3 of book 8 of the *Discoverie*. In some cases, Scot seems in the published version to have broken a reason up into multiple chapters (as with reason 85). Sometimes this editorial process resulted in rather artificial chapter divisions, as in the break between chapters 18 and 19 in book 3, which interrupts the flow of Scot's argument (see the excerpts from the *Discoverie* presented with reason 71 below). As has already been noted, Scot apparently did this without making many changes to the order in which these reasons had originally appeared, but new material has often been woven into the newly formed books and chapters.

Most scholars writing on Scot have tended to emphasise the evidence for a later date for the *Discoverie*, and tend to assume that Scot wrote it in a relatively short period of time. At least part of the book was written in 1583, as Notestein pointed out, since Scot refers at one point to a book published during 'this present yeare 1583'.[102] Kapitaniak has suggested that the entire *Discoverie* was written between April 1582 and the late spring of 1584. Pointing to the pamphlet by W. W. as the likely impetus for the book, Kapitaniak claims that '[a]s W.W.'s pamphlet was published in April 1582, it is safe to assume that Scot did not start working on the *Discoverie* before that date'.[103] But the treatise suggests that the draft version of the *Discoverie* may not have mentioned W. W.'s pamphlet at all, and there is no reason to assume that Scot was entirely uninterested in the subject of witchcraft before 1582; indeed, his obvious interest in and knowledge of the 1581 trial of Margaret Simons suggests otherwise. Even allowing for Scot's dependence on Weyer for much of his material, to have written such an enormous book and seen it through the publication process in this brief time, in addition to his duties as surveyor of Romney Marsh and playing an important role in the rebuilding of Dover harbour in 1583, seems improbably fast.[104]

It has been suggested that Scot might have written parts of the *Discoverie* much earlier than 1584. Simon Davies noted the existence of an entry in the Stationers' Register in September 1576 for a book entitled 'A warninge againste the superstition of wytches and the madnes of magicians', and hypothesised that this might have been an early version of the *Discoverie*. Davies points out in favour of this suggestion the similarity of both topic and language, and argues further that:

> The 1576 entry comes before the Windsor witch-trial of 1579 and the St Osyth witch-trial of 1582 (and their accompanying news pamphlets), and

---

102 Notestein, *A History of Witchcraft in England, 1558–1718*, p. 58; Scot, 6.7, p. 124.
103 Kapitaniak, 'From Grindal to Whitgift', paras 6, 9.
104 Kapitaniak, 'From Grindal to Whitgift', para. 7; Raphael Holinshed, *Chronicles*, vol. 6 (1587), p. 1541.

before the publication in 1581 of *De La Demonomanie Des Sorciers* by Jean Bodin—Scot's great antagonist. Perhaps these works delayed the publication of Scot's own work, possibly inspiring him to substantially lengthen it.[105]

There is no direct external evidence to support this suggestion, but the evidence of the treatise likewise suggests alterations made as a result of events recent at the time of publication.[106] Davies' view, that Scot's work on witchcraft began early and evolved in the early 1580s, cannot be proven, but it is strikingly consistent with the evidence of the treatise – and perhaps also with the evidence of the *Discoverie* itself, in which Scot felt moved to write 'I see my booke groweth to be greater than I meant it should be.'[107]

A final question is whether Scot ever actually read the treatise, and, if so, whether he made alterations to the *Discoverie* based on what he had read. At first sight, there seems to be little evidence of this. Passages in Scot's published *Discoverie* are obviously identical with large chunks of the draft to which the treatise responds; it is precisely this that makes it possible to identify the treatise as a response to Scot. However, a careful reading reveals occasional hints that some changes in the published *Discoverie* may have been made in response to feedback from the author (or to similar feedback from another respondent to the draft, or perhaps merely by coincidence). To take one example, in response to Scot's interpretation of Deuteronomy 18:10–11, the author states that 'here I must put you in remembrance the text speaketh not of raising the dead but of asking counsel of the dead' (fol. 86v, reason 83). In the published *Discoverie*, this point seems to have been taken into account, as Scot writes about one 'that asketh counsell of the dead, or (as some translate it) that raiseth the dead.'[108] There are other faint signs that changes and corrections might have been made on the basis of the author's comments; some of these are pointed out in footnotes to reasons 14, 41, 43, 50, 69, and 86 below. If Scot did see the treatise before publishing the *Discoverie*, however, the changes he made as a result were minor. But the treatise might have helped bring Scot to a realisation that his theological arguments and treatment of continental demonology were insufficiently developed and needed to be

---

105 Simon F. Davies, 'A Possible Stationers' Register Entry for Scot's *Discouerie of Witchcraft*', *Notes and Queries* 59:1 (2012), 41–3 (p. 42).
106 Kapitaniak regards Davies' suggestion as 'impossible', or perhaps merely 'far-fetched' [Fr. *impossible*], on the grounds that the *Discoverie* borrows its structure from the 1577 edition of Weyer. But the structure of the *Discoverie*, as the treatise demonstrates, changed significantly in its published form from Scot's earlier draft version. See *La Sorcellerie Démystifiée*, p. 19, note 58.
107 Scot, 12.15, p. 207 [256].
108 Scot 6.2, p. 91 [113–14].

strengthened and expanded – even if he did not alter his fundamental positions on these questions.

Scholarly understanding of Reginald Scot and the *Discoverie* has undergone a number of modifications over the past fifty years or so. In the 1970s, Sidney Anglo expressed what was then probably the dominant view when he described Scot as a 'secret Sadducee', endorsing James VI and I's judgement of him as a crypto-atheist who went through the motions of paying respect to religious belief while in reality basing his views on a relentless (and godless) empiricism.[109] This view accorded a great deal of significance to Scot's claims to have investigated witchcraft, made at greatest length in book 13 of the *Discoverie*, and shared much common ground with earlier ideas of Scot as a rationalist who was ahead of his time in standing up to witchcraft belief.

Leland Estes, in an important article on the subject, was the first to seriously contest this long-standing view.[110] Estes sometimes exaggerated in the course of what was then a revisionist reading. In downplaying Scot's reputation as an empirical investigator of witchcraft, Estes states that some of Scot's discussion of conjuring tricks 'is copied word for word from books to which Scot very gladly directs the reader's attention', and provides a reference to 13.33 in Scot.[111] There is in fact nothing in this chapter to support Estes' contention; the books to which Scot refers in 13.33 have no writing in them, but feature multi-coloured pages used in a trick exploiting an optical illusion. Scot merely points out that such books are available for sale in Paul's churchyard in London. More generally, however, Estes was surely right to argue that the 'empirical' character of the *Discoverie* had been exaggerated. As Estes points out, Scot is an author 'under the spell of the printed word', relying primarily not on empirical research but on written authority for his arguments.[112]

Less persuasively, Estes found in Scot not a godless rationalist but a 'deeply religious man', who 'found in [his] religion strong reasons for believing that witches did not really exist.'[113] The view of Scot as driven to argue against witchcraft on the basis of his religious convictions has found

---

109 Sydney Anglo, 'Reginald Scot's *Discoverie of Witchcraft*: Scepticism and Sadduceeism', in *The Damned Art*, edited by Sydney Anglo (London: Routledge & Kegan Paul, 1977), pp. 106–39.
110 Leland L. Estes, 'Reginald Scot and his *Discoverie of Witchcraft*: Religion and Science in the Opposition to the European Witch Craze', *Church History* 52:4 (1983), 444–56.
111 Estes, 'Reginald Scot and his *Discoverie of Witchcraft*', p. 445.
112 Estes, 'Reginald Scot and his *Discoverie of Witchcraft*', p. 455.
113 Estes, 'Reginald Scot and his *Discoverie of Witchcraft*', pp. 446, 450.

support among many subsequent writers on the subject, often in spite of disagreement on the exact nature of those convictions.[114] David Wootton, in the course of his attempt to demonstrate that Scot was a sympathiser with or member of the Family of Love, claims that Scot presents, for example, allegorical readings of the Bible and exclusively spiritual demons '[b]ecause this was orthodox Familism', identifying Scot's rhetorical strategy with his personal religious beliefs.[115] Philip Almond, while disagreeing with Wootton about Scot's alleged Familist sympathies, has recently characterised Scot as adopting 'a radical theological position' which 'necessitated ... a radical re-reading of the Scriptures'.[116]

Sometimes, Scot's reading of the Bible is radical, or at least troubling, from the perspective of the treatise. Wootton, as noted above, has pointed out the similarities with arguments advanced by the Family of Love, and Scot's use of allegorical readings would in general have troubled many Reformed Christians at this time. The author of the treatise also expresses disquiet when Scot raises inconsistencies in the Bible, writing of two seemingly conflicting passages that 'except we hold the one to be true as well as the other, we must make the holy ghost a liar in the one of them, which to avoid, the true sense of the places is to be sought out whereby they may be reconciled without any such reproach or blasphemy to the holy ghost' (fol. 101v, reason 106). Here the treatise author seems to reveal his own anxieties about the Bible, and proposes an approach to it which is in line with that of religiously conservative Christians today: reading a rigorous consistency into a book (or anthology of books) which simply does not possess that quality.[117] However, such moments are rare, and much more frequently, the treatise reveals in great clarity and detail that Scot's re-reading of the Bible is not so much radical as simply mendacious.

Scot's interpretation of scripture is frequently called into question in the treatise, and it is apparent not only that the author knows the Bible and theological and exegetical writings much better than Scot, but also that he treats these writings with much greater respect. While he is consistently

---

114 See, for example, Clark, *Thinking with Demons*, p. 242; Wootton, 'Reginald Scot / Abraham Fleming / The Family of Love', in *Languages of Witchcraft*, edited by Stuart Clark (Basingstoke: Macmillan, 2001), pp. 119–38, pp. 121–4. Pierre Kapitaniak summarises the various suggestions that have been put forward from Estes onwards: Scot has been called, among other things, an Erastian, a puritan, a puritan turncoat, a Familist, and a spiritualist: see *La Sorcellerie Démystifiée*, pp. 50–1.
115 Wootton, 'Reginald Scot / Abraham Fleming / The Family of Love', p. 132.
116 Philip Almond, *England's First Demonologist* (London: I. B. Tauris, 2011), p. 179.
117 John Barton, *A History of the Bible* (New York: Penguin, 2019), pp. 7–12.

generous in interpreting Scot's interpretations of scripture as merely erroneous rather than as wilful distortions, this generous attitude strains credulity at times. Scot, commenting on a passage from Corinthians, writes that:

> [Paul] saith, That which is spirituall onelie discerneth spirituall things: for no carnall man can discerne the things of the spirit. Why then should we thinke that a divell, which is a spirit, can be knowne, or made tame and familiar unto a naturall man; or contrarie to nature, can be by a witch made corporall, being by God ordeined to a spirituall proportion?[118]

The passage from Corinthians and the following verse, in the Geneva Bible, are as follows:

> But the naturall man perceiueth not the things of the Spirit of God: for they are foolishnesse vnto him: neither can hee knowe them, because they are spiritually discerned. But hee that is spirituall, discerneth all things: yet he himselfe is iudged of no man. (1 Corinthians 2:14–15)

Scot's claim, that this passage provides evidence that 'natural' men (which he apparently takes to mean all people, as creatures of flesh and blood) cannot have any contact with spirits, is an obvious distortion of its meaning, which distinguishes between 'natural' and 'spiritual' men. The author points this out very mildly, writing merely that 'how any of these words may be applied to your purpose I see not' (fol. 98r, reason 102), before outlining a more orthodox – and more plausible – interpretation of the passage.

This tolerant attitude is in contrast to another manuscript response to Scot by George Wyatt, a grandson of the poet Thomas Wyatt and biographer of Anne Boleyn. The Wyatt and Scot families – both from Kent – had some close links; Scot's cousin Charles Scot married Jane Wyatt.[119] Despite the family ties, however, Wyatt is perturbed by Scot's apparently wilful misinterpretation of Calvin's commentary on Job:

> Truly a man would hardly think that a gentleman that in all things professeth faithfulness and especially a Kentishman where there are so many able to discern what is right should so far corrupt his pen to take so many sentences scattered so diversely in so few sermons of Job and yet to be carried with so contrary an opinion to the plain words of the author[.][120]

---

118 Scot, 17.12, p. 427 [508].
119 The couple's son was another author, William Scott, who wrote the manuscript treatise *The Model of Poesy*, published in an edition by Gavin Alexander (Cambridge: Cambridge University Press, 2013), a major early modern work of literary criticism (p. xix).
120 London, British Library, Add. MS 62135, fols 416–23 (fols 421r–421v). Spelling has been modernised.

Wyatt was outraged by Scot's selective quotation and his abuse of Calvin's great authority – a point also made in the treatise, for example in reason 77.

Much of the hostility directed towards Scot's book may have resulted as much from his disrespectful treatment of his sources as from his opposition to witchcraft prosecutions. Scot's bitterest enemies, such as Holland, certainly took exception to his approach as much as to his conclusions, but even one of his friends (less harshly, but also much more thoroughly) felt the need to criticise his style of argument, and in particular his abuse of the Bible and other religious authorities. It is clear that, as the author of the treatise points out, Scot repeatedly mischaracterises the positions of St Augustine and Calvin, often quoting in a selective and misleading manner, and presenting readings of the Bible which are plainly distortions. It is, of course, impossible to prove that these distortions were intentional, but it is also extremely difficult to believe that they were not.

None of this is to say that Scot was, in fact, the secret Sadducee that Anglo described; his friend the author, who actually knew Scot, certainly does not seem to have seen him this way. Disagreeing with Scot about the nature of demonic possession as represented in the New Testament, the author writes that 'I dare assure myself that (yourself excepted) you are not able to nominate one man learned and of sound religion that is of that opinion' (fol. 99v, reason 104), tactfully making clear that Scot himself is not only learned, but also of sound religion. But whatever Scot's private religious beliefs may have been, they do not seem to have stood in the way of some very tendentious argumentation, as the treatise so thoroughly demonstrates. Scot's overriding concern was to combat witchcraft belief. In order to do so, he was prepared to blatantly misrepresent the authority of revered theologians like Calvin and Augustine, and play fast and loose even with the Bible itself. Scot, when read in the light of the treatise, appears to have been an essentially polemical author, certain of his cause and uninterested in scholarly and doctrinal niceties. He decided on his conclusion before he began his research, and everything he read and wrote was made to fit that conclusion.

The Scot that is reflected in the mirror of the treatise is not one that is easily recognisable in much recent work by historians of witchcraft. This Scot's work is not based on a particular view of spirit which has led him to his position on witchcraft; it adopts this view, understandably but perhaps rather carelessly, as the most convenient way to reach his predetermined position on witchcraft. There seems little reason to doubt that his desire to prove the unreality of witchcraft (as it was usually understood by his contemporaries) depended not on intellectual or theological grounds, but on the distaste for witchcraft prosecutions that he so frequently and colourfully expressed in the *Discoverie*. This Scot may lack the intellectual sophistication he is often credited with, but he is recognisably the author of his previous work *A Perfite*

Platforme of a Hoppe Garden (1574), who wrote the book, in part, because he felt that it would help to alleviate the suffering of the poor.[121]

Sources

An exhaustive account of the sources used in compiling the treatise is unnecessary and possibly impracticable, but some brief remarks may be helpful. The author of the treatise refers to, and quotes from, a number of early modern theologians and patristic writers. Some of these are mentioned because Scot cites or quotes them in his arguments, but many are utilised in arguments the author constructed himself. By far the most frequently cited authorities, unsurprisingly given the period and what has already been said about the author's religious inclinations, are Calvin and St Augustine, and frequent mention is also made of Peter Martyr Vermigli. Other Reformed theologians are also cited in the treatise, including Theodore Beza, Heinrich Bullinger, and Wolfgang Musculus. Some of the older authors referred to include Cyprian and Chrysostom, who is quoted at some length. There is a brief citation of Tertullian, and the Church historians Epiphanius, Eusebius, and Theodoret are mentioned. Authors who wrote in Greek, such as Chrysostom and Cyprian, are always quoted in Latin rather than the original Greek. Nevertheless, the author evidently had at least some knowledge of Greek, as he discusses the meaning of the Greek word ἀποστασία in disputing the precise signification of the word 'apostasy' (fol. 79v, reason 71). The treatise author also refers to more recent Catholic writings. He cites writers on the lives of the popes – Cardinal Benno, Bartolomeo Platina, and Giovanni Stella – albeit only in order to criticise the papacy. The treatise also refers to Gratian's *Decretum*, a twelfth-century compilation of canon law, in order to discuss the canons known (after their opening words) as *Nec mirum* and *Episcopi*, both of which were especially relevant to the later Renaissance debate on witchcraft.[122]

The Bible is quoted in both Latin and English, raising the question of which versions the author used. In the case of the English Bible, it seems

---

121 Scot, *A Perfite Platforme of a Hoppe Garden* (London, 1574), sigs B2r–B2v. Scot lists a large number of sources in the *Discoverie*, suggesting very wide reading on his part. However, Pierre Kapitaniak has suggested that Scot may actually have consulted less than a third of these sources, and credits Scot's editor Abraham Fleming with providing many of the notes and indirect sources listed: *La Sorcellerie Démystifiée*, p. 28.

122 See Alan Kors and Edward Peters (eds), *Witchcraft in Europe, 400–1700: A Documentary History*, 2nd ed. (Philadelphia, PA: University of Pennsylvania

likely that he was most familiar with the most popular version at the time, the Geneva text; quotations or paraphrases from the Bible are typically very similar to this version. In referring to the story of Cain and Abel in Genesis 4, for instance, the author writes that 'it is said of Cain that he, being exceeding wroth, his countenance fell down' (fol. 61v, reason 19). This is very close to the Geneva text: 'Kain was exceeding wroth, and his countenance fell downe', but different from the same passage in most other English bibles that were available at the time. Both the Bishop's Bible of 1568 and the Great Bible of 1539 say that Cain's countenance 'abated', while the Coverdale translation of 1535 has 'changed'. Many other passages are similarly close or identical to the Geneva text – the quotations from the apocryphal Wisdom of Solomon in reason 51 seem to have been copied from it word for word – and for this reason I have used this version throughout in quoting from the Bible, unless otherwise stated. It should be noted, however, that the author also seems to paraphrase the text of the Bible quite frequently, perhaps indicating that he quoted from memory at least some of the time.

The Latin text used by the author presents a more difficult question. The most popular Latin text of the Bible in print in England in the early 1580s, judging by the number of editions on the Early English Books Online database, was the Old Testament of Immanuel Tremellius together with either his Latin translation of the Syriac New Testament or the Latin New Testament of Theodore Beza, or (in some editions) both. But the author's Latin quotations typically do not match the text found in these editions, nor do they match the New Testament of Erasmus (Basel, 1516), the Latin texts used in the various editions of Calvin's commentaries, the translation of Sebastian Castellio (Basel, 1551), or that of the Dominican scholar Santes Pagnino (Lyon, 1527).

The Vulgate was still the most widely available version of the Latin Bible in the late sixteenth century, and there are signs that the author may have used some version of it. However, textual variations within the Vulgate text were so common that it is perhaps misleading to speak of it as a 'version' of the Bible prior to the Clementine edition of 1592. This edition, named after Pope Clement VIII, standardised the text within the Catholic Church and replaced the previous attempt to do so – the controversial version published under the previous pope, Sixtus V, in 1590.[123] Nevertheless, the treatise

---

Press, 2001), pp. 72–5; on the canon *Episcopi*, see also Stephens, *Demon Lovers*, pp. 127–37 and the discussion in the 'Significance' section above.

[123] For an overview of the variety of Latin editions of the Bible during the early modern period see Josef Eskhult, 'Latin Bible Versions in the Age of Reformation and Post-Reformation', *Kyrkohistorisk årsskrift* 106:1 (31–67). See also Bruce Gordon, 'Latin Bibles in the Early Modern Period', in *The New Cambridge History of the Bible* (Cambridge: Cambridge University Press, 2016), pp. 187–216.

author's paraphrase of Jeremiah 17:9, which appears in reason 38, resembles an unusual wording that was used in the Sixtine text of 1590.

The author writes '*pravum et inscrutabile est cor hominis*'; 'The heart of man is shrewd and vnsearchable', according to the translation in a 1612 study of 'contradictions and contrarieties' in the two Vulgate Bibles by the scholar Thomas James.[124] All of the other Latin bibles from the period that I have consulted use the word *omnium* ('[above] all things') rather than *hominis* ('human'/'of man'), and in the Geneva text this passage is translated as 'The heart is deceitful and wicked above all things'. Obviously the treatise author could not have used a printed edition of the 1590 Sixtine Vulgate since it had yet to be published when he wrote in the early 1580s, and it is in any case unlikely that it was ever widely available in England. But this textual variant clearly predates the publication of the Sixtine edition and may have come from an earlier version of the Vulgate.

In addition, in his marginal references to the Bible the author uses the numbering system found in the Vulgate, which refers to the two books of Samuel as the first and second books of Kings, and the two books of Kings as the third and fourth (see reason 48 below). That the author uses this older system is curious, since the division now used was first introduced in Protestant Bibles (including the Geneva Bible) and came into use from the start of the Reformation. This may therefore reflect use of an older Vulgate text on his part. The numbering of Psalms in the author's references, however, does not match the numbering in the Vulgate and Septuagint (the earliest Greek translation of a version of the Hebrew Bible), but the Hebrew numbering system which was preferred in Protestant Bibles (see the footnote to reason 49 below).[125]

On the basis of what is known about early modern scholarly practice, it is quite likely that the author consulted a commentary (or commentaries) on the Bible while writing the treatise, and a commentary may have been the source of some of the Latin quotations from the Bible as well.[126] The most widely available and popular biblical commentary during the sixteenth

---

124 Thomas James, *A treatise of the corruption of Scripture, councels, and fathers, by the prelats, pastors, and pillars of the Church of Rome* (London, 1612), part 3, p. 25. Similar wording is also used elsewhere, however, such as in the 1577 Lutheran Formula of Concord: see *Concordia Triglotta*, edited by F. Bente (St Louis, MO: Concordia Publishing House, 1921), p. 886.
125 On the origins of the Septuagint and its divergence from the Hebrew Bible as it is known today, see Barton, *A History of the Bible*, pp. 437–42.
126 Katrin Ettenhuber, 'The Preacher and Patristics', in *The Oxford Handbook of the Early Modern Sermon* (Oxford: Oxford University Press, 2011), pp. 34–53 (p. 40).

century was still the *Catena Aurea*, a compilation put together in the fourteenth century by the great medieval theologian Thomas Aquinas.[127] There is good reason to suspect that the author used this commentary, or one heavily indebted to it, in compiling the treatise. In his discussion of the term 'generation of vipers' used in the gospel of Matthew, the author quotes from both 'the ancient father Remigius' and Chrysostom. Both of the passages he reproduces are presented in the relevant section of the *Catena Aurea*, and another of the author's references to Chrysostom also appears in the *Catena* (see fols 66v and 105r in reasons 36 and 107 and the relevant footnotes). The Latin translation of Chrysostom used in the treatise matches that in the *Catena*, which is the twelfth-century text of Burgundio of Pisa (d. 1194).[128]

It may seem unlikely that a decidedly Protestant Elizabethan clergyman would be willing to use the works of a man Martin Luther described as 'the source and foundation of all heresy, error, and obliteration of the gospel'.[129] But in fact, English puritans – Reformed rather than Lutheran Protestants – were not necessarily as anti-Thomist as might be assumed. David Sytsma has recently shown that the highly regarded anti-Catholic polemicist William Whitaker made extensive use of Aquinas' commentaries in his *Disputatio de Sacra Scriptura* (Cambridge, 1588), and regarded them as essentially consistent with Protestant perspectives on scripture.[130] The *Catena*, as a compilation of commentary from earlier theologians and patristic authors rather than Aquinas' own writings, would in any case have raised fewer concerns of this nature.

The author was evidently a working clergyman with practical responsibilities, and was not in a position to dedicate himself solely to scholarship. His probable use of commentaries is, perhaps, one indication of this, but he also shows himself to be unaware of (or perhaps unconvinced by) the scholarship of Erasmus; he refers to pseudo-Chrysostom's *Opus Imperfectum in Matthaeum*, an unfinished commentary on the gospel of Matthew, as Chrysostom's work, a long-standing misconception that was first shown

---

127 Carl Trueman, 'Preachers and Renaissance and Medieval Commentary', in *The Oxford Handbook of the Early Modern Sermon* (Oxford: Oxford University Press, 2011), pp. 54–71 (p. 59).
128 James A. Weisheipl, *Friar Thomas D'Aquino* (Oxford: Blackwell, 1974), p. 122.
129 Quoted in the introduction to *Aquinas Among the Protestants*, edited by Manfred Svensson and David VanDrunen (Oxford: Wiley, 2018), p. 1.
130 David Sytsma, 'Thomas Aquinas and Reformed Biblical Interpretation: The Contribution of William Whitaker', in *Aquinas Among the Protestants*, edited by Manfred Svensson and David VanDrunen (Oxford: Wiley, 2018), pp. 49–74 (pp. 60–1).

to be wrong by Erasmus in 1530.[131] The treatise reveals that the author also believed the passage of text included in canon law as *Nec mirum* to have been composed by St Augustine; it is actually from Hrabanus Maurus' ninth-century *De Magicis Artibus*, which paraphrases Augustine and others.[132] Another pseudo-Augustinian work containing a different version of *Nec mirum*, the *Quaestiones Veteris et Novi Testamenti*, is also mistakenly attributed to Augustine. The inaccuracy of this attribution, which again was first pointed out by Erasmus, was known to the Bishop of Winchester, Thomas Bilson, by 1599, when he wrote that 'the questions of the olde testament vnder the name of S. Austen, cited in the Canon law … though they be not Austens, are verie ancient.'[133] These errors, however, are on relatively obscure matters and do not seriously undermine the author's claim to expertise on exegetical matters.

Notes on the text

This edition is arranged in the same way as the manuscript – as a list of numbered 'reasons', which are responses to the reasons presented in a draft version of Scot's *Discoverie*. In order to highlight the relationship between the two texts, I have included excerpts from the printed *Discoverie* before the text of each reason in the treatise in all cases where it has been possible to connect the arguments in the treatise with passages in the *Discoverie*. In a small number of cases these excerpts are suggestions as to what *might* have prompted the response in the treatise, but very frequently there are clear verbal parallels between the two passages which, in my view, allow for a confident connection to be made between them. The excerpts from Scot are distinguished from the text of the treatise typographically. Since some of the treatise's 'reasons', as discussed above, respond to several points in the printed *Discoverie*, these reasons are presented together with extracts from multiple chapters. I have provided references to the relevant book and chapter of Scot for each extract; the *Discourse upon divels and spirits* appended to the 16 books of the *Discoverie* is numbered as book 17.

The text is presented with modernised spelling in order to make it as accessible as possible. This decision was prompted by the fact that the

---

131 See the introduction to the *Incomplete Commentary on Matthew*, translated by James A. Kellerman, edited by Thomas C. Oden (Downers Grove, IL: InterVarsity Press, 2010), p. xix.
132 Kors and Peters (eds), *Witchcraft in Europe, 400–1700*, p. 73.
133 Thomas Bilson, *Certaine sermons touching the full redemption of mankind by the death and bloud of Christ* (London, 1599), p. 210.

treatise is unusually dense and hard to follow at times, even by the standards of early modern manuscripts, owing to its nature as a working document produced by an author who must have had many other demands on his time. Punctuation in the original is notable mainly by its absence; the few punctuation marks that are present are often placed in seemingly random positions within the author's interminable sentences. The word 'and', rather than any kind of punctuation, often introduces what is effectively a new sentence. Minimal punctuation, in accordance with modern expectations, has been added, including some quotation marks where this was felt to be helpful, and the author's own punctuation has sometimes been moved or deleted in the interests of clarity. Nevertheless, the author's sentences remain rather cumbersome. Capitalisation has also been standardised in accordance with modern practice, and the author's spaces have been removed from what are now familiar compound words, such as 'can not' and 'in deed' – here rendered as 'cannot' and 'indeed'.

There are numerous interlineal additions to, and deletions from, the text: these are silently added or removed as appropriate in order to provide a clean and uninterrupted text for the reader, who is assumed to be interested primarily in the content of the treatise. I have silently corrected some obvious minor slips of the pen and a few minor grammatical errors. I have in some cases deleted superfluous words that were obviously written in error, and have added words (in square brackets) where they have been omitted. Latin quotations and phrases have been italicised. There are a few instances in the text of unpaired brackets – an opening bracket without a closing bracket. In these cases I have silently added the missing bracket in the, or at least an, appropriate place.

The most significant textual problem with the treatise is that some words in the original manuscript are illegible, owing either to tight binding, damage to the edge of some pages, weathering to the paper, or badly faded ink. This is especially so on the first page, but in the large majority of cases these missing words do not seriously obscure the author's intended meaning. In these cases, conjectural readings of the words have been provided in curly brackets. Where part of a word is clearly visible, the relevant letters have been provided outside of the curly brackets, with the conjectured word ending following inside. For example, if the ending of a word conjectured to be 'witches' were not legible, but the first three letters were, the word would appear in the text as 'wit{ches}'.

It was felt to be desirable to retain the flavour of the original as far as possible, notwithstanding the modernised spelling. In accordance with this aim, early modern verb endings and familiar early modern words such as 'doth', 'leaveth', and so on have been kept, as has the early modern genitive form seen, for example, in the phrase 'Ulysses his followers'. Obsolete words have not been modernised, although their spelling has been; I have preserved terms such as 'sith', while modernising the spelling from the author's usual 'sythe', rather than changing it to 'since', and words like 'unpossible', 'holden', 'drunken' (as a past tense verb rather than an adjective), and 'throughly' have likewise been left as they are. Definitions from the OED are provided in footnotes in the case of less familiar obsolete words. Latinised forms of names are in general preserved; where, for example, the demonologist Lambert Daneau is mentioned, the author's form Danaeus is kept. An exception has been made with names from characters in the Bible; the Old Testament prophet is 'Elias' in the treatise, but has been changed to the now much more familiar 'Elijah' in this text in the interests of clarity.

The author has made numerous marginal notes to his main text. Usually these are references to his sources; most frequently books of the Bible, but also other works. These references are often provided in Latin; for example, the books of Kings would usually be referred to as 'regu[m]' in the margin. I have moved these authorial notes to footnotes in my text, preserving in these cases the original spelling, and providing more exact references in addition to the author's notes, which usually specify chapter but not verse when citing the Bible. Quotations from other sources, including Reginald Scot, have not been modernised, since they are much less difficult to comprehend in their original form than the treatise would be. Footnotes providing marginal references are not placed on the basis of where the marginal note appears in the text, but are placed after the relevant sentence, in accordance with modern practice.

Passages in Latin in the main text have been transcribed with scribal abbreviations rendered as letters. Spelling has not been otherwise altered, but passages of Latin works have been checked against modern or early modern printed editions, which are listed in the bibliography, and any significant differences are pointed out in footnotes. Very often, however, the author appears to have accurately copied passages from books. English translations are provided for Latin quotations and phrases, wherever possible from published translations identified in the relevant footnote. In a few cases, the translations are mine or have been adapted. In most of these cases, my Latin has been checked, and where necessary corrected, by Dr Victor Wahlström, to whom I am extremely grateful for his assistance; any remaining errors are certainly mine.

The treatise

A defence of witchcraft belief

[f. 57r] Reason 5

Neither hath God given remedies to sicknes or greefes, by words or charmes, but by hearbs and medicines; which he himselfe hath created upon earth, and given men knowledge of the same; that he might be glorified, for that therewith he dooth vouchsafe that the maladies of men and cattell should be cured, &c. And if there be no affliction nor calamitie, but is brought to passe by him, then let us defie the divell, renounce all his works, and not so much as once thinke or dreame upon this supernaturall power of witches; neither let us prosecute them with such despight, whome our fansie condemneth, and our reason acquiteth: our evidence against them consisting in impossibilities, our proofes in unwritten verities, and our whole proceedings in doubts and difficulties. (Scot, Epistle to the readers)

Though there be no affliction nor calamity but it is bro{ught} to pass by the Lord, yet may we think upon the supernatural power of witches and impute many things thereunto, because it may please God (who at his pleasure useth as well the evil as the good for his instruments to pla{gue}, punish, and afflict) by witches and such like to do s{uch} supernatural things upon those whom he will have p{uni}shed or afflicted, even as well as it pleased him to {use} the ministry of their master the devil in afflicting Job, as shall be further proved when I come to the answering your discourse upon Job, and as he used the ministry of {the} man in whom an evil spirit was in punishing the sons of Sceva, &c.[1]

Reason 6

[See excerpt to reason 5 above]

The evidence against witches consisting upon impossibilities to natural wit and reason is not material to take away the strange effects imputed to them. For why may not they through Satan (God so giving leave) work wicked signs and wonders above reason and nature as well as the false Christ, false prophets, and Antichrist of whom mention is made (as before I have showed) that they should show great signs, wonders, and power &c. And as for the proofs against witches which you say consisteth in unwritten verities: if by unwritten verities you mean all that is not written in the scriptures, it may be said how could the things in these days ascribed to witches

---

1 Author's notes: 'Job 1. 2'; 'acts 19'. Books 1 and 2 of Job are discussed at length in reason 65 below. The seven sons of Sceva ('a Iewe, the Priest') are described in the Geneva bible as 'exorcistes' in Acts 19:13–16.

be mentioned in the scriptures, they being things done and practised so long since the scriptures were written? But if you will not reject the writings of the most sort, yea of all the most learned and godly writers in all times and ages as unwritten verities, then have you better proof {...} of their doings to be very strange and beyond reason as {...} self will not deny. Howbeit my meaning is not {...} justify the evidence or proof of Malleus Mall. or of Bodin or such like fabulous and papistical writers, neither will I justify all to be true which is testified of witches by the most learned and godly writers, though I do credit much more thereof than you do, if it were but in this one respect: that I think it much more like and probable for you alone to be deceived in this case or in any other than for all the most learned, wise, and godly of all times and ages.

Reason 7

> I have read in the scriptures, that God maketh the blustering tempests and whirlewinds ... But little thinke our witchmongers, that the Lord commandeth the clouds above, or openeth the doores of heaven, as *David* affirmeth; or that the Lord goeth forth in the tempests and stormes, as the Prophet *Nahum* reporteth: but rather that witches and conjurers are then about their businesse. (Scot, 1.1)

Your scriptures alleged to prove that God is the raiser up of rain, hail, tempests, &c is not of force to prove these things not to be done by witches or devils unless you could prove that God doth these things always immediately and never by means or second causes which I d{o} suppose you cannot prove. And the story of Job proveth [f. 57v] the contrary; also hereof is proved in the Apocalypse by that which is there spoken of the beast (whereby some understand Antichrist, the pope) which should do great wonders insomuch as he should make fire come down from heaven in the sight of men.[2]

Reason 8

> The *Martionists* acknowledged one God the authour of good things, and another the ordeiner of evill: but these make the divell a whole god, to create things of nothing, to knowe mens cogitations, and to doo that which God never did; as, to transubstantiate men into beasts, &c. (Scot, 1.1)

To impute that unto witch or devil which God never did is I suppose no absurdity but great piety. Therefore though God never did transubstantiate

---

2 A reference to Revelation 13:13. The author does not provide a note.

a man into a beast, it would not hereof follow but that devils or witches might do it as well as they do other wicked things and miracles which God doth not otherwise than by allowing them power to do the same. But as touching the manner how devils and witches do or may transubstantiate, as it is held of the best sort of writers is, as I think, no great matter to be granted. For they hold not that there is any true but only a fantastical and illuding transubstantiating of one thing into another and this, you confess, may be done by natural magic, for in your entreating thereupon you say a man may thereby make a man seem to have the head of an ass, a horse, &c.[3] Yea, you confess a true transubstantiating of wood into stones by the quality of certain waters here in England, and that coral of herbs in the sea become stones being taken thence.[4] And why then cannot he that gave this force to these insensible things give (if he please) the like force of transubstantiating things from that they were into things which before they were not to witches or devils? Whether God did ever transubstantiate a man into beast it shall be considered after in the obje{ction} of God's dealings with Nebuchadnezzar by you spok{en} of, and in the mean season I would not have you to think that I do believe that devils or witches do o{r} have done such transubstantiatings as are true and without illusion, though I say it lieth in God to give them such power, as shall be further se{en} afterwards.[5]

[f. 58r] Reason 9

> But if all the divels in hell were dead, and all the witches in *England* burnt or hanged; I warrant you we should not faile to have raine, haile and tempests, as now we have. (Scot, 1.1)

It is to be confessed that we should not fail to have rain, hail, and tempests though there were neither devil nor witch. For the Lord of hosts that hath all creatures at his commandment to do his will is not tied to work the same more by one creature than by another, yea he is tied to no creature or second means at all but may do what pleaseth him immediately and without all means. But hereof to gather that God doth not send sometimes the said things by the devil or by witches, because he would and could send though they were not existent, is in my opinion an argument of no more validity than if a man would say that Christ's disciples did not with a loud voice praise God (as is reported by St Luke) because it is there said to the

---

3 See Scot, 13.19.
4 See Scot, 13.5 and 13.6.
5 On Nebuchadnezzar, see reason 76 below.

Reason 10

> I am also well assured, that if all the old women in the world were witches; and all the priests, conjurers: we should not have a drop of raine, nor a blast of wind the more or the lesse for them. (Scot, 1.1)

The 10th reason is answered in the answer of the 37th reason, where it is showed that neither witch nor devil hath any power to do these or other things imputed unto them but of God, and therefore no marvel though it lie not in them at their pleasure to send a drop of rain more or less, &c. Neither do I think any man to be so senseless as to say they can at their pleasing send rain or tempest &c, for then would it not be confessed (as you say it is by Bodin) that not two of their witchings amongst an 100 take effect: 18 Reas.[7]

Reason 11

> The wind of the Lord, and not the wind of witches, shall destroie the treasures of their plesant vessels, and drie up the fountaines; saith *Oseas*. (Scot, 1.1)

That which is done by the Lord's will and appointment, whether it be done by witch or devil, may well be said to be done by the word of the Lord; that is to say by his power and commandment, which also is more at large showed in the answer of the 3 reason, and so is the place of Hosea to be answered.[8]

Reason 12

> The Imperiall lawe (saith *Brentius*) condemneth them to death that trouble and infect the aire: but I affirme (saith he) that it is neither in the power of witch not divell so to doo, but in God onelie. Though (bes des *Bodin*, and all the popish writers in generall) it please *Danaeus, Hyperius, Hemingius, Erastus,* &c. to conclude otherwise ... S. *Augustine* saith ... We must not thinke that these visible things are at the commandement of the angels that fell, but are obedient to the onelie God. (Scot, 1.1)

---

6 Author's note: 'Luc 19'; Luke 19:37–40.
7 In the printed version of the *Discoverie*, this appears in Scot, 1.3: '*Bodin* himselfe confesseth, that not above two in a hundred of their witchings or wishings take effect'. See also reason 18 below.
8 The reference is to Hosea 13:15.

To your 12 reason there needeth no other answer than is made to the former reason, saving that you say that Danaeus, Hyperius, and Hemmingus do other{wise} conclude of the power of witches than Brentius doth who attributeth all to the power of God, to the which I answer that as touching this point I dare wager with you a gallon of wine that Brentius and the other three do agree in one, all attributing the like power unto God and the like unto witches if they be rightly understood and construed. And now whereas you begin by the authority of men to confirm and strengthen your [f. 58v] part (sith you have in your book confessed that all sort of writers, even of the best credit, are against you) it may be said that you must not look to advantage yourself by any human authorities, except you would have the best writers to give place to others of less credit.[9] But I do not purpose thus to cut off the answering of all your human authorities, for as I shall see cause I will answer them in other sort. But as for the authority of Brentius and St August here alleged, they are not as I think gainsaid by any, neither do they anything at all abridge the power of witches &c otherwise than every man will confess, so far as I know to the contrary.

Reason 13

> Finallie, if witches could accomplish these things; what needed it seeme so strange to the people, when Christ by miracle commanded both seas and winds, &c. (Scot, 1.1)

It might as well be demanded why many of those miracles which Moses did in Egypt should seem strange sith the sorcerers and enchanter[s] of Pharaoh did the like, yea if there be (as you write) stones that turn aside tempests, provoke rain, darken the sun, and preserveth from lightning, and if there be herbs or stones that restoreth eyes or sight to the swallows that have their eyes picked out with instruments and that restore dragons and men (being dead) unto life, and finally if there be in some men's sides force to make all doors to fly open, why then should it seem strange that Christ stilled tempests, giveth rain, darkened the sun at his death, restored the blind to their sight or the dead to life, or finally that he came in to his Apostles the

---

9 This comment could refer to various passages in the printed *Discoverie*. In the epistle to Roger Manwood, Scot writes of authors promoting belief in witchcraft that 'these (my Lord) that fall into so manifest contradictions, and into such absurd asseverations, are not of the inferior sort of witers; neither are they all papists, but men of such accompt, as whose names give more credit to their cause, than their writings.' Scot also writes dismissively of all previous writers on witchcraft in 2.10; see the excerpt from Scot in reason 101 below.

doors being shut and none in the house opening them unto him?[10] If it be answered that these stones, herbs, &c have the said force and virtues from God, so you see by the premises it will be said that whatsoever strange effect shall be said to have been done by witches that they did it not by their own force and power, but by that force and power which it pleased God to allow unto them either for the trial of his children, or for the punishment of the wicked, or for some other good and just respect best known to his divine majesty.

Reason 14

> But the world is now so bewitched and over-run with this fond error, that even where a man shuld seeke comfort and counsell, there shall hee be sent (in case of necessitie) from God to the divell; and from the Physician, to the coosening witch, who will not sticke to take upon hir, by wordes to heale the lame (which was proper onelie to Christ; and to them whom he assisted with his divine power) yea, with hir familiar & charmes she will take upon hir to cure the blind: though in the tenth of S. *Johns* Gospell it be written, that the divell cannot open the eies of the blind. (Scot, 1.2)

It is not so proper to Christ to heal the lame or to do any other miracles but that he imparteth this property and power to others, else could not the prophets or Apostles have healed the lame or done any miracle. And that the power to do miracles is given as well to the wicked as to the godly the scriptures quoted in the 2 Reason, besides many other, do testify.[11] Therefore the allegation [f. 59r] of this property in Christ may not serve your turn unless you prove that which is required of you in my answer to your 7th reason, vz. that Christ doth all miracles immediately by himself and never by means, &c. And as touching your place in the 10 of John where you say it is written that it is not in the devil to open the eyes of the blind, I find not any such assertion there, but only a question propounded thereof by some of the Jews, saying 'can the devil open the eyes of the blind?'[12] But admit

---

10 The author here refers to several passages found in book 13 of the printed version of the *Discoverie*. The stones referred to are Heliotropius and Hyacinthus (Scot 13.6); the dragon restored to life with a herb is described in Scot 13.8; and the 'force' in men's sides is in Scot 13.9, which cites the theologian, philosopher, and reputed magician Albertus Magnus (d. 1280).
11 Scot's mention of 'them whom he assisted with his divine power' in the excerpt from the printed *Discoverie* might suggest that he took part of this response into account.
12 John 10:21: 'Others said, These are not the wordes of him that hathe a deuil: can the deuil open the eyes of the blinde?'

this had been no question but a plain affirmation, and that not by the Jews but by Christ himself, yet would it easily be answered by saying that the devil cannot indeed open the eyes of the blind or do any other miracle by his own virtue and power as Christ did, no more can also any other creature, and therefore if any miracle be done by any creature good or evil, the power of God must still be acknowledged to have some place in the same.

Reason 15

[This reason is not possible to connect with certainty to a specific passage in Scot, but probably responds to part of 1.2, as do the preceding and following reasons.]

To your 15 Reason I answer as to the 3, 7, and 5 reasons is before answered and as I have also answered to the 14 reason.

Reason 16

S. *Paule* fore-sawe the blindnesse and obstinacie, both of these blind shepheards, and also of their scabbed sheepe, when he said; They will not suffer wholsome doctrine, but having their eares itching, shall get them a heape of teachers after their own lusts; and shall turne their eares from the truth, and shall be given to fables. And in the latter time some shall depart from the faith, and shall give heed to spirits of errors, and doctrines of divels, which speake lies (as witches and conjurers doo) but cast thou awaie such prophane and old wives fables.[13] In which sense Basil saith; Who so giveth heed to inchanters, hearkeneth to a fabulous and frivolous thing. (Scot, 1.2)

Your restraining of St Paul's words bidding us to cast away profane and old wives' fables to the only forbidding of witchcraft is a restraining of a general to a particular, as it were of *genus* to *species*, or rather of *genus* to *individuum*, for St Paul in those words indefinitely pronounced meaneth the forbidding not of any one or two profane and old wives' fables but generally of all profane, false, and fabulous doctrines and speeches contrary and repugnant to the sincere doctrine of the gospel without exception, so that his indefinite sentence hath here (as the best interpreters do gather) the nature of a universal sentence as touching the thing therein forbidden. As touching the saying of Basil, it is very good to dehort[14] men from trusting to enchanters, but whether he meant by these words (vain and frivolous)

---

13 Scot paraphrases some of the early verses of 1 Timothy 4.
14 OED: 'To use exhortation to dissuade (a person) from a course or purpose; to advise or counsel against (an action, etc.).'

that enchanters could do no such things as are imputed to them it may be doubted. And if he so meant, yet he spoke in that sense being perhaps himself ignorant what they could do, as one not much studied or occupied in those kind of studies or practices. If you had quoted the place legibly it might be I should have made some further answer to it by perusing it {?}

[f. 59v] Reason 17

> But whatsoever is reported or conceived of such maner of witchcrafts, I dare avow to be false and fabulous (coosinage, dotage, and poisoning excepted:) neither is there any mention made of these kind of witches in the Bible. If Christ had knowne them, he would not have pretermitted to invaie against their presumption, in taking upon them his office: as, to heale and cure diseases; and to worke such miraculous and supernaturall things, as whereby he himselfe was speciallie knowne, beleeved, and published to be God; his actions and cures consisting (in order and effect) according to the power by our witchmoongers imputed to witches. (Scot, 1.5)

Touching Christ's not speaking or inveighing particularly against the particular actions imputed to witches the answer made to your 2 Reason might suffice. Yet will I add somewhat more thereunto, asking of you that if Christ had known that old silly women should be falsely accused for witches and most unjustly tormented and put to death for witchery (as you think they be) why did he not inveigh against this unjust and cruel dealing, which yet he doth not? If you will say there was no such dealing with silly old women in his time, it may be answered that as this dealing hath happened since his time so likewise might there be in our time such witches as we now speak of though there were no such in Christ's time, and that by as good reasons, as there are now and were from Christ's time many sorts of idolatries, sects, and heresies which were not in his time and against the which he never inveighed otherwise than in general words, saying beware of false prophets &c, in which general sort he hath inveighed and forewarned of witches and all other devilish workers of false and wicked miracles, saying namely of witches and sorcerers and generally of all other unbelieving, abominable, and lying persons and murderers that they shall have their part in the lake that burneth with fire and brimstone &c.[15] And by the holy apostle St Paul there is special mention made of witchcraft amongst the wicked deeds of the flesh as of

---

15 Author's note: 'Apocal 21'; Revelation 21:8. The Geneva Bible, which the author often seems to follow, does not in fact mention 'witches' specifically, although it does refer to 'sorcerers', as well as 'liars', 'the abominable' and 'murderers'.

one of those sins which excludeth the practicers of it out of the heavenly inheritance of the kingdom of heaven, so that our witches and the witches of all other times and ages, of what sort or condition soever they be, together with their craft of witching, whatsoever it is or hath been, are here manifestly condemned and spoken against by Christ and by his apostle St Paul, for these their words of witches, sorcerers, and witchcraft are general and not to be restrained more to any one sort of witches or witchcraft than to another.[16] Further, it may be said that Christ was not ignorant of this commandment of God given in Deuteronomy to his people, vz. let none be found amongst you that maketh his son or his daughter to go through fire, or that useth witchcraft, or a [f. 60r] regarder of times, or a marker of the flying of fowls, or a sorcerer, or a charmer, or that counseleth with spirits, or a soothsayer, or that asketh counsel of the dead.[17] And notwithstanding Christ did know that there were in the world all these sorts of people, yet can you not (I think) show that he did particularly inveigh against these more than he hath done against witches. Whereof you may consider that Christ did know of many sorts of wicked persons and practices which he did not particularly reprove or speak of, so that his not speaking particularly of our witches and of their witching practices is no good argument to prove that there be none such. Now whereas in this reason you say Christ was only known, believed, and published to be God by curing and healing disease and by the working of such miraculous and supernatural things as are to our witches imputed, in this I think you are much overseen[18] or rather very greatly out of the way, and that for two especial respects. The one is because Christ did many miracles and supernatural things (testifying him to be God) which no man ever thought or affirmed to be done by witches, as his fasting 40 days and 40 nights without being once hungered, his giving sight to blind born and others, his raising of the dead, his true feeding of 5000 with a few loaves and fishes, his own rising again, his ascending into heaven, his sending of the holy ghost and many such like. Therefore he was not known, believed, and published to be God only by such miracles and supernatural doings as are to our witches imputed. The second respect why I think you out of the way in the foresaid saying is because neither the miracles and supernatural things which you mean of, neither yet any other miracles done by Christ, was the only thing whereby he was known, believed, and published to be God, for there be many and sundry ways

16 Galatians 5:19–21; no note is provided in the treatise.
17 Author's note: 'deutro 18'; Deuteronomy 18:10–11.
18 OED: 'Mistaken, deceived, deluded; betrayed into error; imprudent, hasty, or rash in action.'

besides whereby Christ was thus known, believed, and published. As first the voice of his heavenly father pronouncing him to be the son of God. Secondly the testimony of John Baptist pointing him out as it were with his finger and saying 'behold the Lamb of God which taketh away the sins of the world'. Thirdly the message of the Angel Gabriel to the Virgin Mary signifying to her that she should conceive with child by the holy ghost and that that child should be called the son of God.[19] Likewise the message of an Angel appearing to the shepherds and saying 'behold I bring you tidings of great joy that shall be to all people for un{to} [f. 60v] you is born this day in the city of David a saviour, one which is Christ the Lord'.[20] Fourthly, the publishing of the same message by the shepherd. Fifth, the fact and song of Simeon and the confession of Anna the prophetess.[21] Sixthly, the coming and worshipping of the wise men of the East and, to be short, the whole scriptures of Moses and the prophets chief{ly} tended to this end: to make Christ to be known and believed on, for the which cause Christ speaking of those scriptures (for the New Testament was not then written) said to the Jews, 'search the scriptures in which ye suppose to have life, for they are they which bear witness of me'.[22] For the same cause also did Peter say that all the prophets bear witness unto Christ &c.[23] Thus you see, and may in the scriptures further see that Christ was many and sundry ways made known, published, and believed on as God besides his miracles and supernatural doings. And yet have I not spoken of the doctrine which Christ himself preached, nor of the inward workings of the holy ghost which are principally to be numbered amongst the ways and manner whereby Christ is chiefly known, believed, and published, but these and all the foresaid ways you do utterly exclude in this case by saying that Christ was only by his miracles and supernatural dealings thus known, believed, and published. Yea, in saying this it might be inferred that his apostles and all other true believers were more declared thereof to be gods than he was, for that they might not only do such supernatural things and miracles as you ascribe unto Christ but also greater, as it is testified by Christ himself, saying to them 'verily, verily, I say unto you he that believeth in me, the work that I do he shall do also, and greater than these shall he do for I go unto my father'.[24]

---

19 Author's notes: 'math 3', 'John 1', 'Luc 1': Matthew 3:17, John 1:29, Luke 1:35.
20 Author's note: 'Luc 2'; Luke 2:10–11.
21 Luke 2:25–38.
22 Author's note: 'John 5'; John 5:39.
23 Author's note: 'acts 10'; Acts 10:43.
24 Author's note: 'John 14'; John 14:12.

[f. 61r] Reason 18

> It will not suffice to dissuade a witchmonger from his credulitie, that he seeth the sequele and event to fall out manie times contrarie to their assertion; but in such case (to his greater condemnation) he seeketh further to witches of greater fame. (Scot, 1.5)

> If witches could doo anie such miraculous things, as these and other which are imputed to them, they might doo them againe and againe, at anie time or place, or at anie mans desire: for the divell is as strong at one time as at another, as busie by daie as by night, and readie enough to doo all mischeefe, and careth not whom he abuseth. (Scot, 1.6)

That things do not commonly fall out as witches promise is (as I said before) a very good argument to prove that Bodin and his followers hold not that it is in witches at their pleasure to do strange and supernatural things.[25] It is also a good argument to prove them to be abusers and deceivers of the people, which you in one part of your book do deny them to be if I be not deceived.[26] But where you say if they can at any time do such things they might do them when and as often as they should be desired, because the devil is as strong as busy &c to do mischief at one time as at another, it is in no wise to be granted unto you that the devil hath at all times like strength as he hath readiness to do mischief or miracles. For if he had then no doubt he would plague all godly men as well as ever he plagued Job, and still possess men as in Christ's time and carry all men's swine headlong into the seas as he did to the swine of the Gergesites.[27] He would make all men blind and dumb as he did the man mentioned in Matthew, he would enter into all men's hearts as he did into the heart of Judas and make us all traitors to Christ. Finally, whatsoever mischief or devilish deed he hath done from the beginning of the world to this present time he would daily do the same if he had at all times the like strength, for it is in deed most true which you confess, that he is as busy and as ready hereunto at one time as at another and careth not whom he abuseth, so that there can be no cause rendered why he doth not now such notable mischiefs and strange matters as heretofore he hath done but that he hath not at all times the like strength. Which also is plainly testified in the Apocalypse, where it is showed that he is at some times bound and cast into prison and at other times let loose again.

---

25 See reason 10 above.
26 Scot, 3.19: 'they would have them executed for seducing the people. But God knoweth they have small store of Rhetorike or art to seduce; except to tell a tale of Robin good-fellow be to deceive and seduce.' See reason 71 below.
27 Matthew 8:28; no note provided in the original.

Likewise in other places of the scriptures, as where it is said for this purpose appeared the son of God that he might destroy the work of the devil. Item that Jesus through his death destroyed him that had the power of death, that is, the devil.[28] Item that he [f. 61v] hath spoiled the principalities and powers and hath made a show of them openly and hath triumphed over them in his cross.[29] Now how could these things be true, that Christ hath destroyed the works and power of the devil and made a spoil of him &c, if he were still of the same strength which once he was of? And finally, if this were so, then should the devil be as strong in all those that are regenerated and new born by the word and spirit of God as he was in them before their regeneration and new birth. Therefore I conclude that it cannot be true which you have said as touching this point, and so consequently not true that the devil or his ministers can do the same at all times which they can do at some times.

Reason 19

> And in so much as it is confessed, by the most part of witchmoongers themselves, that [the devil] knoweth not the cogitation of mans heart, he should (me thinks) sometimes appeere unto honest and credible persons, in such grosse and corporall forme, as it is said he dooth unto witches: which you shall never heare to be justified by one sufficient witnesse. For the divell indeed entreth into the mind, and that waie seeketh mans confusion. (Scot, 1.6)

The devil in deed doth not know the cogitations of any man's heart if we shall speak of a sure, certain, and infallible knowledge, for that is only proper to God (as the scriptures everywhere testify). But forasmuch as many times the thoughts of the heart are in some sort expressed and bewrayed by certain outward actions and impressions of the body, the devil may thereby aim[30] and construe at the thoughts of the heart as we, if we see a man look with a stern and furious countenance, may conjecture that man to be in his heart angry or cruel, or if we hear a man often talking lasciviously we may thereof conjecture that he is of an unchaste mind. *Quia ex abundantia cordis os loquitur*,[31] and so of the former example it is said of Cain that he, being exceeding wroth, his countenance fell down, whereby

---

28 Author's notes: 'Apoca 20', '1 John 3, Hebreus 2, Colos 2'; Revelation 20:3, 1 John 3:8, Hebrews 2:14.
29 Author's note: 'Colos 2'; Colossians 2:15.
30 OED: 'to conjecture, guess; to guess at'.
31 Author's note: 'Math 12'. Part of Matthew 12:34: 'For of the abundance of the heart the mouth speaketh'.

is meant that he did in his countenance bewray the wrath of his heart.[32] So is it to this effect said in the Maccabees that they which looked the high priest in the face were wounded in the heart because his countenance and the changing of his colour declared the sorrow of his mind.[33] And by the prophet Isaiah it is said of the wicked Jews that the trial or changing of the countenance did testify against them, wherefore the devil being a most diligent and perspicuous observer of all things making to his purpose may by these and such like extern and outward actions, speeches and impressions of the body somewhat discern who be the fittest persons for him to deal withal.[34] But this I write not as confessing with you that he never appeareth to honest and credible persons in some gross or corporal form. For if I should confess that, I must deny and condemn as false and fabulous the histories and testimonies of most credible historiographers and writers, [f. 62r] yea the scriptures themselves, for I am of opinion that the devil appeared to Christ himself in a corporal shape when he tempted him: to which opinion the very context[35] of the scripture and also the consent of the most interpreters thereof do lead me, as further shall be showed afterwards. The like also I hold of the devil's appearing to Eve in the shape and body of a serpent as shall be also further showed afterwards, and likewise for the devil or devil{s} which (in the bodies of the two men possessed with them) did meet Christ in the land of the Gergesenes and cried out unto him, 'Jesus you son of God what have we to do with thee?'[36] This as I think was an appearing in a corporal form as are many other the like in the scriptures, so that there is no want of sufficient witness for this matter, which also serveth sufficiently to prove that the devil doth not only enter into the minds of men (as you seem to hold) but also into their bodies, whereof it may be more shall be spoken in some other place.

Reason 20

> The art [sic] alwaies presupposeth the power; so as, if they saie they can doo this or that, they must shew how and by what meanes they doo it; as neither the witches, nor the witchmoongers are able to doo. (Scot, 1.6)

The act doth not evermore presuppose such a power as that the doers of the act should always be able to show how and by what means they do it, if you mean the showing thereof in every point particularly. As for example

---

32 Author's note: 'Gen 4'; Genesis 4:5.
33 Author's note: '2 macab 3'; 2 Maccabees 3:16.
34 Author's note: 'Esay 3'; Isaiah 3:9.
35 OED: 'The connection or coherence between the parts of a discourse.'
36 Matthew 8:29.

mention is made by Epiphanius, Eusebius, and other of the ecclesiastical writers that Montan the heretic and his fellows Alcibiades, Theodolus, Prisca, and Maximilla &c, did *praeter morem aliorum prophetarum in ecstaci et stupore et quae alienatione mentis furore corrupti prophetare*.[37] They were not therefore able to show as I think any reason how and by what means they did prophesy, being in such a case. But if you will doubt of the verity of their prophesyings in this sort, how say you to the prophecy of Cayphas prophesying that it was expedient for the Jews that one man should die for the people &c.[38] Do you think he could render any reason how and by what means he, being a wicked priest, become so true a prophet? The like might be asked of the prophecies of Balaam, who could render no other reason for his blessing of God's people when he should and would have cursed them but that he did it by the motion, direction, and power of God, and even so can our witches show how and by what means they do their feats, by saying they do them by the motion, direction, and power of the devil. To be short, the most exquisite philosophers who laboured all that they might to find out the causes and reasons of all things do confess that many things are done of the which no reason can be rendered how and by what means they be done.

[f. 62v] Reason 21

> For to everie action is required the facultie and abilitie of the agent or dooer; the aptnes of the patient[39] or subject; and a convenient and possible application. (Scot, 1.6)

---

37 'Contrary to what is usual with other prophets, they prophesy in ecstasy and in a trance, deranged with frenzy' [my translation]. The authors referred to are Eusebius, Bishop of Caesarea (c. 260–c. 340), and Epiphanius, Bishop of Salamis (c. 315–403). Eusebius wrote a history of the Church, while Epiphanius was known for his *Panarion*, a catalogue and refutation of various heresies. The Montanist movement of the second century originated in Phrygia in modern Turkey. Some of its leading figures were women, including Maximilla and Priscilla (or Prisca). Christine Trevett points out that much of the criticism aimed at the Montanist movement took aim at the ecstatic nature of the prophecies of its exponents: *Montanism: Gender, Authority and the New Prophecy* (Cambridge: Cambridge University Press, 1996), pp. 87–8. An early modern English translation of Eusebius' *Ecclesiasticall Historie* (London, 1577) gives a similar description of Montanus' style of prophecy: 'being madde and sodainly estraunged, and berefte of his witts, [he] waxed furious, and published straunge doctrine, contrary to the tradition, and custome, and auncient succession (now receaued) vnder the name of prophecy' (p. 87).
38 Joseph Caiaphas, the high priest who prophesies the death of Jesus: John 11:49–51.
39 OED: 'Undergoing the action of another; passive; (also) achieved or acquired inwardly. Chiefly in contrast with active, agent.'

If you mean here by these general words ('every action'), as well extraordinary and supernatural actions as ordinary and natural, then is all that you do in this reason set down to be denied. For to supernatural and miraculous actions done by God or by [the] devil and his ministers (of which sort of actions the strange doings of witches are to be accompted) there is no need of such natural and ordinary faculty, aptness, application or power as you speak of either in the agent or in the patient, for then should not the actions be so strange and miraculous as they are. Before therefore you can gain anything by this reason, you must first prove that witches never do or can do more than is in them to do by ordinary means and by their own natural strength and power, which thing will not be granted unto you, because the scriptures, which speak of women that worked by spirits, together with the histories, censures,[40] and experience of all ages are against it.

Reason 22

> Now the witches are mortall, and their power dependeth upon the analogie and consonancie of their minds and bodies; but with their minds they can but will and understand; and with their bodies they can doo no more, but as the bounds and ends of terrene sense will suffer: and therefore their power extendeth not to doo such miracles, as surmounteth their owne sense, and the understanding of others which are wiser than they; so as here wanteth the vertue and power of the efficient.[41] And in reason, there can be no more vertue in the thing caused, than in the cause, or that which proceedeth of or from the benefit of the cause. (Scot, 1.6)

Though it be granted you that there can be no more virtue in the things caused than in the causer &c, yet will it not be granted you that witches are the cause of incantations and charms if you understand them to be either the only or the chief causes thereof, for they are rather instruments whereby the devil doth work such things rather than the causes thereof. And therefore are such wicked persons called the children of the devil in sundry places of the scriptures: so did Paul call Elimas the sorcerer, so also doth St John call all other that do continue under the lore[42] of the devil in committing sin and wickedness without faith or repentance, for so must St John be understood.[43] For the more full answering of this reason I refer you to the answer of the former reason.

---

40 OED: 'Judgement; opinion, *esp.* expressed opinion; criticism.'
41 OED: 'The cause which makes effects to be what they are.'
42 OED: 'A form of doctrine, a creed, religion.'
43 Author's notes: 'acts 13', '1 John 3'; Acts 13:6–8, 1 John 3:10.

Reason 23

> For alas! What an unapt instrument is a toothles, old, impotent, and unweldie woman to flie in the aier? Truelie, the divell little needs such instruments to bring his purposes to passe. (Scot, 1.6)

As you say the devil needeth not such instruments to bring his purpose to pass as our old and toothless women are, so I may say God needeth not any man, woman or other creature to bring his purposes to pass, and yet we know that God, in infinite of his actions and purposes, useth the help and means of sundry his creatures, yea he useth every one of them to the setting forth of his praise and glory. And even so, likewise that I should grant you that the devil needeth neither men or women old or young to work his villainies withal, yet doth it well serve his turn to use as many as possibly he can get to be at his commandment for that it is his chief design and practice to draw from God and from the way of salvation as many as possibly he can. And for that old silly women being brought up in all ignorance and blindness of God, and being by nature the weakest vessels are more apt to be entrapped in his snares than others, what marvel is it if he more work by them than by others?

[f. 63r] Reason 24

> It is strange, that we should suppose, that such persons can worke such feates: and it is more strange, that we will imagine that to be possible to be doone by a witch, which to nature and sense is impossible; speciallie when our neighbours life dependeth upon our credulitie therein; and when we may see the defect of abilitie, which alwaies is an impediment both to the act, and also to the presumption thereof. (Scot, 1.6)

The strangeness of the imagination here spoken of is taken away sufficiently in my answer to your 21 and 22 reasons to the which I do in this point refer you, wishing you withal to consider better of the woman of Endor and of the maid which had a spirit of divination mentioned {in} the acts 15 in whom (as in many others) you may find things done as strange and as much beyond the possibility of nature and sense as are to be found in our witches.[44] And whereas you mislike such credulity whereupon the life of our neighbour doth depend, I say such incredulity is much more to be misliked whereby such wicked and horrible persons should be deemed innocent against many most apparent facts and presumptions, and so consequently be at liberty, boldly and without danger to serve the devil's turn in using his

---

44 Author's note: '1 sam 28 acts 15'; 1 Samuel 28, Acts 15:16.

direction to the taking away of life, limb, and goods of many their honest neighbours as no doubt too too apparently they do and have done, the lord in his secret but yet just judgement so permitting, or rather (for respects to him best known) so allowing it who yet so little alloweth the doers thereof that he hath commanded that no witch should be suffered to live, which commandment doth not only import that there are such persons, but also that their doings and practices are most heinous and devilish.[45]

Reason 25

> And bicause there is nothing possible in lawe, that in nature is impossible; therefore the judge dooth not attend or regard what the accused man saith; or yet would doo: but what is prooved to have beene committed, and naturallie falleth in mans power and will to doo. For the lawe saith, that To will a thing unpossible, is a signe of a mad man, or of a foole, upon whom no sentence or judgement taketh hold. (Scot, 1.6)

Where the law of God hath appointed death or other punishment to any sin or sinner (as to witches it hath done), there we are not to regard what the law of man sayeth to the contrary, how impossible soever the sin be in nature or to the power proper and natural of him that commiteth it. For if you will have the judge do no more in judging upon any sin or sinner than you here prescribe, then neither witches nor enchanters nor sorcerers, nor counsellors with spirits nor any such like (whose practises are to nature and to their own proper power impossible) shall ever be put to death and punished as the law of God hath appointed them to be. And as for that law which sayeth that to will a thing impossible is a sign of a fool or of a mad man &c, if it say this absolutely and without exception, I say and will prove it to be a foolish or rather a mad law. For even the wisest men that ever were have a will to do and practise many things which at the first they hoped to be in their powers to bring to pass, but in the end have given them over as things not possible for them by their wits, power, strength, or learning to be brought to pass. [f. 63v] Yea I say further, the best and wisest men in the world have and ought to have a will unto many things which they know to be merely impossible for them to bring to pass, as for example there is no godly and wise magistrate but he hath and ought to have a will to keep all his subjects in due order and obedience. There is no godly or wise minister but he hath and ought to have a will to reduce[46] his flock to

---

45 Author's note: 'exod 22'; Exodus 22:18.
46 OED: 'To lead or bring back (a person) from error, sin, immorality, etc.; to restore to the truth or the right faith.'

the true knowledge and love of God and of their own salvation. There is no good or wise physician but he hath and ought to have a will to recover the health and good estate of his patients. To be short, there is no godly or wise Christian but he hath and ought to have a will to forsake all sin and wickedness and to please God in all his thoughts, words, and actions, but how unpossible it is for any magistrate, minister, physician, or Christian to bring these things to pass which they so earnestly do and ought to desire you know as well as I. Here also might I speak how all sorts of men in their several sciences, arts, and faculties have a will to excel one another, which yet is merely impossible to be done, for that in every science, art, and faculty there can be but one only of all the professors and practicers of the same that can excel and be most excellent. So likewise when two nations join together in battle one against another, or two persons in suit one against another, there is an earnest will and labour of both parties to obtain the victory, yet is this, we know, merely impossible. And therefore it is to be concluded that either the said law is (as I said before) a foolish and a mad law, or else all the people of the world are foolish and mad men. But were that law sound and not to be controlled[47] yet would it make nothing for your turn against witches and their practices, for the things which they cannot do by their own proper power naturally may be done by the power which the devil doth communicate and commit unto them, and therefore are not merely impossible as you would have them to be thought.

Reason 26

> Seeing therefore that some other things might naturallie be the occasion and cause of such calamities as witches are supposed to bring; let not us that professe the Gospell and knowledge of Christ, be bewitched to beleeve that they doo such things, as are in nature impossible, and in sense and reason incredible. (Scot, 1.6)

Here me thinketh you speak very contrary to yourself, for if other things might naturally be the cause and occasion of those calamities which are surmised to be brought in by witches (as you say they may) why then do you call these things in nature impossible and in sense and reason incredible? I cannot see how any thing may be done naturally which is in nature impossible. Besides, if you will not have witches charged when they confess a fact to be done by them (which fact is evident to be done) because it might be done by some natural means otherwise, then I see no reason why

---

47 OED: 'To challenge, find fault with, censure, reprehend, object to (a thing).'

a murderer confessing himself to have strangled [f. 64r] a man unto death (who is suddenly found dead, and whereof there be divers presumptions that it was the fact of him that confessed it) should be impeached or found guilty of the death forasmuch as the same might naturally come to pass by some apposthume,[48] apoplexy or other disease. How weak a case it is to deny a thing to be done by one means because the same might be done by another I will not persecute[49] to declare as I might. Only this one thing I will note: that if there were any force in this reason, then might a man call in question some of Moses' miracles done in Egypt as not to be done by the power of God, because the like were done of Pharaoh's sorcerers by sorcery and enchantments.

Reason 27

> Such mischeefes as are imputed to witches, happen where no witches are; yea and continue when witches are hanged and burnt: whie then should we attribute such effect to that cause, which being taken awaie, happeneth neverthelesse? (Scot, 1.6)

To this reason I have answered somewhat in my answer to the 9th reason, and yet for more full answer hereof I say it is hard for any man to know where witches be not, and more hard to know when they be all burnt up or hanged. For though there be as many thieves and other felons in every part of this realm taken and either imprisoned or executed as can be justly found and charged, yet we see by the often and daily felonies from time to time committed that there are many thieves and felons still remaining and lurking amongst us, and some of these such as we would take to be right true and honest men. And why may not the like be said of witches and sorcerers? But turn, I pray you, to my foresaid answer.

Reason 28

> Surelie the naturall power of man or woman cannot be so inlarged, as to doo anie thing beyond the power and vertue given and ingrafted by God. But it is the will and mind of man, which is vitiated and depraved by the divell: neither dooth God permit anie more, than that which the naturall order appointed by him dooth require. Which naturall order is nothing else, but the ordinarie power of God, powred into everie creature, according to his state and condition. (Scot, 1.7)

---

48 OED: 'A gathering of purulent matter in any part of the body; a large deep-seated abscess.'

49 OED: 'To follow up, pursue, prosecute (a subject); to carry out, go through with.'

If you would have it true (which here you affirm) that the natural power of man cannot be enlarged so as &c, and that God doth not permit any more than that which the natural order appointed of him at the beginning doth require, which natural order (you say) is nothing else but the ordinary power of God poured into every creature according to his estate and condition: then must it of necessity follow by this your assertion (for any thing I can see to the contrary) that the prophets, apostles, and other holy men never did or possibly could do any of those miracles which in the scriptures and in other ecclesiastical writings are imputed unto them. for miracles cannot be done by the natural order and ordinary power, beyond the which you say God doth not permit anything to any creature. Neither can any of us by that power believe in God or think so much as a good thought. For flesh and blood (that is to say natural wit, power, strength, and knowledge) did not reveal unto Peter or cause him to believe and confess Christ to be the son of the everliving God but as Christ sayeth, it was his heavenly father which revealed this to Peter {and} wrought this faith and confession in him.[50] The natural man, sayeth Paul, doth not perceive the things that are of God's spirit for they are foolishness unto him &c.[51] If therefore our natural power were not [f. 64v] enlarged (and that by an extraordinary power of God working in us by his holy spirit a further faith, knowledge, holiness, and sanctification than we have naturally in us) we were in a most desperate and damnable estate and condition, as the said apostle further showeth, saying that by nature we are the children of God's wrath.[52] Now where you say here again (as before in your 19th reason you said) that it is the will and mind of man that is vitiated and depraved by the devil, if you mean (as I think you do) only the will and mind, I have in the said place spoken somewhat to the contrary thereof and now will speak a little more, and thus I reason. As God and the devil are most contrary, so are their actions and doings most contrary.[53] Wherefore as God in his actions and doings is not only beneficial to our souls but also to our bodies, so contrarily (by an argument *a contrariis*)[54] it doth undoubtedly follow that the devil in his actions and doings is hurtful (as much as he may) not only to our wills and

---

50 Author's note: 'Math 16'; Matthew 16:17.
51 Author's note: '1 Corinth 2'; 1 Corinthians 2:14.
52 Author's note: 'Ephes 2'; Ephesians 2:3.
53 Author's note: '2 Corinth 6' – perhaps a reference to 2 Corinthians 6:14: 'Be not vnequally yoked with the infideles: for what felowship hathe righteousnes with vnrighteousnes? and what communion hathe light with darkenes?'
54 *Argumentum a contrario* is a type of argument deriving unstated rules from stated rules which exclude them; in this case, the goodness of God implies the harmfulness of the Devil.

minds but also to our bodies. Again, sith God hath created not only our souls but also our bodies for his glory and hath required that we should glorify him in both, saying by the apostle, glorify God in your body and in your spirit, for they are God's.[55] How can we think otherwise but that the devil (being in all things the enemy of God and of his glory) will as well seek the dishonour of God in our bodies as in our minds and wills, and if he be able to corrupt and vitiate our wills and minds which far excel our bodies in strength and quality, who will doubt but he is able to corrupt and vitiate our bodies also? Apocal 2 you shall see that Satan procureth bodily hurt unto us and to what end.[56]

Reason 29

> And this I have also noted, that when anie one is coosened with a coosening toie of witchcraft, and maketh report thereof accordinglie verifieng a matter most impossible and false as it were upon his owne knowledge, as being overtaken with some kind of illusion or other (which illusions are right inchantments) even the selfe-same man will deride the like lie proceeding out of another mans mouth, as a fabulous matter unworthie of credit. It is also to be woondered, how men (that have seene some part of witches coosenages detected, and see also therein the impossibilitie of their owne presumptions, & the follie and falsehood of the witches confessions) will not suspect, but remaine unsatisfied, or rather obstinatelie defend the residue of witches supernaturall actions: like as when a juggler hath discovered the slight and illusion of his principall feats, one would fondlie continue to thinke, that his other petie juggling knacks of legierdemaine are done by the helpe of a familiar: and according to the follie of some papists, who seeing and confessing the popes absurd religion, in the erection and maintenance of idolatrie and superstition, speciallie in images, pardons, and relikes of saints, will yet persevere to thinke, that the rest of his doctrine and trumperie is holie and good. (Scot, 1.7)

Here you reason a *secundum quid ad simpliciter*[57] which is as bad a kind of reasoning as may be. By this kind of reason I might say all men are liars in

---

55 Author's note: '1 Corinth 6'; 1 Corinthians 6:20.
56 A reference to Revelation 2:10: 'Feare none of those things which thou shalt suffer: behold, it shal come to passe, that the deuil shal cast some of you into prison, that ye may be tried, and ye shal have tribulation ten days: be thou faithful vnto the death, and I wil giue thee the crowne of life.'
57 A type of logical fallacy which involves mistaking a generalisation or rule of thumb for a rule without any exceptions.

some things (for the scripture sayeth *omnis homo mendax*)[58] *ergo* no man is to be believed in any thing that he shall speak. Or if you will not have your reason here to be answered in this sort it must then be answered thus: some part of magistrates' dealings have been detected to be corrupt and unlawful, *ergo* we must thus think of all other dealings of all magistrates. But to leave the absurdity of this argument and to come to the matter: you know the devil and his ministers are very false and subtle fellows[59] who know it is far from good policy in all things to lie and to deceive, and therefore to win them credit they use sometimes to transform themselves into angels of light; that is to say and do those things that are true and honest, as we see the devils spake the truth when they confessed Christ to be the son of God, and when by the possessed maid the devil confessed Paul, Silas, Timotheus to be the servants of the most high God which showed the way of salvation.[60] So also do the papists when they confess with us the articles of our belief and have epistle and gospel and some good prayers [f. 65r] in their most abominable mass and other services. Wherefore (as I may again return to your reason) if it be a good argument to say all the doings of the devil and his ministers are to be taken for mere cozenage because some of them have been detected so to be, why should it not on the contrary prove a good argument to say the devil and his ministers have been found in some of their words and doings to speak and to do true and good things, *ergo* why should we not so think of all other their speeches and doings?

Reason 30

> If all be true that is alledged of their dooings, why should we beleeve in Christ, bicause of his miracles, when a witch dooth as great wonders as ever he did? (Scot, 2.10)

Indeed, if there were no other cause or thing to induce us to believe in Christ but only his miracles you had put forth a hard question, but yet no harder than this, vz: why should we believe in Christ because of his miracles rather than in his apostles, or so much as in them, sith they did not only as great but also greater miracles than he, as is before showed in my answer to your

---

58 The author does not provide a reference, but is quoting from Psalm 116:11 (or 115:2 in the Vulgate).
59 OED: 'A person who joins with another specified person in committing a particular crime or other wicked act; an accomplice.'
60 Author's notes: '2 corinth ii operarij dolosi', 'math 8 marc 3 acts 16'. 2 Corinthians 11:13 refers to 'deceitful workers' (*operarii dolosi*); the scriptural episodes described are in Matthew 8:29, Mark 3:11, Acts 16:17.

17th reason, where you may see a more full answer to this present reason, which also you may see in my answer to your 13 reason.

Reason 31

> It were a mightie temptation to a seelie old woman, that a visible divell (being in shape so ugglie, as *Danaeus* and others saie he is) should assalt hir in maner and forme as is supposed, or rather avowed; speciallie when there is promise made that none shall be tempted above their strength.[61] (Scot, 2.12)

The promise of God that none shall be tempted above their strength pertaineth only to the children of God, which wholly depend upon him in all assaults and temptations and not to the wicked and faithless despisers of God (as all witches are), neither yet to the chosen and faithful children of God if at any time they put any trust or confidence in their own strengths, as we may see by the example of Peter, who was in this respect suffered to be tempted above his strength when he denied his master. So were Adam and Eve in paradise when they began to doubt of God's word and to hearken to Satan. To be short, if this saying of Paul should appertain generally to all sorts of men without exception (as you seem to take it), then see not I how any one can be damned, no nor how any could sin.

Reason 32

> If the league be untrue, as are the residue of their confessions, the witchmongers arguments fall to the ground: for all the writers herein hold this bargaine for certeine, good, and granted, and as their onelie maxime. But surelie the indentures, conteining those covenants, are sealed with butter; and the labels are but bables. What firme bargaine can be made betwixt a carnall bodie and a spirituall? (Scot, 3.4)

It is written in Gen. that God made a covenant or league with Abraham, for God said there unto Abraham I will make my covenant between me and thee.[62] The prophet, or rather the high priest Zachary speaketh both of this covenant (which he calleth God's holy covenant) and also of another which God did swear to our father Abraham.[63] And other infinite places there be in the scriptures which speak of covenants between God and his people, whereof we may consider that there is no impossibility of

---

61 The 'promise' referred to is made in 1 Corinthians 10:13.
62 Author's note: 'Gen 17'; Genesis 17:2.
63 Author's note: 'all sacrame[n]t[es] are seales of god[es] Covena[n]t[es] to vs {?} Luc 1'; Luke 1:72.

covenanting between a carnal body and a spiritual essence, which also our profession in baptism and the vows made unto God in the Old Testament by the godly of that time doth sufficiently witness. But whether there be any extern league or covenant made with the devil I will not say, I only stand upon this: that it is possible, whereunto also I am induced by the apostle's words, which sayeth 'I would not that ye shouldst have fellowship with devils ye cannot drink [f. 65v] of the cup of the lord and the cup of the devils, ye cannot be partaker of the lord's table and the table of devils'.[64] These words (as I think) go very near to prove that there was some special league and fellowship between the devils and the gentiles there spoken of, which made sacrifices to the devils. And the same apostle speaketh of some in another place which were in the snare of the devil in such sort as they were taken of him at his will, so that if it were the devil's will to have them coupled unto him by an extern league or covenant, I see no cause but that it might be so.[65]

Reason 33

> For the beginning of the credit hereof, resteth upon the confession of a baggage yoong fellow condemned to be burnt for witchcraft; who said to the inquisitors, of likelihood to prolong his life (if at leastwise the storie be true, which is taken out of *Nider*;) If I wist (quoth he) that I might obteine pardon, I would discover all that I knowe of witchcraft. (Scot, 3.4)[66]

It will not be granted you (neither do you prove it at all) that the beginning of the credit given to that league resteth upon the confession of that baggage[67] young fellow you there speak of. I myself (as little as I have travelled[68] in that matter) can show better and more ancient matter for the credit thereof, but I say not I can show matter sufficient for the same.

Reason 34

> [See the excerpt to Reason 32 above]

How certain soever it is holden that there is such a league, yet do I not see any just cause why all arguments used for the proof of witches' devilish

---

64 Author's note: '1 Corinth 10'; 1 Corinthians 10.20–21.
65 Author's note: '2 Tymo 2'; 2 Timothy 2:26.
66 Scot refers to a story published in Nider's *Formicarius* about a man who confessed that he and his wife were both witches; his wife refused to confess even under torture. See Kors and Peters (eds), *Witchcraft in Europe, 400–1700*, pp. 157–8.
67 OED: 'Of persons: morally worthless, good-for-nothing, vile, "scurvy".'
68 OED: 'To work as a student, to study (*in* a subject or author).'

practices shall go to the ground if there were no such league. For if in times past the devil by himself and by his ministers, both men and women, did work as great effects and miracles as are now imputed to witches (as certain it is by the scriptures and other credible writings they did) why may they not now also do the like without the said league if then they were done without the same?

Reason 35

> That the joining of hands with the divell, the kissing of his bare buttocks, and his scratching and biting of them, are absurd lies; everie one having the gift of reason may plainlie perceive: in so much as it is manifest unto us by the word of God, that a spirit hath no flesh, bones, nor sinewes, whereof hands, buttocks, claws, teeth, and lips doo consist. (Scot, 3.6)

The holy angels of heaven are spirits as well as are the devils and so consequently are as void of flesh and bones as they are. Yet can you not deny but the holy angels have appeared in bodies of men to Abraham, Lot, and others, and have eaten and drunken and lodged with them and laid hands upon men, as upon Lot to pull him into his house, upon Habakkuk to carry him to Daniel, upon Jacob to wrestle with him, upon Peter to smite him on the side when he delivered him out of prison &c.[69] Wherefore though spirits have naturally no flesh and bones, yet by a supernatural means they may, and have them at God's pleasure, will, and appointment. But whether they have them truly or but apparently that is another question which here I will not stand upon, because it is not to the present purpose, [f. 66r] but if you think the evil angels or spirits do not nor may not likewise assume bodies and so appear unto men you may remember what is said thereof in my answer to your 19th reason and what shall further be said afterwards. In the mean season that which I have said here in this present place of the good angels is alone sufficient to disprove your reason here used.

Reason 36

> What credible witnesse is there brought at anie time, of this their corporall, visible, and incredible bargaine; saving the confession of some person diseased both in bodie and mind, wilfullie made, or injuriouslie constrained?

---

69 Author's notes: 'Gen 18. 19': Abraham and Sarah are visited by angels in human form in Genesis 18, as is Lot in Genesis 19. 'Gen 32': in Genesis 32:24, Jacob wrestles with an angel in human form. In the deuterocanonical additions to Daniel (14:35), an angel carries Habakkuk by the hair to Babylon. 'acts 12': Peter is released from prison by an angel in Acts 12:7.

It is mervell that no penitent witch that forsaketh hir trade, confesseth not these things without compulsion. (Scot, 3.6)

How can there be any credible witness brought of that league whenas none be admitted to the sight or knowledge thereof but the leaguemakers and their good master the devil himself? It is, you know, the purpose of all sorts of sinners not to have witnesses of their sinful deeds if by any means they can avoid them. And whereas you would annihilate[70] their confessions which either are extorted or wilfully made in respect they are diseased both in body and mind, it will never be granted you that all or the most sort of witches are in this sort diseased, but are in mind and body to the outward appearance (beyond which we cannot judge) as sound and as sensible as other women are which be not of their sort. And not one amongst a thousand of them shall you meet withal which willingly will confess anything of their secret practices but will deny them with more vehement oaths and protestations than any other sort of malefactors use to make in their defence, whereof I myself have had very great experience. And as for constraint used towards them, with us there is none that may be complained of, and I would think that in other countries there is not any used by the most sort of magistrates (though all perhaps be not excusable) except they see great circumstances and vehement presumptions to move them thereunto. And, to be short, if the confessions of malefactors (such especially as proceed voluntarily from them) should be of no force then would it not have been said *ex ore tuo judico te*.[71] And you are not ignorant how David caused the Amalekite (who confessed himself to have slain Saul) to be slain upon that confession, though it were most false which he confessed, saying unto him thy blood be upon thine own head for thine own mouth hath testified against thee &c.[72] This fact of David, as it is not reprehended in the scriptures, so is it of all the godly writers thereupon allowed and averred for lawful and well done. And amongst other Peter Martyr bringeth this dilemma for it, saying if the confession had been true then the Amalekite deserved to be slain for that, contrary to God's law, he had shed man's blood; on the other side if it were false, then was he a bearer of false witness against himself in a cause of murder and so by the civil [f. 66v] law (which imposeth upon false witnesses *paenam talionis*) to be put unto death for the same.[73] And I for my

---

70 OED: 'To treat as non-existent, set at nought.'
71 The author provides no reference, but this is a version of part of Luke 19:22; in the Geneva text, 'Of thine owne mouth wil I iudge thee'.
72 Author's note: '2 Sam 1'; 2 Samuel 1:8–10.
73 Author's note: 'm ff ad lege[m] cornelia[m] de sicarijs'. The reference is to legislation enacted in the Roman republic in 81 BC, the *Lex Cornelia de Sicariis et*

part do the more incline to the allowing of voluntary confessions in corporal punishment because our saviour Christ doth allow of them in his eternal punishment at the day of Judgement, saying thereof: by thy words thou shalt be justified and by thy words thou shalt be condemned.[74] Of which saying Mr Calvin's judgement is that it was then used as a common proverb amongst the people and by Christ (by that citation) applied to his purpose, neither do I doubt (sayeth Mr Calvin) but that this saying was very famous or common in the people's mouth.[75] And Chrysostom writing hereupon sayeth that for a man to be judged and have sentence given against him not upon other men's words but upon his own words is no heavy or cruel kind of judgement but of all other most just.[76]

Reason 37

> Mee thinketh their covenant made at baptisme with God, before good witnesses, sanctified with the word, confirmed with his promises, and

---

Veneficis: Clyde Pharr, 'The Interdiction of Magic in Roman Law', *Transactions and Proceedings of the American Philological Association* 63 (1932), 269–95 (p. 279). The principle of *paenam talionis*, or 'penalty of retaliation', was enshrined in English law in 37 Edward III c. 18, which states that 'Though that it be contained in the Great Charter, that no Man be taken nor imprisoned, nor put out of his Freehold, without Process of the Law; Nevertheless divers People make false Suggestions to the King himself, as well for Malice as otherwise, whereof the King is often grieved, and divers of the Realm put in Damage, against the Form of the same Charter; wherefore it is ordained, That all they that make such Suggestions, be sent with the same Suggestions before the Chancellor, Treasurer, and his Grand Council, and that they there find Surety to pursue their Suggestions, and incur the same Pain that the other should have had if he were attainted, in case that this Suggestion be found evil.'

74 Author's note: 'math 12'; Matthew 12:37.
75 Author's note: 'Harmonia'; i.e. Calvin's commentaries on the gospels, published as *Harmonia ex Evangelistis* (Geneva, 1555). Calvin's commentary on Matthew 12:37 begins as follows: 'This was a common proverb, which he applied to the present subject; for I have no doubt that this was a saying which the people had frequently in their mouths, that "every man is condemned or acquitted by his own acknowledgment." But Christ turns it to a meaning somewhat different, that a wicked speech, being the indication of concealed malice, is enough to condemn a man.' Calvin, *Commentary on a Harmony of the Evangelists, Matthew, Mark, and Luke*, vol. 2, translated by William Pringle (Edinburgh: Calvin Translation Society, 1845), p. 82.
76 Author's note: 'prima in math ex pos Homil 43'. One possible source for this quotation, Thomas Aquinas' *Catena Aurea* (see the discussion of sources in the introduction above), includes the following excerpt from Chrysostom's homilies on Matthew in its commentary on this verse: '*Vide autem quia non est onerosum hoc*

established with his sacraments, should be of more force than that which they make with the divell, which no bodie seeth or knoweth. For God deceiveth none, with whom he bargaineth; neither dooth he mocke or disappoint them, although he danse not among them. (Scot, 3.6)

Here you fall into another contrariety against yourself, confessing that we in baptism make a covenant with God whereas before in your 32 reason you ask what firm bargain there can be made between a carnal body and a spiritual essence, as who should say there could be none. And where you say this one covenant made with God in baptism should be of more force than that made with the devil, no man can or will deny it to be most true; so also may we say that the word spoken by God unto Adam and Eve should be of more force then the word spoken unto them by the devil, so also should the love of virtue be of more force than the love of vice and the love of heavenly joys and treasures of more force than the love of earthly joys and treasures, but yet we know that the things of the lesser force were and are preferred even of the most before the things of the greater force. Wherefore it is not to the purpose to show what should be but what is, and in so doing there is more likelihood against you than with you, as by these instances you may perceive, as also by infinite other which you may easily find out the rather if you remember this saying of St John: *totus mundus in maligno positus est*,[77] or this of Christ: *intrate per augustam portam quoniam lata est porta et spaciosa via quae adduxit ad exitium et multiquae sunt qui introeunt per eam quia angusta est porta quae ducit ad vitam et stricta via et pauci sunt qui inveniant eam.*[78]

---

judicium. Non ex quibus alius dixit de te, sed ex quibus ipse locutos es, sententiam judex feret'; *Catena Aurea in Quatuor Evangelia*, in *Opera Omnia*, vol. 11 (New York: Musurgia, 1949), p. 160; 'See that this sentence is not a burdensome one. The Judge will pass sentence not according to what any other has said concerning you, but according to what you have yourself spoken'; *Catena Aurea: Commentary on the Four Gospels*, translated by John Henry Newman (Oxford: John Henry Parker, 1841), p. 465. However, missing from the Catena (or at least from this version of it) is the following clause, which the author seems to be aware of: 'which is of all things the very fairest: since surely with thee it rests, either to speak, or not to speak'; Chrysostom, *Homilies on the Gospel of St Matthew*, vol. 2, translated by George Prevost (Oxford: John Henry Parker, 1854), p. 589.

77 Author's note: '1 John 5'; 1 John 5:19: 'the whole worlde lyeth in wickednes'.
78 Author's note: 'Math 7'; Matthew 7:13–14: 'Enter in at the streicte gate: for it is the wide gate, and broad waye that leadeth to destruction: and manie there be which go in thereat, Because the gate is streicte, and the way narowe that leadeth vnto life, and fewe there be that finde it.'

Reason 38

> Their oth, to procure into their league and fellowship as manie as they can (whereby everie one witch, as *Bodin* affirmeth, augmenteth the number of fiftie) bewraieth greatlie their indirect dealing. Hereof I have made triall, as also of the residue of their coosening devices; and have beene with the best, or rather the woorst of them, to see what might be gathered out of their counsels; and have cunninglie treated with them thereabouts: and further, have sent certeine old persons to indent with them, to be admitted into their societie. But as well by their excuses and delaies, as by other circumstances, I have tried and found all their trade to be meere coosening. (Scot, 3.6)

It may be (and I am persuaded so) that there be both better and worse of that sort than ever you have met withal, but admit you were not in this deceived; yet will it not follow that there is no other thing in their practices that you do speak of because you could try and find out no other by such means as you used, and by such delays and circumstances as you marked in them for *pravum et inscrutabile est cor hominis*[79] and they [f. 67r] in this business serve a crafty master and (as the Apostle termeth him for his singular subtleties) an old serpent, by whom they are made too crafty wise to bewray the secrecy of their practices so long as by any means they can conceal them.[80] Yea and in other kind of malefactors it hath been often seen that no examination, trial, or torment could wring from them the bewraying of their dealings, were they never so wisely and politicly handled.

Reason 39

> I praie you what bargaine have they made with the divell, that with their angrie lookes beewitch lambs, children, &c? Is it not confessed, that it is naturall, though it be a lie? (Scot, 3.6)

The making of a bargain with the devil is no let or prejudice to natural means of hurting, for the devil is very willing that hurt should be done by all manner of means, and if there were any such natural force in eyes that with looks hurt might be done, it is to be thought that silly women (void of natural philosophy) should never have known the same if the devil had not

---

79 A paraphrase of Jeremiah 17:9, which is not cited in the treatise: 'The heart of man is shrewd and vnsearchable'; Thomas James, *A treatise of the corruption of Scripture, councels, and fathers, by the prelats, pastors, and pillars of the Church of Rome* (London, 1612), part 3, p. 25. See the discussion of this quotation in the 'Sources' section of the introduction.

80 Author's note: 'Apoc 12, 20'; Revelation 12:9, 20:2.

bewrayed it unto them. Whether it be true or false that there is in eyes and looks such force I will not stand to dispute but sure I am, and you know it as well as I, that many great learned men hold it for a truth.

Reason 40

> What bargaine maketh the soothsaier, which hath his severall kinds of witchcraft and divination expressed in the scripture? Or is it not granted that they make none? How chanceth it that we heare not of this bargaine in the scriptures? (Scot, 3.6)

How it chanceth that you hear not of the soothsayer's bargain in the scriptures you may see sufficiently by that which is answered to your 2 Reason and 17 reason, and me thinketh you do herein very well answer yourself in your 96 reason following, where you ask of the witchmongers whether it be expedient for the holy ghost of necessity (for the satisfying of his curiosity) to make mention of every particular thing that he imagineth may be bewitched.

Reason 41

> It is confessed (saie some by the waie of objection) even of these women themselves, that they doo these and such other horrible things, as deserveth death, with all extremitie, &c. Whereunto I answer, that whosoever consideratelie beholdeth their confessions, shall perceive all to be vaine, idle, false, inconstant, and of no weight; except their contempt and ignorance in religion: which is rather the fault of the negligent pastor, than of the simple woman.
>
> First, if their confession be made by compulsion, of force or authoritie, or by persuasion, and under colour of freendship, it is not to be regarded; bicause the extremitie of threts and tortures provokes it; or the qualitie of faire words and allurements constraines it. If it be voluntarie, manie circumstances must be considered, to wit; whether she appeach not hir selfe to overthrow hir neighbour, which manie times happeneth through their cankered and malicious melancholike humor: then; whether in that same melancholike mood and frentike humor, she desire not the abridgment of hir owne daies. (Scot, 3.7)

I do not hold with compulsory or extorted confessions neither in this case nor in any other unless the fact be very apparent and no cause why the malefactor doth not confess it but only his obstinate and perverse stubbornness, in which case I think it lawful by tortures to compel him to confess, especially in such countries where by the laws none can be put to death without confession, though he were never so guilty and the same most apparently known.[81] And as for voluntary confessions I have said my mind before in the answer to your 36 reason, and in this I do with you agree that all circumstances should be duly considered, which I doubt not most magistrates do observe, howsoever the Inquisitors' *Haereticae pravitatis*[82] do the contrary.[83]

Reason 42

> And as they sometimes confesse impossibilities, as that they flie in the aire, transubstantiate themselves, raise tempests, transfer or remoove corne, &c: so doo they also (I saie) confesse voluntarilie, that which no man could proove, and that which no man would ghesse, nor yet beleeve, except he were as mad as they; so as they bring death wilfullie upon themselves: which argueth an unsound mind. (Scot, 3.7)

They which voluntary confess matter of death or that else would not be believed against themselves are rarely to be found, as before I have noted in the 36 reason. And when any such are found it doth not as I think so much argue the unsoundness of their minds as that it argueth a guilty conscience, by the force whereof not only witches but other heinous malefactors do sometimes bewray themselves contrary to all expectation, as perhaps shall be further showed afterwards, and you have partly showed it in your example of Bessus, Reason 51.

[f. 67v] Reason 43

> Also sometimes (as else-where I have prooved) they confesse that whereof they were never guiltie; supposing that they did that which they did not, by meanes of certeine circumstances. (Scot, 3.7)

Whether they suppose a guiltiness in themselves where none is and so confess an untruth against themselves is a matter that cannot be known and therefore not to be affirmed for a certainty so to be. I would rather think (if at any time they confess that which they did not) that the same

---

81 This was not the case in England, according to present-day legal historians: extracting confessions by torture was only permitted if a warrant was issued by the monarch or her privy council. While it could conceivably have happened anyway, there is little evidence for this: Orna Alyagon Darr, *Marks of an Absolute Witch* (Farnham: Ashgate, 2011), p. 9.
82 *Inquisitio Haereticae pravitatis* is the Latin name given to the Inquisition.
83 The specific 'circumstances' listed by Scot in the printed *Discoverie* may not have been mentioned in the draft to which the treatise responds, since the author suggests them himself in another response to Scot – see reason 43 below.

proceedeth of a desperate weariness of their lives or of malice to some others whom they would entangled in the like danger by that confession rather than otherwise, and I have in deed both known and read of some (not being witches nor that way suspected) which have upon these respects accused themselves.[84] But such an extraordinary matter must not be drawn to a general defence or excuse for all voluntary confessions. In this case our common saying, better is a mischief than an inconvenience, must take place as in many other things it doth.[85]

Reason 44

> But if this their confession be examined by divinitie, philosophie, physicke, lawe or conscience, it will be found false and insufficient. First, for that the working of miracles is ceased. Secondlie, no reason can be yeelded for a thing so farre beyond all reason. Thirdlie, no receipt can be of such efficacie, as when the same is touched with a bare hand, from whence the veines have passage through the bodie unto the hart, it should not annoie the poisoner; and yet reteine vertue and force enough, to pearse through so manie garments and the verie flesh incurablie, to the place of death in another person. *Cui argumento* (saith *Bodin*) *nescio quid responderi possit*. Fourthlie, no lawe will admit such a confession, as yeeldeth unto impossibilities, against the which there is never any lawe provided; otherwise it would not serve a mans turne, to plead and proove that he was at *Berwicke* that daie, that he is accused to have doone a murther in *Canturburie*; for it might be said he was conveied to *Berwicke*, and backe againe by inchantment. Fiftlie, he is not by conscience to be executed, which hath no sound mind nor perfect judgement. (Scot, 3.7)

Touching the impossibilities of their confessions, as also what is to be thought of these words and charms, looks &c, enough hath been said before in my answers to your 4, 6, 13, and 21 reasons. And as for your present assertion of divinity, of philosophy, of physic, of law, and of conscience to be against their confessions, it may (as I think) be easily answered and taken away. And first to this point of divinity, that miracles are now ceased to be wrought: I may not acknowledge any such divinity unless I will manifestly impugn the scriptures, especially if we speak of false and wicked miracles,

---

84 Cf. the excerpt from Scot, 3.7 quoted with reason 41 above.
85 This was a legal principle applied by common law judges from as early as the fourteenth century, which held that it was better for a single person to suffer an injustice than for legal rules to be undermined by making exceptions to them: John Baker, *The Oxford History of the Laws of England*, vol. 6 (Oxford: Oxford University Press, 2003), p. 41.

as now we do, for that such kind of miracles shall be most rife and common towards the latter end of the world (in which time we are), the places of scripture quoted in my answer to your 2 Reason do most plainly testify.[86] To the which you may add others out of the Apocalypse, as where it is said of the second beast (in way of prophecy for the time to come) that he did great wonders, so that he made fire come down from heaven on the earth in the sight of men.[87] Where also it is said that when the 1000 years were expired Satan shall be loosed out of his prison and shall go out to deceive the people which are in the 4 quarters of the earth.[88] And as this may suffice to prove that false and wicked miracles are not ceased, so also I say for true and godly miracles that although we are not now to require or look for any for the confirmation of our faith because the miracles already done and mentioned in the scriptures are sufficient, yet is there nothing that I know in divinity to persuade us that God hath so utterly determined to cease from all such miracles that he will never show any after Christ's time and the time of his Apostles, for if we will not discredit the histories of all times and ages, we cannot (as I said in another [f. 68r] place before) deny but that God hath showed some miracles in all ages both immediately and by means. Yea, and even in our age and time, as what can we think of the wonderful preservation of Rochelle from famine or yielding by the strange and extraordinary coming and departing of the fishes reported in the late French histories but that it was a mighty good miracle?[89] What shall we also think of the strange, sudden, and extraordinary punishments which fell upon many of the blasphemous persecutors in Queen Mary's days, whereof report is made by Mr Foxe in his martyrology, but that God did miraculously lay his hand upon them for their horrible blasphemy and tyranny?[90] To be short (let other men

---

86 Author's notes: 'se more of ceasing of miracles to your 86 Reas.'; 'se more of this in St August de civitate dei li 20 ca 16 et li 21 ca 5 6 et 7' [Augustine's *City of God* 20:16 and 21:5–7]. The author discusses these chapters at greater length later in the current reason.

87 Author's note: 'Apoca 13'. The beast out of the earth, which follows the beast out of the sea, is described in Revelation 13:11–15.

88 Author's note: 'Apoca 20'; Revelation 20:7.

89 La Rochelle was besieged in 1572–73 during the French wars of religion. According to one of the 'French histories' referred to here, *The fourth parte of Co[m]mentaries of the ciuill warres in Fraunce* (London, 1576), 'it is wonderful which certaine honest and credible persons do report, which were at that siege, how that a certaine kinde of fishe came into the haven in such plentifull maner, contrary to their wonted custome, that the poorer sorte used to eate them in steade of breade, and that the same plentie went away almost the same day, when the kings army departed upon the conclusion of peace' (p. 85).

90 The reference is to John Foxe's *Actes and Monuments*, the first edition of which was printed in 1563.

think as they will) I for my part think our earthquakes, especially the first of them, to be a great miracle of God to advise us of his wrath and to call us to repentance, of which mind I am the rather first because I find in the scriptures threapnings[91] of God's shaking the earth, secondly for that earthquakes are numbered amongst the miracles which happened at Christ's death and also amongst the miraculous signs which shall precede the second coming of Christ, and thirdly because all the philosophers of all ages could never agree upon any natural cause thereof, some affirming fire, some water, some winds, some the ponderosity, age, and concavity of the earth, some one thing and some another.[92] And yet if they had all agreed in one upon one cause (as they do most notably dissent) yet would I still take earthquakes for miracles by reason of the authority of scripture, which are already and might be more at large alleged, and here I have made mention of the philosophers not only for the purpose aforesaid but also thereby to answer in part your authority of philosophy here alleged. For when they can give no true or certain reason for so an apparent matter as earthquakes are, why should we look at their hands for a reason of the secret and miraculous practices of witches? [f. 68v] It nothing appertaineth (as I think) to philosophy to render reasons for miracles nor of any other practices of the devil, for whether there were a devil or devils they did not know, and how then should they know the reasons of his practices? Yea, I dare affirm that all the philosophers in the world were never able to render any reason for the natural effects of those herbs and stones and bodies of men which you in your treatise of magic natural have mentioned, or of those that are mentioned by St August in one of his books *De Civitate Dei* vz. libro 21 ca. 5, 6, *et* 7, to the which places for avoiding prolixity I do refer you, where you shall not only read of many strange effects of natural things, but also be satisfied in this: that a reason is not to be required for everything which we should believe to be true, and especially in the said 5 chapter, which is entitled thus: *Quanta sunt qua non possunt rectem agnosci, et tamen eadem esse non sit ambiguum.*[93] In this chapter he greatly reproveth those that will not believe miraculous matters except they may be proved by reason, and against such he opposeth (as I do now unto you) the incredible effects of natural things for the which no reason can be delivered, and yet are they

---

91 OED: 'To rebuke, reprove, chide, scold, blame.'
92 This must be a reference to the Dover Straits earthquake of 6 April 1580, which was followed by a powerful aftershock on 1 May: see the 'Date' section in the Introduction above. On the earthquakes preceding the second coming of Christ, see, for example, Matthew 24:3–7; no references are given in the treatise.
93 Augustine, *City of God*, 21.5: 'Of such things as cannot be assuredly known to be such, and yet are not to be doubted.'

believed. And whereas the believers of them answer that they believe them (and not other miraculous matters) saying (as you may see in the foresaid 7th cap) *vis haec est naturae natura eorum sic se habet* &c,⁹⁴ he there showeth that some of the said effects of natural things are rather against nature than according to the same, proving according to the title of that chapter that *in rebus miris summa credendi ratio sit in omnipotentia creatoris*.⁹⁵ And lest you should think that all this treatise of St August tendeth only to the defence of divine miracles, and for the believing of them, if you read the said 6 chapter you shall see that he doth acknowledge also devilish miracles in that chapter, thus entitled: *Quod non omnia miracula naturalia sint, pleraque humano ingenio modificata pleraque autem daemonum arte composita*.⁹⁶ Herein I have now (and somewhat also before in my answer to your 20 reason) said the more because you do very much and often harp upon this string; vz. that witches' doings and their confessions of the same are not to be credited [f. 69r] because there can be no reason delivered for them. And now to your authority of physic, I answer that he is not worthy the name of a physician who knoweth not that there be many sorts of *antidotum* against the force of poisoning. And if physicians were ignorant hereof (as they are not) yet you yourself cannot be ignorant hereof having showed divers stones whose nature is to deliver the users of them from poisoning. But St August also in the places here quoted doth at large answer this matter first by the example of the scorpion, who with the poison of his body poisoneth all other living things to whom the same is applied, but yet is so far from taking any hurt himself by that poison that his life is thereby preserved most especially. For if the same poison should be taken from him (as St Aug. there sayeth) he would without all doubt perish and be slain thereby.⁹⁷ Secondly St August showeth there an history of a certain wicked

---

94 A reference to 21:7 of *De Civitate Dei*: '*uis est ista naturae, natura eorum sic se habet, propriarum sunt istae efficaciae naturarum. tota itaque ratio est, cur Agrigentinum salem flamma fluere faciat, aqua crepitare, quia haec est natura eius.*' In this passage, Augustine quotes the hypothetical arguments of people with whom he disagrees: '"It is nature; nature has given it this quality." So then it was nature that made the Agrigentine salt melt in the fire, and crackle in the water.' Augustine goes on to sarcastically describe this explanation as 'A good brief reason verily, and a sufficient' (*City of God*, 21.7).
95 'God's omnipotency the ground of all belief in things marvelled at'.
96 'All strange effects are not nature's. Some are man's devices; some the devil's' (*City of God*, 21.6).
97 Author's note: 'de morib[us] manichoru[m] li 1 ca 8'. The reference is to Augustine's *The Way of Life of the Manicheans*. Here Augustine writes: 'For one of the leaders of your heresy, whose informal discussions we frequently attended, used to say by way of an answer to anyone who maintained that evil is not a substance: "I would like to

woman of Athens which being with other wicked persons condemned to die by drinking of poison used before by a little and a little to drink poison: by the customable use whereof when the time was come that she with the other should drink that measure of poison which was by order appointed to condemned persons to bring them to their deaths, she alone did drink up the same without any hurt to her health, all the other presently dying by their drinking of the like measure, insomuch that the escape of this woman being holden for a miracle she was not after put to death but banished.[98] This history St Aug. doth set down to show thereby the same to be possible which you do here think impossible; vz. that poison may be so used and applied by the temperature of one body more than of another, that it may hurt the one and not the other, which also he showeth by the divers use and application of *Elleborum,* saying there *Elleborum nonne alio modo cibus est, alio medicamentum, alio venenum?* and let this suffice for this

    put a scorpion in that man's hand and see whether he would not draw his hand away. If he did so, he would have proved conclusively, not by words but by the act itself, that evil is a substance since he would not deny that the animal is a substance." He did not say this in front of the person himself, but to us when we, being disturbed by what the man had said, reported it to him. Thus, as I said, he gave a childish answer to children. For who, with a modicum of knowledge, cannot see that such creatures are harmful because they are incompatible with our bodily composition, and that when the conditions are compatible, they do not harm and can even be quite beneficial? If the poison were evil in itself, the scorpion would be the first to suffer. Actually, however, if it were deprived of all its poison, the scorpion would most certainly die. Therefore, what it is evil for the scorpion to lose, it is evil for us to receive, and what it is good for the scorpion to have, it is good for us to be without.' *The Way of Life of the Manicheans,* translated by Donald A. Gallagher and Idella J. Gallagher (Washington, DC: Catholic University of America Press, 1966), pp. 72–3. The story about the female criminal follows immediately afterwards in the same chapter (see following and note below).

98 Author's note: '& here I have somwhat holpen Bodyn w[ho] sayth *Huic argumento quid responderi possit nescio*'. This, like Scot's rendering, seems to be a paraphrase or variant of the 1581 Basel edition: '*cui argumento non video quid responderi possit*': *De Magorum Daemonomania,* 2.8 (p. 220). The full passage, in the original French edition, reads: '*Il est tout notoire, que les plus grandes Sorcieres font quelquesfois mourir en souflant au visage, comme Daneau a bien remarqué en son petit dialogue: mai ie n'approuve pas que c'est par le moyen des poisons qu'elles ont en la bouche, comme dit Daneau: Car les Sorcieres en mourroient les premieres, qui est vn argument auquel ie ne voy point de response*': *De la Démonomanie des Sorciers* (Paris, 1580), p. 114v; 'It is notorious that the greatest witches sometimes kill by blowing on the face, as Daneau has well remarked in his little *Dialogue*. But I cannot agree that this is by means of poison held in the mouth, as Daneau says: for then the witch would die first, an argument to which I can see no answer' [my translation].

point.[99] To your allegation of law I say I know not what law you mean of, but sure I am the law of God appointed death to all witches, sorcerers, and such like without exception or regard had to the impossibility of their doings.[100] The law also under the which we in England live accepteth and alloweth the confession of witches in cases of death (as it doth the confessions of all other malefactors in the like case) no less than it doth accept and allow an 100 witnesses against them insomuch as if a witch or any other malefactor be arraigned of witchery &c (which is by law capital) and do confess herself guilty, there needeth no other evidence or trial to condemn her. The Canon law also doth the same, as you are not ignorant by the proceedings of the Inquisitors [f. 69v] by force of that law, neither are you ignorant that the law of the 12 tables (which was the first and most reverenced law of the Romans) doth appoint death to witches and such like in cases of as great impossibilities as may be to man's reason and nature. Finally, how the civil law doth allow of voluntary confessions, whether they be true in the things which they do confess or whether they be false in bearing false witness against themselves, I have before showed in my answer to your 36 reason, so that you have no reason to allege against this matter law so absolutely and so indefinitely as you do. Yea, indeed so generally as you do, for you say no law will admit such a confession as doth yield to impossibilities, and herein also you are contrary to yourself for in your 12 reason you show how Brentius replieth against the imperial[101] which condemneth them to death that trouble and infect things. For how can such troublers as are by that law condemned to death be known to have done such things otherwise than by their own confessions? Now resteth your reason of conscience to be answered, wherein you use *petitio principii*,[102] grounding your assertion upon a thing presupposed to be true and granted so to be, which is indeed both untrue and ungranted. Your ground is this: that our witches or old women confessing themselves to be witches are not by conscience to be executed upon their confessions because they have no sound or perfect judgement. But that they are void of such judgement I have before in my answers to your 36, 42, and 43 reasons denied, showing reason to the contrary more than you have showed for your part, for as yet you have showed none nor can (as I think) unless you can prove all or the most sort of our suspected witches to be either natural idiots or drunken or lunatics or frantic when they confess, for these only be the persons whom

---

99 Augustine, *The Way of Life of the Manicheans*: 'And is not hellebore sometimes a food, sometimes a medicine, and sometimes a poison?' (p. 74).
100 Author's note: 'exo 22 deutro 18'; Exodus 22:18, Deuteronomy 18:10.
101 OED: 'A decree or statute of an emperor'.
102 circular reasoning, or 'begging the question'.

we accompt to have no sound or perfect judgement, except you will add unto these (as you may) infants and those that be not come to mature years, as those also that are decrepit and dote through old age, and those likewise that have their senses taken from them by paralyses, apoplexies, and other sicknesses. As for the melancholy persons whom you have described and spoken of, they may well go amongst the lunatic and frantic. But the most of our suspected witches cannot be numbered with them or with any of the other sort more than any other sort of honest and sober women, for that they have (as before I have said) their reason, sense, understanding, and judgement to outward appearance as sound and as perfect as any other woman have of their age and education, which surely is not to be denied, sith by common trial and experience in talking and conferring with them and in all other their affairs it will so be found in the most of them.

[f. 70r] Reason 45

> Alas! if they were so subtill, as witchmongers make them to be, they would espie that it were meere follie for them, not onelie to make a bargaine with the divell to throw their soules into hell fire, but their bodies to the tortures of temporall fire and death, for the accomplishment of nothing that might benefit themselves at all: but they would at the leastwise indent with the divell, both to inrich them, and also to enoble them; and finallie to endue them with all worldlie felicitie and pleasure: which is furthest from them of all other. (Scot, 3.8)

To espy the avoiding of hellfire is not in the subtlety of human wit or reason but in the gift and grace of God, which he bestoweth upon his elect children outwardly by the preaching of his word and inwardly by the working of his holy spirit, from the which gift all the ungodly that continue in their ungodliness without true faith and repentance are utterly secluded.[103] And therefore no marvel it is if witches, which are said to forsake the faith of Christ and to bind themselves by league or otherwise by free and glad consent of mind unto the devil, should neither see nor yet believe hellfire to be due unto them. St Paul bids us mark our calling, how not many wise are called &c, and Christ thanketh his heavenly father that it pleased him to reveal unto babes and infants those things which he had hidden from the wise and prudent of the world.[104] And by common experience we see an infinite number of most wise men (as the world esteemeth them) to run headlong to the devil by their manifold sins and wickedness. Wherefore of the subtlety

---

103 OED: 'To shut off, obstruct the access to (a thing).'
104 Author's notes: 'i corinth I', 'math 11'; 1 Corinthians 1:26, Matthew 11:25.

and wit of the wicked, I say with the prophet they are wise to do evil, but to do well they have no knowledge.[105] And why the wicked have no knowledge to do well the same prophet showeth after in another place saying, 'Lo they have rejected the word of the Lord, and what wisdom can be in them?'[106] Now as touching the throwing of their bodies into temporal death and tortures, I think of them in this as I do of other malefactors; vz. that as thieves, murderers, and traitors &c do think nothing less than to come to death and tortures when they attempt their villainies, but are in good hope (the devil together with the corruption of their own natures so persuading them) that they shall escape and have their desired success, even so is it with witches to think and hope of their practices. And these rather than the other for that their practices are more secret and hard to be found out than are those of thieves, murderers, and traitors. And where you say they do all this for nothing that might benefit them, there is no doubt but they do it upon hope of great benefit promised by the devil unto them and to many of them performed. The story of Christ's temptation may suffice to teach us what great and fair promises the devil will make to have men serve and worship him. For there he promised to Christ all the kingdoms of the world, and the glory of them, to win worship at his hands, and to our first parents he promised they should be like unto gods and not die if they would be ruled by him.[107] That also he doth sometime yield benefits where he taketh footing may appear by the great advantage which she gat unto her master that was possessed with a wicked spirit by which she did divine.[108] And if the pope's own historiographers and secretaries do not belie those most unholy fathers, divers of them gat possession of Peter's chair (as they call their popedom) by the devil's help and promise, with whom they dealt and consulted by their sorceries, [f. 70v] especially Benedict the 9, Gregory the 6, Gregory the 7, Sylvester the 2, who by the authors quoted and by divers other are recorded to have been notable conjurers and sorcerers.[109] And of the said Sylvester it is recorded that he being a monk did in his youth leave his monastery and gave himself wholly to the devil upon condition that he should obtain at his hands what he would desire and so in the end came to the popedom by the devil's help, with this condition: that after he was dead

---

105 Author's note: 'Jeremy 4'; Jeremiah 4:22.
106 Author's note: 'Jeremy 8'; Jeremiah 8:9.
107 Author's notes: 'math 4', 'Gen 3'; Matthew 4:8–9, Genesis 3:5.
108 Author's note: 'acts 16'; Acts 16:16.
109 Author's note: 'platina. cardinalis benno. joha[n]es stella venetus &c'. The references are to Benno, an eleventh-century cardinal who sided with the antipope Clement III and wrote a highly critical biography of Clement's rival Gregory VII, and Bartolomeo Platina and Giovanni Stella, both of whom wrote lives of the popes.

the devil should for that benefit bestowed upon him possess him both body and soul. Divers histories mo[110] might be here remembered for proof of the devil's large liberality extended to many others his servants. But admit he did nothing else for them but only help them to be revenged of those who they most deadly hate and would hurt. Do you think this to be esteemed but for a small benefit amongst the godless envious persons? Then are you very ignorant and unexpert in the force of envy, and I would we were all most ignorant thereof as touching the experience of it in our own persons. But I will give you an example or two of the force of this venomous vice in the persons of other. Was not this vice, think you, of most great force in the heart of Herodias and her daughter when they did choose rather to be revenged of John Baptist with the cutting off his head (for the malice they did bear him) than to have the one half of Herod's kingdom which they might have had instead of the other?[111] Was not this vice also (think you) of most great force in the heart of wicked king Ahab against Elijah the prophet when as there was no nation or kingdom whither that king did not send and by oath enquire for Elijah, that finding him he might kill him thereby to wreak his malice upon him?[112] To be short, was not (think you) the force of this vice very great in the heart of Constantius an Arian Emperor towards good Athanasius, the chief enemy of that horrible heresy, when as this heretic Emperor did command (as the story telleth *ingenti mercede proposita*)[113] that Athanasius (being then fled from his furious hands) should be found out and killed and brought unto him dead or alive, saying that he had not so hearty a desire to enjoy any success as the removing and ridding of Athanasius out of the way from ecclesiastical affairs.[114] Here might I remember the force of envy in Cain, in Esau, in the sons of Jacob towards their own natural brethren whom through envy they handled most villainously, especially Cain, of the force of whose envy St Cyprian speaketh

---

110 OED: 'A greater number; more individuals of the kind specified or implied.'
111 Author's note: 'math 14 marc 6'; the story of the beheading of John the Baptist is told in Matthew 14:1–12 and Mark 6:14–29 (and mentioned in Luke 9:9).
112 Author's note: '1 regu[m] i8'; 1 Kings 18:10. Ahab enquired 'by oath' in that he required a sworn oath that John the Baptist could not be found.
113 'after a great reward had been offered' [my translation].
114 Constantius II (317–61), Roman Emperor from 337–361; Athanasius (c. 296–373), bishop of Alexandria. Author's notes: 'theodoret[us] li 2 ca 14' and 'theodoret[us] li 2 ca 16'. The references are to the *Ecclesiastical History* of the fifth-century Bishop of Cyrus, Theodoret. In the nineteenth-century English translation of Theodoret's *Ecclesiastical History*, translated by Blomfield Jackson, in *Nicene and Post-Nicene Fathers*, Second Series, vol. 3, edited by Philip Schaff and Henry Wace (Grand Rapids, MI: Wm B. Eerdman, 1953), the reward for Athanasius' capture is offered in chapter 11 (p. 76).

notably well, saying *Tantum valuit ad consummationem* [f. 71r] *facinoris, aemulationis furor ut nec charitas fratris, nec sceleris immanitas; nec timor dei, nec poena delicti cogitaretur.*[115] And no less notably doth he write of this vice of envy generally in the same place, saying *non est autem quod aliquis existimet malum istud una specie contineri, aut brevibus terminis et angusto fine concludi. Late patet caeli* [sic] *multiplex et faecunda pernicies, radix est omnium malorum, et fons cladium, seminarium delictorum, materia culparum* &c.[116] Again he sayeth *mala caetera habent terminum, et quodcumque delinquitur delicti consummatione finitur. In adultero cessat facinus perpetrato stupro, in latrone conquiescit scelus homicidio admisso, et praedoni rapacitatem statuit possessa praeda, et falsario modum ponit impleta fallacia. Zelus terminum non habet, permanens iugit malum et sine fine peccatum est* &c.[117] Thus may you see how great and endless also the force of envy is, whereby you may the more consider that if the wicked do serve the devil for no other thing but to have their malice and envy executed, this alone is unto such persons a most notable benefit. Yea, it is the whole benefit that the devil himself doth win by all his endless and restless travels, for of his envy it was that sin first entered into the world, and of envy only it is that he troubleth and turmoileth himself and this present world with the creatures of the same by such infinite ways and means as he doth. And therefore it is enough for his servants (as it is for Christ's servants) to be in such state and condition as their master is. For this saying of

---

115 Author's note: 'sermonez de Zelo et Livore'. The reference is to Cyprian's *On Jealousy and Envy*: 'So far prevailed the rage of envy to the consummation of that deed of wickedness, that neither the love of his brother, nor the immensity of the crime, nor the fear of God, nor the penalty of the sin, was considered.' St Cyprian, *On Jealousy and Envy*, translated by Ernest Wallis, in *Anti-Nicene Fathers*, vol. 5, edited by Alexander Roberts and James Donaldson, revised by A. Cleveland Coxe (Grand Rapids, MI: Wm B. Eerdman, 1978), p. 492.

116 St Cyprian, *Jealousy and Envy*: 'there is no ground for anyone to suppose that evil of that kind is confined in one form, or restrained within brief limits in a narrow boundary. The mischief of jealousy, manifold and fruitful, extends widely. It is the root of all evils, the fountain of disasters, the nursery of crimes, the material of transgressions' (6); *caeli* ('heaven') seems to be an error for *zeli* ('jealousy') on the author's part.

117 St Cyprian, *Jealousy and Envy*: 'Other ills have their limit; and whatever wrong is done, is bounded by the completion of the crime. In the adulterer the offence ceases when the violation is perpetrated; in the case of the [assassin], the crime is at rest when the homicide is committed; and the possession of the booty puts an end to the rapacity of the thief; and the completed deception places a limit to the wrong of the cheat. Jealousy has no limit; it is an evil continually enduring, and a sin without end' (7) [translation adapted].

Christ, *non est discipulas supra magistri*, with the other *sufficit discipula ut sit sicut magister*, is generally true between all kind of masters and their scholars or servants.[118]

Reason 46

[See excerpt to reason 45 above]

To this 46 reason I have in my answer to the former reason said sufficiently, saving for the matter of indenting here spoken I can say nothing whether it be so or no, no more can you or any man else.[119] But the likelihood is, yea the very certainty is, that the devil either by league or by his secret and subtle suggestions doth in some such sort allure the minds of those that are his servants as they like well of his persuasions and offers. And that he leaveth not all his servants in great excess of penury the examples before showed may suffice to prove the contrary.

Reason 47

Yea, if they were sensible, they would saie to the divell; Whie should I hearken to you, when you will deceive me? Did you not promise my neighbour mother *Dutton* to save and rescue hir; and yet lo she is hanged? Surelie this would appose the divell verie sore. And it is a woonder, that none, from the beginning of the world, till this daie, hath made this and such like objections, whereto the divell could never make answer. (Scot, 3.8)

If they should object and question with the devil as you would here advise them to do, yet do I not think the devil would be so opposed thereby as he should be unable to make answer unto it. We see by experience that false and subtle men do many times deceive those that deal with them and [fol. 71v] yet are not greatly to seek[120] for their answer when they be charged with deceit or breaking of promise, as for example if a blind physician (yea or a cunning) promiseth his patient to restore him to health and fail therein, will he not turn the fault upon his patient and say that he did not in all points observe his prescriptions of diet, warm keeping, walking &c? You know, I am sure, the merry tale which showeth that the blind physician will sooner charge his patient with eating up an ass and surfeiting

---

118 Author's note: 'mattheu 10'; Matthew 10:24–25: 'The disciple is not aboue his master'; 'It is ynough for the disciple to be as his master'.
119 OED: 'To enter into an engagement by indentures; hence, to make a formal or express agreement; to covenant (*with* a person *for* a thing); to engage.'
120 OED: 'At a loss or at fault; unable to act, understand, etc.; puzzled to know or decide.'

thereby rather than he will confess his own ignorance. So also the lawyer (the unlearned and unconscionable especially) if he promise his client good success in his cause and the same fall out contrariwise, will he not cunningly turn the fault of his promise breaking either upon his client, saying he did not throughly inform him, or else upon the jury, saying they were partial? If men then can find pretty shifts to blear the eyes even of wise men when they so deceive them, shall we think that he which is the captain and inspirer of all subtle shifts (and therefore called *mille artifex*)[121] would be to seek of a shift to blear the eyes of such silly and simple women as you make witches be, if they should oppose him with Mother Dutton or any other the like? No, no, it is his special property to excecate[122] and blind the senses and understandings of the unbelieving sort, as the apostle telleth, and therefore have not such either the grace or the wisdom that is fit to catch him in a trip[123] or to put him to his trump.[124]

Reason 48

> But were it not more [sic] madnes for them to serve the divell, under these conditions; and yet to endure whippings with iron rods at the divels hands; which (as the witchmongers write) are so set on, that the print of the lashes remaine upon the witches bodie ever after, even so long as she hath a daie to live? (Scot, 3.8)

It is, I confess, mere madness and more than madness for them to serve the devil under those or any other conditions, and to have such whipping cheer[125] for their guerdon[126] and pains. But this is no such special kind of madness as you mean of, but such as is common to all the devil's servitors (I mean the reprobated) how wise and how prudent soever they are in worldly wit and judgement. The whole nation for the most part of the wicked Jews had this kind of madness in them when they rejected the government which the lord had appointed them under godly and just Samuel, and would need have instead of the same a king to reign over them, though they were told

---

121 This description of the devil (roughly, 'the contriver with a thousand tricks') may have originated in the Auvergne region of France: Priscilla Baumann, 'The Deadliest Sin: Warnings against Avarice and Usury on Romanesque Capitals in Auvergne', *Church History* 59:1 (1990), 7–18 (p. 10, footnote 6).
122 OED: 'To make blind, to blind.'
123 OED: 'A mistake, blunder; a fault; a slip, lapse; a false step; a slip of the tongue. †to take or have in a trip (also †to take trip), to catch tripping, to detect in an error.'
124 Author's note: '2 Corinth 4'; 2 Corinthians 4:4.
125 OED: '(humorous) flogging, flagellation.'
126 OED: 'A reward, requital, or recompense.'

beforehand that they, their sons, their daughters, all that they had shall be under that king most cruelly oppressed and most extremely handled.[127] Yea they proceeded to a further kind of madness than this is, for they offered their sons and their daughters unto devils and shed innocent blood, even the blood of their sons and of their daughters whom they offered to the idols of Canaan.[128] Now if this kind of madness [f. 72r] took footing amongst the Jews which were the chosen and peculiar people of God, which had his law and prophets to instruct them and had seen the great and mighty miracles of God as well in punishing them for their sins as in defending them from their enemies, is it, think you, to be supposed that any other people or nation of the world were free from this or the like madness? No, verily, all histories testify the contrary. For proof whereof and for avoiding of prolixity I refer you to Tertullian, Plutarch, Polydore Vergil &c, where you shall see that throughout all nations as well civil as barbarous, the slaying and sacrificing of men, women, and children to their false gods and idols was often put in use and practised.[129] And not to go from the histories of the scriptures, you may see there how the king of Moab (being overcome in battle by the Israelites) did take his eldest son that should have reigned in his stead and offered him for a burnt sacrifice which no doubt was done to appease the wrath of his false gods whom he thought to be offended with him.[130] There shall you see also that it was a common use of the heathen, yea and of God's people, to make their sons and daughters go through the fire unto Moloch, that is to burn them up with fire unto their false gods for sacrifices unto them, whereof it came that God very often commanded his people to take heed of that wickedness, appointing them to be slain as many as should commit the same.[131] There shall you also read how the priests of

---

127 Author's note: '1 Sam 8'; 1 Samuel 8:1–20.
128 Author's note: 'psal 106'; Psalm 106:38.
129 Author's notes: 'Tertulian in suo scorpiago advers[us] Gnosticos plutarc in parallellia ca 66 et 67 polidor li 5 ca 8 de invent reru[m].' The references are to Tertullian's *Adversus Gnosticos Scorpiace*, Plutarch's *Parallel Lives* (*Vitae Parallelae* or Gr. *Bíoi Parálléloi*) and Polydore Vergil's *De Inventoribus Rerum* (Lyon, 1546). The title of book 5, chapter 8 of this last work begins '*cunctas fere gentes quondam daemonibus malis humanas immolasse hostias*': 'Almost all nations once sacrificed human victims to evil demons' [my translation].
130 Author's note: '4 Regu[m] 3'; 2 Kings 3:27. The author follows the numbering of the books of the Bible found in the Vulgate and the Septuagint, which referred to the two books of Samuel as 1 Kings and 2 Kings and the two books of Kings as 3 Kings and 4 Kings. See also the discussion of sources in the introduction above.
131 Author's notes: '4 Regu[m] 16 Ahas', 'levitic[us] 18. 20 deutro 12 18 4 Regu[m] 17 21'; in 2 Kings 16:3 king Ahaz 'made his sonne to go thorow the fyre, after the abominations of the heathe[n]'. Rules against this practice and the worship of false

112 A defence of witchcraft belief

Baal did miserably cut and lance themselves with knives and lances when they prayed to that, their false god, to be heard of him. Finally there shall you read that there was scarcely any horrible act or cruelty to be devised but the same was done and suffered for the serving of devils, idols, and false gods, as well by the professed people of God as by the heathen which did not know him. And now if a man should ask you what gain or benefit was gotten hereby, more than our witches get by suffering themselves to be whipped with iron rods I suppose you nor no man else can tell wherefore. Let them all that I have now spoken be deemed as mad as our witches, if not much madder.

Reason 49

> But these old women being daunted with authoritie, circumvented with guile, constrained by force, compelled by feare, induced by error, and deceived by ignorance, doo fall into such rash credulitie, and so are brought unto these absurd confessions. Whose error of mind and blindnes of will dependeth upon the disease and infirmitie of nature: and therefore their actions in that case are the more to be borne withall; bicause they, being destitute of reason, can have no consent. For, *Delictum sine consensu non potest committi, neque injuria sine animo injuriandi*; that is, There can be no sinne without consent, nor injurie committed without a mind to doo wrong. (Scot, 3.8)

I suppose our witches are by no other means brought to confess their witcheries than other malefactors are brought to confess other their sins and wickedness, and with us there are not applied to our witches any such tortures as are applied to other malefactors, yea they are put to no tortures at all for anything I know or have heard of. As for their disease and unsoundness of mind it is before sufficiently answered in Reas. 36, 42, 43, and 44. Where you say *peccati sine consensu non potest committi*,[132] I will not here urge against you original sin which dwelleth in the least infant without consent, but I will take your meaning to be (as I think it is) of actual sins. And although I am not ignorant of this saying of St [f. 72v]

---

gods are given in Leviticus 18:21 and 20:2–5, and in Deuteronomy 12 and 18:10. 2 Kings 17 and 21 both describe the commands of God and the continuing idolatry of the Israelites at length.

132 'sin cannot be committed without consent'. The quotation given in the treatise differs from that in the published version of Scot's book, although the import of the two phrases is the same. Scot provides a reference to to '*L. si per errorem jurisd, omni cum inde*'; his direct source is Johannes Weyer: Kapitaniak (ed.), *La Sorcellerie Démystifiée*, p. 158, footnote 47.

Augustine (making in appearance with you), vz. *omne peccatum ideo est voluntarium ut nisi sit voluntarium non est peccatum*[133] yet dare I affirm (for certain) that even actual sins may be and daily are committed without consent, if you will accept that to be done without a man's consent which is done without his knowledge, as it I think is not to be denied. For proof of this my purpose[134] I will first use the words of the prophet David where he sayeth *delicta quis intelligit ab occultis meis munda me domine*.[135] Here the prophet confesseth that no man doth understand or know all his sin (for so much importeth his interrogation)[136] and withal he desireth God to cleanse him from those sins which he doth not know of. For by secret or hidden sins in this place he meaneth not (as all interpreters hereof do affirm) those sins which he did commit secretly in his own knowledge from the eyes of others, but he meaneth those sins which he himself did never know or understand of. Again, the wicked Jews which put Christ to death did not know him to be the lord of life, neither was it any part of their mind and consent that the lord of life should be put unto death, as the apostle testifyeth, saying unto them, 'And now brethren I know that through ignorance ye did it'.[137] And Christ himself testifyeth the same, praying unto his heavenly father for them, saying further 'forgive them for they wot not what they do'.[138] Again it is said in another place, they would not have crucified the lord of glory had they known the wisdom of God that was hid in him.[139] Hereof I gather that if sin reach no further than where it hath the consent of the sinner then these Jews in putting of Christ unto death sinned not against him in that he was the lord of life, the son of God, and the messiah of the world, but only in that he was a man as other men are. But yet the scripture is plain to the contrary even in the foresaid place, for in that Christ prayed that they might be forgiven that wherein they sinned ignorantly, and in that the apostle in the forsaid place exhorted them to repent the same, saying 'Amend your lives therefore and turn' &c, it is manifest that they sinned further than

---

133 'But in fact sin is so much a voluntary evil that it is not sin at all unless it is voluntary.' *De Vera Religione*, 14.27. Translation from John S. H. Burleigh (ed.), *Augustine: Earlier Writings* (Philadelphia, PA: The Westminster Press, 1953), p. 238.
134 OED: 'That which is propounded; a proposition, a question, an argument; a riddle.'
135 Author's note: 'psal i9'; Psalm 19.12: 'Who can vnderstand *his* fautes? clense me from secret *fautes*.' This verse is psalm 18.13 in the Vulgate Bible; here the author uses the newer numbering system, following the Hebrew arrangement rather than that of the Septuagint.
136 OED: 'Questioning, or a question, as a form of speech.'
137 Author's note: 'acts 3'; Acts 3:17.
138 Luke 23:34; no note provided in the original text.
139 Author's note: '1 corinth 2'; a paraphrase of 1 Corinthians 2:7–8.

either their knowledge or consent did reach unto.[140] And what think you of Pontius Pilate, of whom it is said in the said place of the Acts that he judged Christ to be delivered, and in another place that in token that he was far from consenting to his death washed his hands before the multitude, pronouncing himself to be innocent from Christ's death and transferring the whole guiltiness thereof unto them, saying 'I am Innocent of the blood of this just man look ye unto it'.[141] Do you think for all this that Pilate was indeed innocent in this matter, though he withheld his assent from it? I trow not. Let this then suffice to show that this is no true principle, vz. *peccatum sine consensu non potest committi*, and this may also serve for to overthrow your other principle: to wit, that an injury cannot be done without a mind to do the same. But this the very moral philosophers do overthrow, as Tully [fol. 73r] in his *Offices* where he sayeth *tam est in vitio qui illatam iniuriam non propulsat (si possit) quam is qui infert iniuriam*[142] and Aristotle in his *Ethics* doth tell us that a man may *agere iusta* which is not *iustus* whereof by the contrary (*quorum eadem est ratio*)[143] we may learn that injury may be done though the doer thereof be no injurious or unjust person. But all this is by the way rather to answer to your said two principles than to the matter, to which I do now return and do say that if both these your principles were true yet do they not aptly agree to our witches, for they are such (as experience teacheth too evidently) which do both wish unto their enemies such hurts as are supposed to come by witchcraft, and when they see they happen unto them according to their malicious wishes they do much rejoice thereat. Wherefore whether our witches be (as sometimes

---

140 Author's note: 'acts 3'; Acts 3:19.
141 Author's note: 'math 27'; Matthew 27:24.
142 'He who does not (if he can) prevent an injury is as much at fault as the one who inflicted the injury.' This seems to be a paraphrase of part of Cicero's *De Officiis*, 1.23. The Loeb text, translated by Walter Miller (Cambridge, MA: Harvard University Press, 1913), reads: '*Nam qui iniuste impetum in quempiam facit aut ira aut aliqua perturbatione incitatus, is quasi manus afferre videtur socio; qui autem non defendit nec obsistit, si potest, iniuriae, tam est in vitio, quam si parentes aut amicos aut patriam deserat*'; 'For he who, under the influence of anger or some other passion, wrongfully assaults another seems, as it were, to be laying violent hands upon a comrade; but he who does not prevent or oppose wrong, if he can, is just as guilty of wrong as if he deserted his parents or his friends or his country'.
143 'act justly', 'just', 'which is the same reason'. Aristotle argues against the idea that 'if we do just and temperate actions, we are already just and temperate', stating instead that virtue involves not only performing virtuous actions but doing so 'with knowledge', 'from rational choice', and 'from a firm and unshakeable character.' *Nicomachean Ethics*, rev. ed., translated by Roger Crisp (Cambridge: Cambridge University Press, 2014) 2.4 (pp. 27–8).

they confess they are) the procurers of those hurts, or whether they do but falsely imagine they did them, yet is it plain that they consent, and that most gladly, to the doing of them, and so consequently they are not by your said principles to be at all excused.

Reason 50

> Yet the lawe saith further, that A purpose reteined in mind, dooth nothing to the privat or publike hurt of anie man; and much more that an impossible purpose is unpunishable. *Sanae mentis voluntas, voluntas rei possibilis est*; A sound mind willeth nothing but that which is possible. (Scot, 3.8)

I would you did show what law you speak of, for if you speak of a law to which we are not tied either by God's law or by the law of this realm then can it have with us no authority and so shall it need no answer.[144] But to say somewhat to the matter, your law (whatsoever it be) is directly against the law and word of God, for thereby evil thoughts and purposes, how secretly soever they be retained in mind, are of themselves both wicked and damnable, as to lust in my heart for my neighbour's wife, or in my heart to hate him.[145] The one is adultery, the other is murder, and so much to a private hurt (if to none other, yet to myself) that it deserveth damnation without God's mercy.[146] And as touching the law of our realm, I suppose there be divers cases wherein the purpose of the heart (if it come by confession unto light) is very punishable, especially if one should purpose (which God forbid) the destruction of our Queen or of her counsellors and after confess the same, no act being done, I trow it should not go unpunished. But more to the matter, I say our witches do not retain their evil purposes in mind only, but they use imprecations, charms, cursings, crossings, and such other outward actions as no man can deny, themselves both confessing the same and also using the same in the presence and hearing of those their neighbours whom they think they may trust, especially when they pretend to do some good thing or cure thereby. As touching the possibility of their doings, as also that they are not unsound of mind which have a will to impossible things, I have said sufficiently in Reas. 44 *et* 25.

---

144 The published version of the *Discoverie* appears to have taken this objection into account, as it does provide two marginal references: 'C. sed hoc d. de publ. &c.' and '*Bal. in leg. &c.*' Again, Scot's direct source is Weyer: Kapitaniak (ed.), *La Sorcellerie Démystifiée*, p. 158, footnote 49.
145 Author's note: 'mathew 5'; Matthew 5:22, 28.
146 Author's note: '1 John 3'; 1 John 3:15.

[f. 73v] Reason 51

> If anie man advisedlie marke their words, actions, cogitations [sic], and gestures, he shall perceive that melancholie abounding in their head, and occupieng their braine, hath deprived or rather depraved their judgements, and all their senses: I meane not of coosening witches, but of poore melancholike women, which are themselves deceived. For you shall understand, that the force which melancholie hath, and the effects that it worketh in the bodie of a man, or rather of a woman, are almost incredible. For as some of these melancholike persons imagine, they are witches and by witchcraft can worke woonders, and doo what they list: so doo other, troubled with this disease, imagine manie strange, incredible, and impossible things. Some, that they are monarchs and princes, and that all other men are their subjects: some, that they are brute beasts: some, that they be urinals or earthen pots, greatlie fearing to be broken: some, that everie one that meeteth them, will conveie them to the gallowes; and yet in the end hang themselves.
> [...]
> Now, if the fansie of a melancholike person may be occupied in causes which are both false and impossible; why should an old witch be thought free from such fantasies, who (as the learned philosophers and physicians saie) upon the stopping of their monethlie melancholike flux or issue of bloud, in their age must needs increase therein, as (through their weaknesse both of bodie and braine) the aptest persons to meete with such melancholike imaginations: with whome their imaginations remaine, even when their senses are gone. (Scot, 3.9)

As are the countenances, gestures, words, and actions of our witches when they come before authority to be examined, such are the same or the very like in the most sort of malefactors (of what quality soever their crime is) if they have guilty consciences. This have I partly showed before in the 19 Reas. by the example of Cain's countenance altered, and by a saying of the prophet Isaiah there quoted, to which I do now add our common experience, which teacheth us what hanging looks thieves and murderers have, and what stickings and unwonted scuttings[147] they use in their answers, their senses and memories many times so failing them that they trip themselves in their tales with manifest contrarieties. And this is the just judgement of God bearing sway in their guilty consciences, even whether they will or nil, rather than a melancholy humour as you would have it. For witches, as I said before in the 42 Reason, where I promised to say

---

147 'Sticking' in the sense 'To stop what one is doing; to cease' and scuttings 'To dock, cut short' (OED).

somewhat more of this matter, and now for promise sake, I say there is no greater force in all the melancholy humours that may be imagined than is in a guilty conscience. This made our first parents flee and hide themselves from the presence of God. This made Cain to say his punishment was greater than he could bear and to repute himself a vagabond and a runagate upon the earth and to fear that everyone that found him would slay him. This enforced the traitor Judas most desperately to hang himself. And how many it hath enforced even in our memories to do the like or to cut their own throats is hard to be numbered for the multitude of them. But as I may omit the innumerable examples hereof, you may have in the wisdom of Solomon a most notable description of the force of a guilty conscience in the wicked of all sorts, for there shall you read how they be troubled with horrible fear, dreams, and visitations[148] in such sort that no art nor physic could help them, no creature comfort them or bring solace unto them, but contrariwise everything was fearful and troublesome to them. Yea, and when no fearful thing did fear them, yet were they afraid of the beasts that passed by them and at the hissing of serpents, so that they died for fear, and said they saw not the air which can be by no means avoided. Whether it were an hissing wind or a sweet song of the birds amongst the thick branches of the trees, or the vehemency of hasty running [f. 74r] water, or a great noise of the falling down of stones or the running of skipping beasts that could not be seen or the noise of cruel beasts that roared or the sound that answereth in the hollow mountains, these fearful things made them to sorrow &c.[149] Now that no man should impute this fearful and restless estate of the wicked, to a choleric [sic] humour or to any other natural cause he showeth very plainly in that chapter that the very cause thereof was the guiltiness of their own hearts and consciences, saying 'For it is a fearful thing when malice is condemned by her own testimony, and a conscience that is touched doth ever forecast cruel things'.[150] And that this horror and distress of conscience proceedeth from the just judgement of God against sinners to punish them for their sins, infinite places of the scriptures do teach us, but none more notably than those of Leviticus and Deuteronomy, where we may read how amongst other plagues and punishments threapned of God unto those that would not hear his word and walk after his commandments, this is threapned unto them: that God would send a faintness

---

148 In the manuscript, this word reads 'vysytions'; a possible alternate reading could be 'visions'.
149 Author's note: 'wysdom 17'; the author quotes extensively from the Wisdom of Solomon, 17.9 and 17.17–18, which was included in the Apocrypha in the Geneva Bible.
150 Wisdom of Solomon, 17:10.

into their hearts and strike them with madness, blindness, and astonying[151] of heart, that they should fear and tremble at the shaking of a leaf and flee when no man pursued them, that also they should have no rest but instead thereof such trembling of heart, such sorrowfulness of mind, such fearful sights as they should fear both night and day, in such sort that when it is day they should wish for night, and when it is night they should wish for day for the fear of their heart which they should fear and for the sight of their eyes which they should see.[152] Wherefore, sith this is the just judgement of God upon sins, you should have some better consideration hereof and not impute the confessions and disguised actions, gestures, and behaviours of wicked women (and so notoriously known to be for the most part of them which are accused and suspected for witches) to melancholy humours altogether as you do, as though there could be no other cause thereof, whereby the just judgement of God in this case is altogether secluded and forgotten, which oft[153] most principally to be remembered. And this I note the rather because I see you so much inclined to ascribe the premises to the force of melancholy without consideration had to the force of a guilty conscience, that you do here reckon up Bessus' confession of his parricide as proceeding from a melancholy humour when as the truth is, and all the writers and interpreters upon it his confession do acknowledge, that the same proceeded from the guiltiness of his wicked conscience.[154] And as for your other examples of melancholy persons confessing and imagining things which are not, how do they agree with this of Bessus who confessed that which indeed was? If you will have this proceed from melancholy then is it

---

151 OED: 'to stun, paralyse, astound, amaze'.
152 Author's note: 'Levitic[us] 26 deuto 28'; Leviticus 26:36–37, Deuteronomy 28:28, 65–67.
153 The OED records 'oft' as an alternate form of 'ought'.
154 Pierre Kapitaniak points out that the direct source of the story of Bessus (originally from Plutarch) is Ludwig Lavater's *Of Ghostes and Spirites*, translated by Robert Harrison (London, 1572), p. 15 (*La Sorcellerie Démystifiée*, p. 159, note 57). Scot regards the story of Bessus as an example of melancholy, but Lavater's version makes no mention of this. The author points out an alternative (and more frequently accepted) explanation, given for example in Montaigne's essay 'Of Conscience': 'The storie of Bessus the Poenian is so common, that even children have it in their mouths, who being found fault withall, that in mirth he had beaten downe a nest of young Sparrowes, and then killed them, answered, he had great reason to doe it; forsomuch as those young birds ceased not falsly to accuse him to have murthered his father, which parricide was never suspected to have beene committed by him; and untill that day had layen secret; but the revengefull furies of the conscience, made the same partie to reveale it' – *Essays*, vol. 2, translated by John Florio (London: Folio, 2006); p. 41.

much against your purpose, for it proveth that howsoever men or women be touched with that humour, yet may their confessions be true as this of Bessus was. And therefore {does} [f. 74v] not the opinion of a melancholy humour excuse our witches, though being possessed therewith they did always belie themselves. Yea and between the effects of melancholy and the effects of a guilty conscience there is commonly this difference: that the one sort do willingly and of their own accord confess false things and stand so stiffly and obstinately to that which they confess or imagine that no persuasion or advice can bring them from the same, as evidently appeareth by your own examples of melancholy persons.[155] The other sort would not in any wise (if otherwise they could choose) confess true things against themselves but use as many shifts and helps as they may to conceal them insomuch (as you very well know and confess) they are most times drawn to the confession of the truth (when the same tendeth to their hurt and peril) by guile, by persuasion, by promise, and by tortures &c. Now seeing it goeth thus with witches rather than after the manner of your melancholy persons, me thinketh there is greater reason why they should [be] numbered with them which through the force of a guilty conscience confess the truth against themselves than with those which through the force of melancholy confess false things and stand by the same in the manner aforesaid. Of such melancholy persons I can make no other reckoning than I do of the lunatics and frantic sort, but of our witches other reckoning is to be made, as before hath been showed in other reasons. And thus as you do here ask why our witches should be thought free from the force of a melancholy humour, so may I with more reason ask why they should be thought free from the force of a guilty conscience. But you allege a natural reason out of physic and philosophy to prove your assertion here, saying by the authority of the same that they must needs incur unto this melancholy humour by reason of their monthly issue which is in their age stopped &c. To which I answer that if there be any necessity in this matter then not only our old witches but also all other women of their age, be they never so wise or honest, should also have the like strange and fantastical imaginations, having the like cause thereof in them as the said witches have for it. What necessarily cometh to pass must needs be and cannot be avoided, as both philosophers and physicians will confess, knowing this to be the definition or description of *necessarium*; vz. *hoc demum est necessarium quod aliter se habere non potest*.[156] But I marvel you do lean to philosophy or physic in this point when as before both against philosophy and physic you denied that women could

---

155 Scot gives several examples, most of which are omitted from the excerpt above.
156 'Necessity is what cannot be otherwise' [my translation].

hurt by their eyes and looks, saying the assertion thereof was a lie. Thus have [I] the more largely debated this matter of melancholy because it is one of the chiefest points you stand upon in the excuse and defence of our witches' innocence.

[f. 75r] Reason 52

> But if they may imagine, that they can transforme their owne bodies, which neverthelesse remaineth in the former shape: how much more credible is it, that they may falselie suppose they can hurt and infeeble other mens bodies; or which is lesse, hinder the coming of butter? &c. But what is it that they will not imagine, and consequentlie confesse that they can doo; speciallie being so earnestlie persuaded thereunto, so sorelie tormented, so craftilie examined, with such promises of favour, as wherby they imagine, that they shall ever after live in great credit & welth? (Scot, 3.9)

How falsely they do imagine the transforming of their own bodies I will not here dispute neither will I deny but that they may falsely imagine the rest here spoken of. But my answer to this reason shall be this: *a posse ad esse non valet argumentum*[157] and further I say the right learned do not impute the foresaid false imaginations of transforming themselves to the force of a melancholy humour as you do, but rather to the subtle practices and illusions of Satan offering matter to their minds and senses, as well sleeping as waking, whereby they are moved so to think, which shall be afterward showed even out of some places by you alleged to another purpose.[158]

Reason 53

> If you read the executions doone upon witches, either in times past in other countries, or latelie in this land; you shall see such impossibilities confessed, as none, having his right wits, will beleeve. Among other like false confessions, we read that there was a witch confessed at the time of hir death or execution, that she had raised all the tempests, and procured all the frosts and hard weather that happened in the winter 1565: and that manie grave and wise men beleeved hir. (Scot, 3.9)

Touching the impossibilities of things confessed enough is answered before in other Reas., vz. 4, 6, 13, 21 reas. To your example of the witch's confession here alleged I might say *una hyrundo non facit ver*,[159] but I rather say

---

157 'From being possible to being is not a valid argument'.
158 See reason 67 below.
159 'One swallow does not make a spring'.

that if there be such virtues in stones, herbs, birds, and beasts as you have described, there is some natural possibility for that matter or [at] the least some of them to be done, and further I say if many grave men did believe her then were not the impossibilities such as no man in his right wits would believe them.

Reason 54

> One *Ade Davie*, the wife of *Simon Davie*, husbandman, being reputed a right honest bodie, and being of good parentage, grew suddenlie (as hir husband informed mee, and as it is well knowne in these parts) to be somewhat pensive and more sad than in times past. [...] Hir poore husband being abashed at this hir behaviour, comforted hir, as he could; asking hir the cause of hir trouble & greefe: who told him, that she had (contrarie to Gods lawe) & to the offense of all good christians, to the injurie of him, & speciallie to the losse of hir owne soule, bargained and given hir soule to the divell, to be delivered unto him within short space. [...] But God knoweth, she was innocent of anie these crimes: howbeit she was brought lowe and pressed downe with the weight of this humor, so as both hir rest and sleepe were taken awaie from hir; & hir fansies troubled and disquieted with despaire, and such other cogitations as grew by occasion thereof. (Scot, 3.10)

Your example of Davie's wife I could fully requite with an example of a woman of Kennington which came to my examination who was altogether in the same case, if not in worse, but not for that crime of witching but for playing false play with her husband, which in the end she confessed, being before that reputed a right honest woman amongst her neighbours.[160] And till she had confessed she could not rest night or day but continued in a most sad, sorrowful, and restless condition and was thereby pined away and brought so near to death's door that there was no hope of life left in her. After the matter confessed she found herself well eased at the heart and so by good counsel confirming[161] her she came by a little and little to health of body and quiet of mind soon after doing public penance for the matter confessed. Now to impute these confessions to a melancholic imagination is as I think some derogation to the judgements of God against sin before spoken of Reas. 51, besides sith the cause resting in the mind of the party is not open to any man's eyes or senses, there is no certain censure to be

---

160 The author's mention of Kennington refers not to the area of London, but to what was at the time a village near Ashford in Kent; see the discussion of authorship in the introduction above.

161 OED: 'To strengthen, invigorate; to make firm, support (physically).'

given of the cause. Only your good opinion of the woman may induce you to judge of the matter as you do, but in a woman you may be deceived as well as Solomon or Samson were. Finally, if voluntary [fol. 75v] confessions may be excused and counted of no force in witches by the pretence of melancholy, why may not the same be pretended for all other malefactors, which confess murders, thefts, and adulteries, which without their confessions could never have been proved but by presumptions. And all the world knoweth there want not most great presumptions of hurts and murders laid to witches' charges.

Reason 55

> But in truth, this melancholike humor (as the best physicians affirme) is the cause of all their strange, impossible, and incredible confessions: which are so fond, that I woonder how anie man can be abused thereby. (Scot, 3.11)

I say as before I have said, [in] Reas. 51 and in other places, that such confessions are more like to spring from the horror of a guilty conscience or from some public practice and illusion of Satan (with whom witches have too much familiarity as it is thought) than from that humour of melancholy, neither do I think that any good and learned physician professing God and his word will ever say the contrary. If other physicians than these say as you it is not much to be marvelled sith it is not possible that they (knowing no more than naturally is to be known) should yield any other than natural reasons for their assertions.

Reason 56

> If our witches phantasies were not corrupted, nor their wils confounded with this humor, they would not so voluntarilie and readilie confesse that which calleth their life in question; whereof they could never otherwise be convicted. (Scot, 3.11; cf. reason 42 above)

This reason is all one with your 42 Reas. and therefore my answer made to the same shall suffice for answer of this, to which you may also join my answer to your 44 Reas. and 51, 55, in which places the unsoundness of their mind is at large answered and the causes of such confessions imputed to other things more probable.

Reason 57

> But whie should there be more credit given to witches, when they saie they have made a reall bargaine with the divell, killed a cow, bewitched butter, infeebled a child, forespoken hir neighbour, &c: than when she confesseth

> that she transubstantiateth hir selfe, maketh it raine or haile, flieth in the aire, goeth invisible, transferreth corne in the grasse from one field to another? &c. If you thinke that in the one their confessions be sound, whie should you saie that they are corrupt in the other; the confession of all these things being made at one instant, and affirmed with like constancie, or rather audacitie? (Scot, 3.11)

You would have the devil and his ministers always to lie or always to speak the truth, which thing is so far from their nature to do, and also from their purpose, as you shall always find the contrary in them, as hath been before showed sufficient in my answer to your 29 which may serve for answer to this reason.

Reason 58

> But I saie, both with the divines, and philosophers, that that which is imagined of witchcraft, hath no truth of action; or being besides their imagination, the which (for the most part) is occupied in false causes. For whosoever desireth to bring to passe an impossible thing, hath a vaine, an idle, and a childish persuasion, bred by an unsound mind: for *Sanae mentis voluntas, voluntas rei possibilis est*; The will of a sound mind, is the desire of a possible thing. (Scot, 3.11)

I suppose few divines will say thus knowing that God by his word doth so often and so vehemently condemn witches and witchcraft as it doth. And I suppose God would rather have sent witches to the physicians to be cured rather than to tormenters to be executed with death if there was no more in them and in their doings but their vain and melancholy imaginations. The rest of this reason is often answered before, in reason 25 most specially. As for philosophers they are seldom well coupled with good divines, and in matter handled in the scriptures (as this is) we are not to regard what they say. Yet if I had seen their saying and reasons touching this matter I would have said more to them than now I do or can do.[162]

[fol. 76r] Reason 59

> But it is objected, that witches confesse they renounce the faith, and as their confession must be true (or else they would not make it:) so must their fault be worthie of death, or else they should not be executed. Whereunto I

---

162 Scot cites a variety of authorities in the margin of the printed *Discoverie* (see Kapitaniak, (ed.), *La Sorcellerie Démystifiée*, p. 164, footnote 75), but provides no quotations.

> answer as before; that their confessions are extorted, or else proceed from an unsound mind. Yea I saie further, that we our selves, which are sound of mind, and yet seeke anie other waie of salvation than Christ Jesus, or breake his commandements, or walke not in his steps with a livelie faith, &c: doo not onlie renounce the faith, but God himselfe: and therefore they (in confessing that they forsake God, and imbrace sathan) doo that which we all should doo. (Scot, 3.12)

There be degrees in forsaking of God and in breaking of his commandments. Some forsake him utterly and sin desperately and with greediness, others forsake God but in some points and sin of frailty or ignorance rather than of malice or set purpose, as our papists do not utterly forsake Christ though they seek salvation by other things as well as by him.[163] And there is none so godly but he breaketh God's commandments daily, yea sometime the very elect fall into as great sins as the most reprobate, as Lot into incest, David into adultery and murder, Peter into denying of Christ, Paul into horrible persecution of God's Church, but yet for that these sinned partly of frailty, partly of ignorance, and did believe and repent, it is not in any wise to be said of them that they did no less forsake God and embrace Satan than the other sinners which at the first I spake of, in which number I see none more meet to be placed than witches are, especially if they do renounce their faith in Christ and enter into league with Satan, as the most sort think they do.

Reason 60

> As touching that horrible part of their confession, in the league which tendeth to the killing of their owne and others children, the seething of them, and the making of their potion or pottage, and the effects thereof; their good fridaies meeting, being the daie of their deliverance, their incests, with their returne at the end of nine monethes when commonlie women be neither able to go that journie, nor to returne, &c; it is so horrible, unnaturall, unlikelie, and unpossible; that if I should behold such things with mine eies, I should rather thinke my selfe dreaming, dronken, or some waie deprived of my senses; than give credit to so horrible and filthie matters. (Scot, 3.12)

What you would believe or not believe you best know, but I do believe that there is nothing so horrible, or so unnatural, or so unlikely or impossible in wicked things which Satan will not procure to be done by his ministers, and the which he will not also bring to pass if [it] please God to give him

---

163 Author's note: 'Ephes 4'; Ephesians 4:19.

leave and liberty, as many times he doth in as great impossibilities as there are and in matters as horrible. Sufficient causes of this my believing I find (besides common experience in the actions of this world) in the scriptures as Rom. 1, Ephes. 2, 2 Thes. 2 &c, to the which may be added the horrible deeds and practices of the wicked kings and others set out in the histories of the Old Testament, as well of heathen as of God's professed people whereof somewhat hath been spoken before in Reas. 49. And were but the only wicked acts of Manasseh considered, you should in them find as much horrible and unnatural matter as you have here touched on may in a manner be imagined.[164] And yet must we think the wicked parts and practices of the wicked to be more wicked and horrible than is expressed in the scriptures, because the holy ghost by the mouth of the apostle sayeth it is a shame to name all things done of the wicked in secret.[165]

Reason 61

> How hath the oile or pottage of a sodden child such vertue, as that a staffe annointed therewith, can carrie folke in the aire? Their potable liquor, which (they saie) maketh maisters of that facultie, is it not ridiculous? And is it not, by the opinion of all philosophers, physicians, and divines, void of such vertue, as is imputed thereunto? (Scot, 3.12)

To this question answer is made in the 4 Reas., and I add thereunto that few wise men impute to these extern actions and ceremonies the force of those effects which are here spoken of, no more than we do impute to the hem of Christ's garment, to Peter's shadow, and to Paul's partlets[166] or kerchiefs the effect of healing those diseases in the healing whereof these things were used.[167]

[fol. 76v] Reason 62

> And to speake more generallie of all the impossible actions referred unto them, as also of their false confessions; I saie, that there is none which acknowledgeth God to be onlie omnipotent, and the onlie worker of all

---

164 Author's note: '4 Regu[m] 21 et 2 cro 33'; 2 Kings 21:1–18; 2 Chronicles 33:1–20.
165 Author's note: 'Ephes 5'; Ephesians 5:12.
166 OED: 'An item of clothing worn over the neck and upper part of the chest.' The exact nature of the garment named in the Bible seems uncertain; the King James text has 'handkerchiefs or aprons', while the Geneva version, in Acts 19:12, has 'kerchiefs or handkerchiefs', or, in a gloss, 'napkins'.
167 Author's note: 'math 9 Acts 5 Acts 19'. The references to garments and Peter's shadow are in Matthew 9:20, Acts 5:15, and Acts 19:12.

> miracles, nor anie other indued with meane sense, but will denie that the elements are obedient to witches, and at their commandement; or that they may at their pleasure send raine, haile, tempests, thunder, lightening[.] (Scot, 3.13)

This reason you shall find answered in Reas. 3, 12, 7, and 14. And that no man holdeth that witches can do these things at their pleasure you shall find [in] Reas. 10 and 18. But this I add: that if you will affirm, as here you do, that God is the only worker of miracles, then must you either deny that there be any wicked and false miracles, or else you must make God to be the only worker of them as well as he is of the good and true miracles, but neither may that be denied nor this affirmed simply and properly. But according to some respects (as appeareth in my answer to the 3 Reas.) the doing of evil things may be ascribed to God, vz. not as to the author of any evil things but as to the disposer, governor, ruler and director of them to his will and pleasure, howsoever the wicked doers of them mean them directly to the contrary. And when any wicked thing is done by the wicked, they are properly to be said the workers thereof though God do order and direct the work as pleaseth him.

Reason 63

> If they could indeed bring these things to passe at their pleasure, then might they also be impediments unto the course of all other naturall Ordinances appointed by God: as, to cause it to hold up, when it should raine; and to make midnight, of high noone: and by those meanes (I saie) the divine power should beecome servile to the will of a witch, so as we could neither eat nor drinke but by their permission. (Scot, 3.13)

Indeed if it were granted that witches could at their pleasure send rain, hail, tempests &c (which no man that I know doth or ever did grant) many mo things would also be granted unto them, but yet would it not follow that they should be able to do the contrary things how spoken, or to keep us from meat and drink at their pleasure. For he that hath power to kill a man hath not power to make a man alive; but by your kind of reasoning if it should be granted that witches can by their witcheries kill men, children or cattle it must also be granted that they can make them alive by the same means. It is not therefore true (you see) that whoso can do one thing can also do the contrary thing thereunto, and again to reason from particulars to generals (as you seem here to do) is as far from good order of reasoning as may be, whereof more is spoken before to your 29 Reas. And last of all, if all this should be granted you yet would it not thereof follow that the divine power should (as you say) become servile by these means to the will of a witch, for it resteth in the divine power so to order the wills and hearts of all witches as they should never have any pleasure to do any of these things but when it should please the divine power to have them done, so that the servility should still remain in the witches and not in the said power.

Reason 64

> Me thinks *Seneca* might satisfie these credulous or rather idolatrous people, that runne a whorehunting, either in bodie or phansie, after these witches, beleeving all that is attributed unto them, to the derogation of Gods glorie. He saith, that the rude people, and our ignorant predecessors did beleeve, that raine and showers might be procured and staied by witches charmes and inchantments: of which kind of things that there can nothing be wrought, it is so manifest, that we need not go to anie philosophers schoole, to learne the confutation thereof. But *Jeremie*, by the word of God, dooth utterlie confound all that which may be devised for the maintenance of that foolish opinion, saieng; Are there any among the gods of the gentiles, that sendeth raine, or giveth showers from heaven? Art not thou the selfe same our Lord God? We will trust in thee, for thou dooest and makest all these things. (Scot, 3.13)

The answer made to your 3 and 7 Reasons doth fully answer the authorities of Seneca and Jeremy here alleged by you. And no man as I think professing God did ever in any such sense as you mean it impute to witches or their charms any such power over rain or showers &c, wherein see my next answer.

[f. 77r] Reason 65

> And whereas the storie of *Job* in this case is alledged against me (wherein a witch is not once named) I have particularlie answered it else-where. And therefore thus much onelie I say heere; that Even there, where it pleased God (as *Calvine* saith) to set downe circumstances for the instruction of our grosse capacities, which are not able to conceive of spirituall communication, or heavenlie affaires; the divell desireth God to stretch out his hand, and touch all that *Job* hath. And though he seemeth to grant sathans desire, yet God himselfe sent fire from heaven, &c. Where, it is to be gathered, that although God said, He is in thine hand: it was the Lords hand that punished *Job*, and not the hand of the divell, who said not, Give me leave to plague him; but, Laie thine hand upon him. (Scot, 3.13)

To prove that it was the hand of God and not the hand of the devil that punished Job you do here lean to the devil's words rather than to God's words. The devil in deed desired God to lay his hand upon Job, and God also did therein grant the devil's request, but how and by what means God should lay his hand upon Job the devil's words did not express. But the words of God do express the same so plainly as no man can doubt but that God did punish Job by the hand of the devil and his devilish ministers. For did not God say unto the devil (making his first request that Job might be touched in all that he had) 'lo, all that he hath is in thy hand, only upon himself shalt thou not stretch out thy hand'?[168] And again, did he not say to the devil (making his second request that God would stretch out his hand to touch Job's bones and his flesh) 'lo, he is in thine hand, but save his life'?[169] Do not both these sayings of God most plainly show that God did not immediately by himself punish Job in any of his punishments, but did wholly commit the execution of the same to the devil? For how was Job else put into the devil's hand to be punished, or for what cause did God limit the devil how far he should go in punishing Job if God had reserved to his own immediate hand these punishments and not left them to the hand of Satan? If this be not plain enough, then consider the text further and you shall there find it set down in most plain words that Job was punished by the hand of the devil. For after God had said unto the devil, 'lo he is in thine hand, but save his life', it followeth immediately in the text: 'So Satan departed from the presence of the lord and smote Job with sore boils from the sole of his foot unto his crown.' Now whereas you use the authority of Mr Calvin as if he did make with you in ascribing these punishments of Job to the hand of God and not to the hand of the devil, I cannot peruse Mr Calvin's words upon that place because I have not his homilies upon the book of Job. But at adventure I dare wager with you the price of that book that you are deceived in his opinion as touching that point, and for your better satisfaction herein I will show his words in another place where he confesseth the punishments of Job to have been executed by the hand and work of Satan, God permitting unto him the execution of the same. Mr Calvin's words be these: *Satanae affligendum servuum suum dominus permittit Chaldaeos quos ad id exequendum delegit ministros illi permittit, ac tradit impellendos: Satan alioqui pravos Chaldaeorum* [f. 77v] *animos venenatis suis aculeis ad perpetrandum id flagitium instigat: illi ad iniusticiam furiosè ruunt omniaque membra scelere obstringunt ac contaminant. Proprie ergo agere dicitur Satan in reprobis in quibus regnum suum (hoc est nequitiae) exercet.*[170] These words of Mr Calvin may as I think satisfy

---

168 Author's note: 'Job 1'; Job 1:12.
169 Author's note: 'Job 2'; Job 2:6.
170 Author's note: 'Cal Insti ca 2 Sectione 69'. In the fifth and final (Geneva, 1559) Latin edition of the *Institutes*, this passage appears in book 2, chapter 4, section 2

you that his opinion touching Job's punishments is otherwise than you take it to be.[171] But yet the words of Job himself seem (as you think) to make with you, for when he being punished said 'the lord hath given and the lord hath taken', that he doth hereby impute to the hand of God and not to the hand of witch or devil the punishments then laid upon him, and this no man will deny to be so. But that Job did in such sort impute his punishments to God's hand as that he would exclude from the same the hand of Satan and his ministers no man will or ever did grant, as you shall well find if you would peruse as many as ever wrote upon this matter. Job did in this case as all good and faithful men do in the like, who, having respect to this, that Satan and all his ministers can do nothing unto them more than it pleaseth God they should do for some good end and purpose to him best known, do not so much respect the mean or second causes and instruments whereby they are afflicted as they respect the will, the purpose, and pleasure of God in the same. And therefore they do rather refer their afflictions to God with thankful and patient hearts than to any second cause or instrument, though of such second causes and instruments they be not ignorant. So we see did Joseph when he said to his brethren that God sent him into Egypt before them: not being yet ignorant that he was by them sold and sent thither.[172] So David, not respecting the second causes or instruments of Shimei his cursing and reviling of him, but the purpose and pleasure of God in the same, would not have those curses and revilings so much referred to Shimei that was the instrument as to God himself, saying

---

(p. 101). The author appears to be using the fourth edition instead (Geneva, 1550), in which the passage does indeed appear in section 69 of chapter 2. In translation, the passage reads: 'The Lord permits Satan to afflict His servant; He hands the Chaldeans over to be impelled by Satan, having chosen them as His ministers for this task. Satan with his poison darts arouses the wicked minds of the Chaldeans to execute that evil deed. They dash madly into injustice, and they render all their members guilty and befoul them by the crime. Satan is properly said, therefore, to act in the reprobate over whom he exercises his reign, that is, the reign of wickedness.' *Institutes of the Christian Religion*, translated by Ford Lewis Battles (Philadelphia, PA: The Westminster Press, 1960), vol. 1, pp. 310–11.

171 Author's note: '& Mr Martir agreinge herein w[i]th Mr Calvin saythe. *In Jobo diabolus deduxit igne[m] de caelo et p[er]didit greges, excitavit ventos et concussit quatuor angulos dom[us] et filios Jobi opp[re]ssit* 1 Sam ca 28': 'In the book of Job, the devil brought down fire from heaven and destroyed flocks of animals, stirred up winds and shook the four corners of the house and brought low the sons of Job' [my translation]. The reference is to Peter Martyr Vermigli's commentaries on the book of Samuel: *In duos Libros Samuelis Prophetae* (Zurich, 1575), p. 166.

172 Author's note: 'Gen 45'; Genesis 45:5.

to Abishai (that would have slain Shimei for his labour) that it was the lord which bade him curse.[173] And even so Job, though he were not ignorant that his hurts and losses in his children and goods came by the fall of the house by fire from heaven, by the Sabeans, and by the Chaldeans (for all this wasted him) yet he leaving the regard of all means and second causes imputeth the whole matter unto God, as he might very well for the respect aforesaid.[174] Whereof also I have spoken more largely to your 3 Reas., showing there how one and the self same work may be imputed to God and also to creatures. To which place I refer you, or rather to the foresaid place of Mr Calvin where this is declared much more learnedly and plainly than lieth in me to declare the same.[175] In that chapter and section shall you see how things in divers respects may be imputed to God, to Satan, and to man, and that in this present example of Job.

[fol. 78r] Reason 66

> ... if that which is conteined in M. *Mal*, *Bodin*, &c: or in the pamphlets late set foorth in English, of witches executions, shuld be true in those things that witches are said to confesse, what creature could live in securitie? Or what needed such preparation of warres, or such trouble, or charge in that behalfe. No prince should be able to reigne or live in the land. For (as *Danaeus* saith) that one *Martine* a witch killed the emperour of *Germanie* with witchcraft: so would our witches (if they could) destroie all our magistrates. One old witch might overthrowe an armie roiall: and then what needed we any guns, or wild fire, or any other instruments of warre? (Scot, 3.14)

> I find another storie written in M. *Mal*. repeated by *Bodin*; that one souldier called *Pumher*, dailie through witchcraft killed with his bowe and arrowes three of the enimies, as they stood peeping over the walles of a castell besieged: so as in the end he killed them all quite, saving one ... But this latter storie I can requite with a familiar example. For at Towne *Malling* in Kent, one of Q. *Maries* justices, upon the complaint of many wise men, and a few foolish boies, laid an archer by the heeles; bicause he shot so neere the white at buts. For he was informed and persuaded, that the poore man plaied with a flie, otherwise called a divell or familiar ... And therefore the archer was severelie punished, to the great encouragement of archers, and to the wise example of justice; but speciallie to the overthrowe of witchcraft. (Scot, 3.15)

---

173 Author's note: '2 Sam 16'; 2 Samuel 16:5–10.
174 Author's note: 'Job 1'; Job 1:21.
175 Author's note: 'institution ca 2 sectione 69'; see note above.

To this Reason I say as before I have said to the like: that I do not think any witch, witchmonger, writer or fable did or will attribute such large power and scope to witches as you do here speak of. If any do, I neither know them nor consent to them, whereof you may see more: Reas. 10, 18. As for your examples here alleged out of Danaeus and other histories touching Martin and the witches used in the wars of the Danes and Huns, because you give no censure of them whether they were true or false there is no cause to reply unto them. And as for the cunning archer of *Malleus Maleficarum* and Bodin, you have so fitly matched him with the cunning archer of Malling that I should be much to blame if I would not agree that one of them should be set against the other.

Reason 67

> Certeine generall councels, by their decrees, have condemned the confessions and erronious credulitie of witches, to be vaine, fantasticall and fabulous ... to wit; their night walkings and meetings with *Herodias*, and the *Pagan* gods: at which time they should passe so farre in so little a space on cockhorsse; their transubstantiation, their eating of childrer, and their pulling of them from their mothers sides, their entring into mens houses, through chinks and little holes, where a flie can scarselie wring out, and the disquieting of the inhabitants, &c: all which are not onelie said by a generall councell to be meere fantasticall, and imaginations in dreames; but so affirmed by the ancient writers.
> [...]
> But bicause the old hammar of *Sprenger* and *Institor*, in their old *Malleo Maleficarum*, was insufficient to knocke downe this councell; a yoong beetle-head called Frier *Bartholomaeus Spineus* hath made a new leaden beetle, to beate downe the councell, and to kill these old women. Wherein he counterfeiting *Aesops* asse, claweth the pope with his heeles: affirming upon his credit, that the councell is false and erronious; bicause the doctrine swarveth from the popish church, and is not authenticall but apocryphall; saieng (though untrulie) that that councell was not called by the commandement and pleasure of the pope, nor ratified by his authoritie, which (saith he) is sufficient to disanull all councels. (Scot, 3.16)

If no general council had condemned the matters here mentioned as parcel of their league yet I think all wise men would never have believed them as things truly done. But what is this to prove the vanity of witches' confessions and of men's credulity in all other parts and practices of witches, which are more probable and apparent and with the which there concur very great and vehement presumptions? Yet this by the way, you have to note that the council here by you alleged doth not impute these confessions of the witches to the force of any melancholy humour as you do, but to the illusions and vain visions whereby they are of Satan seduced and deceived, being made to believe and profess those things; vz. their riding by night with Diana &c there mentioned.[176] Neither doth that council hold and excuse these women for simple and innocent persons as you do but contrariwise pronounces them to be wicked women, such as are turned backward after Satan, also that they are subverted and holden captive of him, and having left their creator do seek the helps and succours of the devil, and are therefore to be by all means dishonested[177] and cast out of the Church by excommunication, that so the Church may be delivered of such pestilence or poison.[178] Which things with many other contained in that place do make very much against your foresaid opinions, and do also in effect confess that there is some special league and society between witches and the devil, though not such a corporal league as is of the gross sort of witchmonger imagined. And where you say that Friar Bartholomeus laboureth to disannul this council (as if it were not authentical) for that the doctrine thereof agreeth not with the popish Church, if you mark it throughly for so much as Gratian doth put down in this place and specially at the end, you shall find it so well to agree with popish doctrine as the poor friar in rejecting of it deserveth the pope's c{?} for his labour.

[fol. 78v] Reason 68

> Alas! what creature being sound in state of mind, would (without compulsion) make such maner of confessions as they do; or would, for a trifle, or nothing, make a perfect bargaine with the divell for hir soule, to be yeelded up unto his tortures and everlasting flames, and that within a verie short time; speciallie being through age most commonlie unlike to live one whole yeare? (Scot, 3.18; cf. 45th reason above)

This reason being altogether like and in effect one with your 45 Reason is in mine answer to the same fully and at large answered.

---

176 Author's note: 'decreta causa 26 quest 5 Episcopi'. The reference is to the version of the canon *Episcopi* recorded in the *Decretum Gratiani*, a twelth-century collection of canon law. See the discussion in the 'Significance' and 'Sources' sections in the introduction above.

177 OED: 'To bring dishonour, disgrace, or discredit upon; to dishonour; to stain with ignominy'.

178 Author's note: 'how they are by the dyvell made to beleave thes thing[es] ys also ther shewed.'

Reason 69

> The terror of hell fire must needs be to them diverslie manifested, and much more terrible; bicause of their weaknesse, nature, and kind, than to any other: as it would appeere, if a witch were but asked, Whether she would be contented to be hanged one yeare hence, upon condition hir displesure might be wreked upon hir enimie presentlie. As for theeves, & such other, they thinke not to go to hell fire; but are either persuaded there is no hell, or that their crime deserveth it not, or else that they have time enough to repent: so as, no doubt, if they were perfectlie resolved heereof, they would never make such adventures. Neither doo I thinke, that for any summe of monie, they would make so direct a bargaine to go to hell fire.
> [...]
> And the lawe saith, that The confession of such persons as are illuded, must needs be erronious, and therefore is not to be admitted; for, *Confessio debet tenere verum & possibile*. But these things are opposite both to lawe and nature, and therfore it followeth not; Bicause these witches confesse so, *Ergo* it is so ... Their confession in this case conteineth an outward act, and the same impossible both in lawe and nature, and also unlikelie to be true[.] (Scot, 3.18)

In my answer whither I have referred you for your former question I have also disappointed you of this prevention, proving that witches do as little think to go to hell, or to the temporal fire or gallows, as thieves and other malefactors do.[179] And therefore I do again refer you to my said answer to your 45 Reas. in this point. And as touching your matter of impossibility to law and nature here mentioned I refer you to my answer of your 4, 6, 13, 21, and 44 Reasons as before I have often done in this case.

Reason 70

To this allegation of law I have at large answered before in my answers to your 36 and 44 Reasons.

Reason 71

> But when these witchmongers are convinced in the objection concerning their confessions; so as thereby their tyrannicall arguments cannot prevaile, to imbrue the magistrates hands in so much bloud as their appetite requireth: they fall to accusing them of other crimes, that the world might

---

[179] Scot, in the printed version of the *Discoverie*, appears to have considered this argument; see the excerpt above.

thinke they had some colour to mainteine their malicious furie against them. (3.18)

First therefore they laie to their charge idolatrie. But alas without all reason: for such are properlie knowne to us to be idolaters, as doo externall worship to idols or strange gods.
[...]
Secondlie, apostasie is laid to their charge, whereby it is inferred, that they are worthie to die. But apostasie is, where anie of sound judgement forsake the gospell, learned and well knowne unto them; and doo not onelie imbrace impietie and infidelitie; but oppugne and resist the truth erstwhile by them professed. But alas these poore women go not about to defend anie impietie, but after good admonition repent.

Thirdlie, they would have them executed for seducing the people. But God knoweth they have small store of Rhetorike or art to seduce; except to tell a tale of Robin good-fellow be to deceive and seduce. Neither may their age or sex admit that opinion or accusation to be just: for they themselves are poore seduced soules. I for my part (as else-where I have said) have prooved this point to be false in most apparent sort.

Fourthlie, as touching the accusation, which all the writers use herein against them for their carnall copulation with *Incubus*: the follie of mens credulitie is as much to be woondered at and derided, as the others vaine and impossible confessions. For the divell is a spirit, and hath neither flesh nor bones, which were to be used in the performance of this action. And since he also lacketh all instruments, substance, and seed ingendred of bloud; it were follie to staie overlong in the confutation of that, which is not in the nature of things. (Scot, 3.19)

But to use few words herein, I hope you understand that they affirme and saie, that *Incubus* is a spirit; and I trust you know that a spirit hath no flesh nor bones, &c: and that he neither dooth eate nor drinke. [...] Item, where the genitall members want, there can be no lust of the flesh: neither dooth nature give anie desire of generation, where there is no propagation or succession required. And as spirits cannot be greeved with hunger, so can they not be inflamed with lustes. (Scot, 4.10)

But in truth, this *Incubus* is a bodilie disease (as hath beene said) although it extend unto the trouble of the mind: which of some is called The mare, oppressing manie in their sleepe so sore, as they are not able to call for helpe, or stir themselves under the burthen of that heavie humor, which is ingendred of a thicke vapor proceeding from the cruditie and rawnesse in the stomach: which ascending up into the head oppresseth the braine, in so much as manie are much infeebled therebie, as being nightlie haunted therewith.

[...]
Hyperius being much bewitched and blinded in this matter of witchcraft, hoovering about the interpretation of *Genesis* 6. from whence the opinion of Incubus and Succubus is extorted [...] *Tertullian* and *Sulpicius Severus* doo interpret *Filios Dei* in that place to be angels, or evill spirits, and to have beene enamored with the beautie of those wenches; and finallie, begat giants by them. Which is throughlie confuted by *Chrysostome, Hom.* 22. in *Gen*: but speciallie by the circumstance of the text. (Scot, 4.11)

Now will I (after all this long discourse of abhominable clokec knaveries) here conclude with certeine of *G. Chaucers* verses, who as he smelt out the absurdities of poperie, so found he the priests knaverie in this matter of *Incubus*, and (as the time would suffer him) he derided their folie and falshood in this wise:

> *For now the great charitie and praiers*
> *Of limitors and other holie friers,*
> *That searchen everie land and everie streame*
> *As thicke as motes in the sunne beame,*
> *Blissing halles, kitchens, chambers & bowers,*
> *Cities, borroghes, castels and hie towers,*
> *Thropes, barnes, shepens, and dairies,*
> *This maketh that there beene now no fairies;*
> *For there as wont to walken was an elfe,*
> *There walketh now the limitor himselfe,*
> *In undermeales, and in mornings,*
> *And saith his mattens and his holie things*
> *As he goeth in his limitatiowne,*
> *Women may go safelie up and downe,*
> *In everie bush, and under everie tree,*
> *There nis none other Incubus but hee, &c.*
> (Scot, 4.12)

Howsoever witches may be excused of having carnal copulation with devils, yet do not I think they can be justly excused of idolatry, apostasy, and seducing of the people. But before I prove this my opinion I must first say somewhat to the reproof of some of your assertions. And first, where you say such are properly idolatrous which do external worship to idols or strange Gods, I do think that they which in their hearts do worship such things are more properly and more worthily to be deemed Idolaters. My reason is this: they are the most proper, truest, and chiefest worshippers of God which worship him in spirit and truth and, inasmuch as he is a spirit, he chiefly requireth such worshippers of him.[180] *Ergo a contrariis*[181] they are the most proper and chief idolaters which turn their hearts and spirit from the worshipping of God to the worshipping of idols and false gods. Again, if they most properly be idolaters which do external worship to idols or strange gods would it *a contrariis* follow that they are properly the true worshippers of God which worship him with external worship, which is directly against the whole scriptures and specially these words of Christ, saying to the Samaritan woman: 'The hour cometh and now is when the true worshippers shall worship the father in spirit and truth, for the father requireth even such to worship him. God is a spirit and they that worship him must worship him in spirit.'[182] [fol. 79r] Secondly I say that idolatry may be stretched further {if} you do here appoint the utmost limits of it, for not only they which seek salvation of idols or of any other than God are idolaters, but they also which in temporal and worldly matters do seek help and defence where they ought and as they ought not. As for example our papists, which do worship and implore the saints departed for to be holpen and defended in such sicknesses and diseases as may fall upon them or their cattle (in which case they have for several diseases several saints) are as I think worthy the name of idolaters, both for that they do hereby abridge the providence of God over his creatures, and also transfer from him that worship and invocation which is only due unto him (as being two principal parts of his true honour and service) unto his creatures, wherein they do indeed make them as gods unto them. Which the godly patriarch Jacob did well consider, and therefore when Rachel his wife requested him to give her children, he was very angry with her (as the text sayeth) for the same, and asked her if he were a god or in God's stead, thereby plainly showing that to pray to a creature for anything temporal which is not in the creature to give is to make a god of the same creature.[183] The like example we have in that king of Israel (which being written unto by the King of Aram and requested to heal Naaman of his leprosy) did upon the reading of the King of Aram's letter rend his clothes and said 'Am I a god to kill and to give life that he doth send to me to heal a man of his leprosy?'[184] But if idolatry reach no further than you set down, it is far enough to bring our witches within the compass of idolatry. For do not they neglect the power of God most horribly when as they do not call upon God in time of trouble and distress as he hath commanded, but do use most wicked charms and sorceries to help both themselves and others in all their

180 Author's note: 'John 4'; John 4:24.
181 'Therefore, on the contrary'.
182 Author's note: 'John 4'; John 4:23–24.
183 Author's note: 'Gen 30'; Genesis 30:1–2.
184 Author's note: '4 Regu[m] 5'; 2 Kings 5:7.

troubles and distress?[185] Yea, not only do they neglect the power of God but utterly contemn and forsake the same, seeking helps and succours at the devil's hands, as the foresaid Aquiren Council by you alleged to another purpose doth plainly affirm, saying as well of all wicked men and women which follow the art of sorcery, witchcraft and such like magical and diabolical practices after this manner: *Subversi sunt et a diabolo captivi tenentur: qui relicto creatore suo, diaboli suffragia querunt*[186] wherefore if you will not refuse the authorities which you yourself bring for your purpose you may not deny witches to be idolaters.[187] Yea, and this is also sufficient to prove them to be apostates, for if the forsaking of the creator to seek help of the devil be not apostasy, what then may be so counted I know not. Howbeit I think their apostasy may appear and be proved otherwise, for the word [**fol. 79v**] ἀποστασία[188] is nothing so narrowly to be restrained as you by your definition thereof do restrain the same, but it reacheth in right signification as well unto those which in worldly and profane matter forsake their fidelity, duty, and profession as to those which do the same in holy and divine matters: insomuch as a servant forsaking his master, a subject forsaking his prince, a soldier forsaking his captain and a friend forsaking his friend &c may right well be called an *apostata* if the said forsakings be committed contrary to duty, promise, or profession.[189] Wherefore if our witches do forsake the faith of Christ, wherein they were baptised and the which they once professed and promised to continue in, this is plain apostasy though none other of the circumstances by you set down in your definition do concur with the same, for in this there is a plain desertion and falling away from a faith professed, in the which by duty they should have continued, and therefore it is an apostasy. Now whether this be an apostasy wittingly or by ignorance committed, that is another question not pertinent to our purpose whilst we reason of this: whether witches be apostates, yea or no. But if we

---

185 Author's note: 'psal 50'; Psalm 50:15: 'And call vpon me in the daie of trouble: so wil I deliuer thee, & thou shalt glorifie me.'
186 From the canon *Episcopi*. 'Those who have been subverted and are held captive by the Devil, leaving their creator, seek the aid of the Devil'; translation from Kors and Peters (eds), *Witchcraft in Europe, 400–1700*, p. 62.
187 Scot, in 3.16 (see reason 67 above) cites 'Concil Acquirens' as the source of the canon *Episcopi*. The canon probably dates from the ninth century but was believed to originate from the Council of Ancyra (modern Ankara) in the fourth century; see Edward Peters, *The Magician, The Witch, and the Law* (Philadelphia, PA: University of Pennsylvania Press, 1978), pp. 72–3 and Stephens, *Demon Lovers*, pp. 127–8. Kapitaniak argues that Scot's direct source was Weyer (*La Sorcellerie Démystifiée*, p. 170, note 104).
188 Gr., 'apostacy'.
189 Author's note: 'Mr Calvin uppo[n] the 3 of Genesis calleth ye serpent an Apostate'.

shall reason whether this ignorant kind of apostasy deserve death, I will not in that point dissent from you, so as it be simple ignorance and not joined with open obstinacy after the truth revealed unto them. Now as touching their deceiving and seducing of the people objected unto witches, they cannot be excused thereof for any of the excuses here by you alleged, for whatsoever they want in rhetoric or art their master the devil can easily supply, and as for their sex or gender it is in common opinion more apt to deceit than the sex of men. Their age also (if they be not come to dotage but have their right wits) doth minister by long practice and experience the more knowledge and cunning how to deceive, and as for your trial it may satisfy yourself but others it cannot. If I shall tell you of my trial that way I must say unto you by reason of the calling and authority I have, I have had to do in the examination of many of them but never did I find more subtle, crafty, and crabbed queans than the most of them were. And where you said before they do not defend any impiety, but do after good admonition repent, I did never yet meet with any of them which did not from time to time continue in their old trade, how well so ever they were admonished to the contrary, or what fair promises so ever they made of amendment when they stood in danger of punishment. As for carnal [fol. 80r] copulation with devils I think thereof as you do, howbeit you are not ignorant that St Augustine and other of the learned whose authorities you use in other points to serve your turn are in this point also of a contrary mind unto you.[190] Neither are your reasons so firm but that they are and may be gainsaid. As first, though the devils have naturally no flesh and bones, yet some hold they do and may assume true bodies for the time, and others as you know hold their taking of seed from men and the transferring thereof to women. Secondly, that they do not eat or drink is doubtful, because the good spirits of God have eaten and drunken, and though they did not yet might they have assumed seed as well as they have assumed bodies. Thirdly, though they had no desire naturally of generation yet would they have a desire thereunto for mischief's sake, I mean to do hurt thereby. And this answereth the 4 reason also. The 5 reason also of you here used is in the premises answered, but of their assuming or not assuming of bodies somewhat is said in answer of your other Reasons and more shall be perhaps said afterward. Your 6 reason I leave to physicians;

---

190 Author's note: 'de civit dei li 15 ca. 23': 'And seeing it is so general a report, and so many aver it either from their own experience or from others, that are of indubitable honesty and credit, that the silvans and fauns, commonly called incubi, have often injured women, desiring and acting carnally with them, and that certain devils whom the Gauls call *dusii* do continually practise this uncleanness, and tempt others to it, which is affirmed by such persons, and with such confidence that it were impudence to deny it' (*City of God* 15.23).

your refutation in the 7 I allow, yet not because Chrysostom is against Tertullian and Sulpitius (for their authority may countervail his) but because of the truth.[191] Your 8 and last reason out of old Chaucer I cannot allow because there was as I think many an incubus (in the sense that Chaucer meaneth) as well as the lewd limitor.

Reason 72

> ... there was one *Bajanus* a *Jew*, being the sonne of *Simeon*, which could, when he list, turne himselfe into a woolfe; and by that meanes could escape the force and danger of a whole armie of men. Which thing (saith *Bodin*) is woonderfull: but yet (saith he) it is much more marvelous, that men will not beleeve it. For manie poets affirme it; yea, and if you looke well into the matter (saith he) you shall find it easie to doo. Item, he saith, that as naturall woolves persecute beasts; so doo these magicall woolves devoure men, women, and children. And yet God saith to the people (I trowe) and not to the cattell of Israell; If you observe not my commandements, I will send among you the beasts of the feeld, which shall devoure both you and your cattell. Item, I will send the teeth of beasts upon you. Where is *Bodins* distinction now become? He never saith, I will send witches in the likenes of wolves, &c: to devoure you or your cattell. (Scot, 5.1)

That the lord threapned in Deuteronomy to send beasts and not witches to destroy the disobedient and their cattle is of no force to prove that there are no witches to hurt or destroy.[192] God is called the lord of hosts because he can fight and destroy his enemies by all or any of the creatures of this world,

---

191 See the excerpt from 4.11 above. The reference is to Genesis 6.2–4, which reads as follows: 'Then the sonnes of God sawe the daughters of men that they were faire, and they toke them wiues of all that they liked. Therefore the Lord said, My spirit shal not alway striue with man, because he is but flesh, & his dayes shal be an hundreth and twentie yeres. There were gyantes in the earth in those dayes: yea, and after that the sonnes of God came vnto the daughters of me[n], and they had borne them children, these were mightie men, which in olde time were men of renoume.' As the author apparently acknowledges, this passage provides the thinnest of grounds for a belief in incubus demons, which did not stop the authors of the *Malleus Maleficarum* from making a rather feeble attempt: 'Certain people say that ... the phrase "the sons of God" signifies "the sons of Seth" and not "the incubus angels," and similarly "the daughters of men" signifies the women whose lineage went back to Cain. Despite this claim, the contrary is claimed by many people, as is clear, and what many people think cannot be altogether false according to the Philosopher [i.e. Aristotle]' (26B–26C, p. 132). Sulpicius Severus (c. 363–c. 425) was an early Christian writer from Acquitaine.

192 Deuteronomy 32:24.

wherefore you may not restrain him to any particular way of punishing (as now you do) unless you can prove that it is always his pleasure to use that one kind of punishing and no other, which you can never prove, the scriptures and common experience teaching us that even one and the self same sin and people {?} hurt or punished sometime by one mean sometime by anoth{er} and for proof hereof you need seek no further but even to the said chapter by you alleged, for there you shall find other means of punishment and destruction threapned to the disobedient than this of beasts.

Reason 73

> [Bodin] mainteineth, as sacred and true, all *Homers* fables of *Circes* and *Ulysses* his companions: inveieng against *Chrysostome*, who rightlie interpreteth *Homers* meaning to be, that *Ulysses* his people were by the harlot *Circes* made in their brutish maners to resemble swine.
> [...]
> Howbeit, *S. Augustine* (whether to confute or confirme that opinion judge you) saith; *Non est credendum, humanum corpus daemonum arte vel potestate in bestialia lineamenta converti posse*: We may not beleeve that a mans bodie may be altered into the lineaments of a beast by the divels art or power. (Scot, 5.1)

No marvel it is if St Chrysostom do thus interpret the transformation of Ulysses his followers and servants, for you know there is nothing more common with Chrysostom in all his works than to make morals and allegories of things most truly done. But I marvel you do here [fol. 80v] add St August to the confirmation of Chrysostom whenas you do in some other places of your book confess that he doth affirm the said transformation to be corporal and that he doth also subscribe to the story of the knight of Rhodes of a man by a witch turned into an ass or to the like.[193] But here I

---

[193] The story ascribed to 'the knight of Rhodes' is taken from the *Malleus Maleficarum* 166C–167C (pp. 432–5), and is sarcastically retold by Scot in 5.3; see the excerpts to reason 76 below. Scot comments on Augustine's view of the story as follows: 'Upon the advantage of this storie [of the Knight of Rhodes] M. Mal. Bodin, and the residue of the witchmongers triumph; and speciallie bicause S. *Augustine* subscribeth thereunto; or at the least to the verie like. Which I must confesse I find too common in his books, insomuch as I judge them rather to be foisted in by some fond papist or witchmonger, than so learned a mans dooings. The best is, that he himselfe is no eiewitnesse to any of those his tales; but speaketh onelie by report; wherein he uttereth these words: to wit, that It were a point of great incivilitie, &c: to discredit so manie and so certeine reports. And in that respect he justifieth the corporall transfigurations of *Ulysses* his mates, throgh the witchcraft of *Circes*[.]'

must put you in remembrance that to make St August the better to agree with St Chrysostom you do not soundly set down St August's words, for his words be these: *Non itaquae solum animum sed nec corpus quidem ulla ratione crediderim daemonum arte vel potestate in membra vel lineamenta bestialia veraciter posse converti.*[194] Here you leave out this word *veracit* whereby you make St August speak so absolutely and without exception of this matter of transformation, as though his opinion were absolutely on your side, which indeed is not so. For even in this present chapter, and immediately after these words he confesseth (and also immediately before them) that the things which are created of the true God may be changed *specie tenus ut videantur esse quod non sunt*[195] and how that may be done he there at large showeth as you know. But as touching the foresaid transformation of Ulysses' followers, I do not find that St August doth affirm the same to be corporal as resolved in the believing thereof, but doth rather doubt whether it were so, yea or no, and therefore here you stretch his words too far as before you did abridge them.

Reason 74

> Generall councels, and the popes canons, which *Bodin* so regardeth, doo condemne and pronounce his opinions in this behalfe to be absurd; and the residue of the witchmongers, with himselfe in the number, to be woorsse than infidels. And these are the verie words of the canons, which else-where I have more largelie repeated; Whosoever beleeveth, that anie creature can be made or changed into better or woorsse, or transformed into anie other shape, or into anie other similitude, by anie other than by God himselfe the creator of all things, without all doubt is an infidell, and woorsse than a pagan. (Scot, 5.3)

---

194 John Healey's 1610 translation of this passage ('Nor do I think the devils can form any soul or body into bestial or brutal members and essences') also ignores this word; Augustine, *City of God*, 18.18 (p. 192). The author's version of this passage varies slightly from that in a modern edition of the Latin text; cf. *De Civitate Dei*, edited by B. Dombart and A. Kalb (Turnhout: Brepols, 1955), p. 608. Author's notes: 'de civit dei li 18 ca 18'; 'thes very words hath August also in Li de spiritu et anima ca 26 w[i]th some other words declaring his opynion in this matter'. *De Spiritu et Anima* is of disputed authorship, but is now known not to be by St Augustine: Gaetamo Raciti, 'L'Autore del *De spiritu et anima*', *Rivista di Filosofia Neo-Scolastica* 53 (1961), 385–401. In the printed *Discoverie*, Scot provides a marginal reference to this work as well as to *City of God*.

195 'in appearance, so that they appear to be what they are not' [my translation]. The quotation seems to have been adapted from the full passage, which in a modern edition reads: '*sed specie tenus, quae a uero Deo sunt creata, commutant, ut uideantur esse quod non sunt*' (Dombart and Kalb (eds), *De Civitate Dei*, p. 608).

The authority now alleged you did call before (Reas. 6) a general council, and now you call it a pope's canon, and yet then you said it was rejected of Friar Bartholomew for disagreeing from the popish doctrine. This is some contrariety as I take it. But to the matter: I understand this canon to mean as St August before meant: to wit, of true transformations and not of fantastical or apparent, for if you do not so understand it then must we say that St August, with many other very learned and godly, is without all doubt an infidel and worse than a pagan. And the reason here added enforceth this sense that I speak of, for when the canon sayeth they attribute to a creature which only belongeth to God the creator, this must needs be understood of true transformations only and not of fantastical, false, and deceitful transformations, unless we will say it doth only belong unto God to make them also, which I suppose he that should say were worthy to be called an infidel and worse than a pagan. This also by the way [fol. 81r] you are to note: that this canon doth allow unto God power to transform creatures into other shapes and similitudes. But you in other places of your book are against this, saying God should do against his ordinance and be contrary to himself if he should make such transformations, insomuch also as you affirm that if God would give a man leave to do this he cannot do it, whereof more perhaps may be said after.[196] So then you see this canon neither now nor before is so much with you as it is against you.

Reason 75

I grant all this. But what if it please God in his providence to give the devil power over the body of men and beasts as many times he doth, which hath been before showed in the example of Job, and may be seen in infinite places of the scripture besides? May not then the devil (think you) do much more unto men's bodies than any human wit or reason can comprehend, or than the order of nature doth allow? I think he may, and if you think otherwise you are surely much deceived. But hereof enough hath been spoken to other your Reasons.

Reason 76

> It happened in the city of *Salamin*, in the kingdome of *Cyprus* (wherein is a good haven) that a ship loaden with merchandize staied there for a short space. In the meane time many of the souldiers and mariners went to shoare, to provide fresh victuals. Among which number, a certaine English man, being a sturdie yoong fellowe, went to a womans house, a little waie out of the citie, and not farre from the sea side, to see whether she had anie

---

196 See reason 76 below, and the accompanying excerpt from Scot 5.5.

egs to sell. Who perceiving him to be a lustie yoong fellowe, a stranger, and farre from his countrie (so as upon the losse of him there would be the lesse misse or inquirie) she considered with hir selfe how to destroie him; and willed him to staie there awhile, whilest she went to fetch a few egs for him. But she tarried long, so as the yoong man called unto hir, desiring hir to make hast: for he told hir that the tide would be spent, and by that meanes his ship would be gone, and leave him behind. Howbeit, after some detracting of time, she brought him a few egs, willing him to returne to hir, if his ship were gone when he came. The young fellowe returned towards his ship: but before he went aboord, hee would needs eate an eg or twaine to satisfie his hunger, and within short space he became dumb and out of his wits (as he afterwards said.) When he would have entred into the ship, the mariners beat him backe with a cudgell, saieng; What a murren lacks the asse? Whither the divell will this asse? The asse or yoong man (I cannot tell by which name I should terme him) being many times repelled, and understanding their words that called him asse, considering that he could speake never a word, and yet could understand everie bodie; he thought that he was bewitched by the woman, at whose house he was. And therefore, when by no meanes he could get into the boate, but was driven to tarrie and see hir departure; being also beaten from place to place, as an asse: he remembred the witches words, and the words of his owne fellowes that called him asse, and returned to the witches house, in whose service hee remained by the space of three yeares, dooing nothing with his hands all that while, but carried such burthens as she laied on his backe; having onelie this comfort, that although he were reputed an asse among strangers and beasts, yet that both this witch, and all other witches knew him to be a man.

After three yeares were passed over, in a morning betimes he went to towne before his dame; who upon some occasion (of like to make water) staied a little behind. In the meane time being neere to a church, he heard a little saccaring bell ring to the elevation of a morrowe masse, and not daring to go into the church, least he should have beene beaten and driven out with cudgels, in great devotion he fell downe in the churchyard, upon the knees of his hinder legs, and did lift his forefeet over his head, as the preest doth hold the sacrament at the elevation. Which prodigious sight when certeine merchants of *Genua* espied, and with woonder beheld; anon commeth the witch with a cudgell in hir hand, beating foorth the asse. And bicause (as it hath beene said) such kinds of witchcrafts are verie usuall in those parts; the merchants aforesaid made such meanes, as both the asse and the witch were attached by the judge. And she being examined and set upon the racke, confessed the whole matter, and promised, that if she might have libertie to go home, she would restore him to his old shape: and being dismissed, she did accordinglie. So as notwithstanding they apprehended hir againe, and burned hir: and the yoong man returned into his countrie with a joifull and merrie hart. (Scot, 5.3)

Concerning the veritie or probabilitie of this enterlude, betwixt *Bodin*, *M. Mal.* the witch, the asse, the masse, the merchants, the inquisitors, the tormentors, &c: First I woonder at the miracle of transubstantiation: Secondlie at the impudencie of *Bodin* and *James Sprenger*, for affirming so grosse a lie, devised beelike by the knight of the Rhodes, to make a foole of *Sprenger*, and an asse of *Bodin*: Thirdlie, that the asse had no more wit than to kneele downe and hold up his forefeete to a peece of starch or flowre, which neither would, nor could, nor did helpe him: Fourthlie, that the masse could not reforme that which the witch transformed: Fiftlie, that the merchants, the inquisitors, and the tormentors, could not either severallie or jointlie doo it, but referre the matter to the witches courtesie and good pleasure. But where was the yoong mans owne shape all these three yeares, wherein he was made an asse? It is a certeine and a generall rule, that two substantiall formes cannot be in one subject *Simul & semel*, both at once: which is confessed by themselves. The forme of the beast occupied some place in the aire, and so I thinke should the forme of a man doo also.
[...]
What lucke was it, that this yoong fellow of *England*, landing so latelie in those parts, and that old woman of *Cyprus*, being both of so base a condition, should both understand one anothers communication; *England* and *Cyprus* being so manie hundred miles distant, and their languages so farre differing? [...] You heare, that at the inquisitors commandement, and through the tormentors correction, she promised to restore him to his owne shape: and so she did, as being thereunto compelled. I answer, that as the whole storie is an impious fable; so this assertion is false, and disagreeable to their owne doctrine, which mainteineth, that the witch dooth nothing but by the permission and leave of God. For if she could doo or undoo such a thing at hir owne pleasure, or at the commandement of the inquisitors, or for feare of the tormentors, or for love of the partie, or for remorse of conscience: then is it not either by the extraordinarie leave, nor yet by the like direction of God; except you will make him a confederate with old witches. (Scot, 5.4)

Bodin saith (his reason onelie reserved) he was trulie transubstantiated into an asse; so as there must be no part of a man, but reason remaining in this asse. And yet *Hermes Trismegistus* thinketh he hath good authoritie and reason to saie ... An humane soule cannot receive anie other than an humane bodie, nor yet canne light into a bodie that wanteth reason of mind. But *S. James* saith; the bodie without the spirit is dead. And surelie, when the soule is departed from the bodie, the life of man is dissolved: and therefore *Paule* wished to be dissolved, when he would have beene with Christ. The bodie of man is subject to divers kinds of agues, sicknesses, and infirmities, whereunto an asses bodie is not inclined: and mans bodie must be fed with bread, &c: and not with hay. [...] And therefore it is absolutelie against the ordinance of God (who hath made me a man) that I should flie like a bird, or swim like a fish, or creepe like a worme, or become an asse in shape: insomuch as if God would give me leave, I cannot doo it; for it were contrarie to his owne order and decree, and to the constitution of anie bodie which he hath made. Yea the spirits themselves have their lawes and limits prescribed, beyond the which they cannot passe one haires breadth; otherwise God should be contrarie to himselfe: which is farre from him. Neither is Gods omnipotencie hereby qualified, but the divels impotencie manifested, who hath none other power, but that which God from the beginning hath appointed unto him, consonant to his nature and substance. He may well be restreined from his power and will, but beyond the same he cannot passe, as being Gods minister, no further but in that which he hath from the beginning enabled him to doo: which is, that he being a spirit, may with Gods leave and ordinance viciat and corrupt the spirit and will of man: wherein he is verie diligent.

What a beastlie assertion is it, that a man, whom GOD hath made according to his owne similitude and likenes, should be by a witch turned into a beast? What an impietie is it to affirme, that an asses bodie is the temple of the Holy-ghost? Or an asse to be the child of God, and God to be his father; as it is said of man? Which *Paule* to the *Corinthians* so divinelie confuteth, who saith, that Our bodies are the members of Christ. In the which we are to glorifie God: for the bodie is for the Lord, and the Lord is for the bodie. Surelie he meaneth not for an asses bodie, as by this time I hope appeareth[.]

[...]

Bodins poet, *Ovid*, whose *Metamorphosis* make so much for him, saith to the overthrow of this phantasticall imagination [...]

> *The Lord did set mans face so hie,*
> *That he the heavens might behold,*
> *And looke up to the starrie skie.*
> *To see his woonders manifold.*

Now, if a witch or a divell can so alter the shape of a man, as contrarilie to make him looke downe to hell, like a beast; Gods works should not onelie be defaced and disgraced, but his ordinance should be woonderfullie altered, and thereby confounded. (Scot, 5.5)

Malleus Maleficarum, *Bodin*, and manie other of them that mainteine witchcraft, triumph upon the storie of *Nabuchadnez-zar*, as though *Circes* had transformed him with hir sorceries into an oxe, as she did others into swine, &c. I answer, that he was neither in bodie nor shape transformed at all, according to their grosse imagination; as appeareth both by the plaine words of the text, and also by the opinions of the best interpreters thereof: but that he was, for his beastlie government and conditions, throwne out of his kingdome and banished for a time, and driven to hide himselfe in the wildernesse, there in exile to lead his life in beastlie sort, among beasts of the field, and fowles of the aire (for by the waie I tell you it appeareth by the text, that he was rather turned into the shape of a fowle than of a beast) untill he rejecting his beastlie conditions, was upon his repentance and amendment called home, and restored unto his kingdome. Howbeit, this (by their confession) was neither divels nor witches dooing; but a miracle wrought by God, whom alone I acknowledge to be able to bring to passe such workes at his pleasure. (Scot, 5.6)

Howsoever I do agree with you for the untruth of this knight's tale, yet your reasons here used to improve[197] the verity thereof seem unto me neither firm nor sound for many of them. As first, that the ass had no more wit than to kneel to a piece of starch, it may be said that he was belike a popish ass and had therein as much wit as the wisest papist in the world had or yet hath.[198] 2ly, there is in the mass or massmonger as little force or honesty as is in the witch and witchcraft and Satan must not be divided against himself lest his kingdom fall. 3ly, neither do witchmongers hold that two substantial forms can be *simul et semel in eadem subiecto* for the form of the ass was not substantial but fantastical. 4ly, it may be the Englishman had remained long enough in that country (though not in that haven) to learn the language and so the one might understand the other, and much might be understood by signs. 5ly, if witchmongers confess thus much then have you done them much wrong in your book in that you do oftentimes lay to their charge that they hold that witches can at their pleasure play their parts in the [**fol. 81v**] witchings.[199] But to the matter, I answer if the witch could either at the time by her appointed or by the inquisitor's commandment unwitch this man, it is to be presupposed that it was by God's leave and permission in that he did not put a let or impediment against the doing thereof. For the which, if he be to be thought

---

197 OED: 'To disprove, refute; to show to be wrong or false.'
198 This 'first' response corresponds to the third point made by Scot in 5.4 of the printed *Discoverie* (cf. the excerpt reproduced above).
199 Cf. Scot's comment in the excerpt from 5.4 above: 'this assertion is false, and disagreeable to their owne doctrine, which mainteineth, that the witch dooth nothing but by the permission and leave of God.'

The treatise 147

a confederate with witches, why then should he not be thought to be a confederate with all other kind of sinners whom he daily suffereth to sin and work wickedness at their pleasures, yea, whom he hath given over into such a reprobate sense and hardness of heart as they can do nothing but sin? Yet God forbid we should speak or think of God so unreverently as to make him a confederate with any sinner. 6ly, whether this saying of Mercurius be true it shall be considered in the story of Nebuchadnezzar, and I confess with St James and St Paul that a body without spirit is dead.[200] But this young man's body had his spirit and his ass's body was without spirit, being only a fantastical body and *specie tenus*.[201] And this shall prove for answer to the 7, 8, 9 reasons next ensuing, saving that hereto I add that if God did transform the body of Nebuchadnezzar into a beast (as some think he did) then are these questions and propositions to be demanded of God and not of man, who can as I think answer no better than to say with God all things are possible. 10ly, you say it is absolutely against God's ordinance that man should fly in the air &c, but I think it not such an absolute ordinance of God as he may not permit to a man the contrary to the same. It is affirmed by all antiquity and even of the best sort that Simon Magus did fly in the air though it were to his cost in the end, and we read in the scriptures of Enoch, of Elijah, and of Christ which were assumpted[202] into heaven in their lifetimes through the clouds and air further than ever any bird was able to make his flight. And every one of us shall at the last day be taken up in the clouds and meet the Lord in the air, therefore whether we may or shall fly like birds in the air is not material, but this I am sure amounteth to as much a matter and to a far better and greater flight in the air than birds ever had or shall have.[203] For swimming like a fish I say no more but that I am sure you know many men that can swim well both under water and above also. As for a man to become an

---

200 Mercurius is the Latin name given to Hermes Trismegistus (see the excerpt from Scot 5.5 quoted above), the putative author of the esoteric texts known as the *Corpus Hermeticum*, which were incorrectly believed to be pre-Christian in the sixteenth century.
201 'appearance'.
202 OED: 'Assumed, taken up, raised, elevated, elected.'
203 Author's note: '4 Regu[m] 2 acts 1 thes 4'; 2 Kings 2:11 ('And as thei went walking and talking, beholde, there appeared a charet of fyre, and horses of fyre, and did separate them twaine. So Elijah went vp by a whyrlewinde into heauen.'), Acts 1:9 ('And when he had spoken these things, while they behelde, he was taken vp: for a cloude toke him vp out of their sight'), 1 Thessalonians 4:17 ('Then shal we which liue and remaine, be caught vp with them also in the cloudes, to mete the Lord in the ayer: & so shal we euer be with the Lord.')

ass, if it would please God to have it so I think as possible and as little contrary to God's ordinance as that Balaam's ass spake after the manner and voice of a man. Neither may God be said contrary to himself or to his ordinance in these cases, for he never promised he would not do these things, nor never tied himself [fol. 82r] to all his ordinances (no, nor to the greater part of them) by any such absolute necessity or condition as he might not at his pleasure alter them. For were it so then he could never have done any miracle sith all miracles are contrary to the common course and natural order of things ordained of God. But to rest in this matter of transformation or transubstantiations of one thing into another, I may say it is as much against the common and ordinary ordinance of God for a rod to be turned into a serpent or a serpent into a rod, for water to be turned into blood or wine &c as it is for a man to be turned into another shape or substance, yet you know that God did alter and transform the said things. You know also and will I am sure confess that Lot's wife was turned into a stone or pillar of salt, and therefore I cannot but marvel that you will make this matter of transformation so impossible to God as you do, or that you will charge him with contrariety to himself in this case, especially sith you confess in the examples of your natural magic that one substance hath been altered into another by force of natural things. 11ly, that the devil hath no other power than that which God from the beginning appointed him consonant to his nature is in no wise to be granted. For first, if you mean that he hath now the same power which he had at the beginning (as your words import you do so mean) then would it follow that he might stand in the grace of God and serve him in doing good and holy actions as other good spirits do, for at the beginning he was of their sort, all being created good. Again, if he has now the same power which once he had in doing mischief he might then bring the whole mass of mankind into that damnable estate and condition to the which he did once bring us through our first parents. To be short, where do you find that it was from the beginning appointed unto the devil to play all these wicked parts and pageants which are in scripture and other histories recorded of him, and which by daily experience are seen and felt? It is written of him that he was from the beginning (vz. of his falling from God) a liar and a murderer (and what he was further from that beginning of his fall I do not presently remember that it is recorded) wherein if my memory fail me not then would it follow that the devil hath no power but to lie and to murder, and so in all other sins he should be clean, as being without power either to do them or to procure them to be done.[204] But I have before showed (Reason 18) that the

---

204 John 8:44.

power and strength of the devil is not always of one sort but sometime greater and sometime less as it pleaseth God to order the matter. And I have also [fol. 82v] showed before (Reason 28) that God doth permit much more to his creatures than the natural order by him at the first appointed doth permit, and there have I also showed (and likewise in your 29th Reason) that the devil's power doth not only reach to the vitiating of men's minds but also to the vitiating and hurting of their bodies, as you may see also in the story of Job and in the evangelical histories, where you shall find that many were bodily possessed of the devil and by him most cruelly hurt and tormented in their bodies. And where you say here the devil's power may be restrained but not enlarged, this is contrary to your assertion in your 18th Reason, where you say the devil is as strong at one time as at another. And in that you say his power cannot be enlarged seemeth contrary to the saying of Christ and of his apostles, which teach that towards the end of the world the times shall be most perilous and the power of Satan then so great in signs and wonders and in all deceitfulness that the very elect should be deceived by him if it were possible, and finally that his wrath should be then the greater for that he had but a short time.[205] 12ly, you say it is a beastly assertion to say that a man whom God hath made to his own image and likeness should be turned into a beast, or that the body of an ass should be the temple of the holy ghost or the child of God &c. First, as touching the image of God, you do I am sure know that man is said to be made according to the same, not in respect of his body (which can have no likeness with God, being a spirit) but in respect of man's spirit or soul and the good qualities wherewith the same was at the first endued by God, in which image and likeness man was by sin so much depraved and made unlike unto God that he became in very deed more like to a beast than unto God. And therefore is the prophet David bold to compare men unto beasts in that they were so far fallen from God's image, saying man being in honour did not regard it but became like unto horse and mule, in whom there is no understanding.[206] Yea, worse than beasts are men called in the scripture for they are there called the children of the devil, yea his servants, slaves, and captives &c. And a far less derogation is it as I think unto man to have his body transformed to the vilest beast that ever was than to have his soul transformed from the image of God to the image of the devil in all abominable sin [fol. 83r] and wickedness as by sin it came to pass, the devil being the first and chief mean thereof, so that if the devil

---

205 Author's notes: 'math 24 2 thes 2 2 Timo 3 Apocal. 12'; Matthew 24:24, 2 Thessalonians 2:3–12, 2 Timothy 3:1, Revelation 12:12.
206 Author's note: 'psal'; Psalm 32.9.

had this power so ugly to transform our best and chiefest part it might seem to be a good argument *a maiora ad minus*[207] that he might much sooner transform our bodies into the shapes of beasts, this being nothing so ill or so great a transformation as the other. Now as touching man's body being the temple of the holy ghost and our being the children of God and he our father, these sayings are not generally to be stretched to all sorts of men but to the elect and chosen children of God, for the reprobate are not in the sense of these places either God's children or their bodies the temples of the holy ghost, but rather the children of the devil and his temples. 13ly, those things you here speak of are as much meant of asses' bodies as they are meant of the bodies of men being reprobates, and more do asses glorify God in their kind than those kind of men. And it were no great absurdity to say that the body of an ass is for the Lord; first because all creatures generally were made and serve to his glory, and secondly in this special sense: that it pleased the Lord to use the body of an ass to carry him to Jerusalem and to say also that he had need of the ass. 14ly, for defacing, altering, and confounding the ordinance of God by making man to look downward to hell, contrary to God's ordinance described by Ovid *pronaque cum spectent animalia caetera* &c,[208] I say if the devil or witch could do this they did no more therein than we see daily to be done by extreme old age and by sundry kinds of sicknesses. Neither is this so great a matter as the devil hath done, by whom we have been brought so far from God's ordinance in our creation as he made us not only to step down to hellward but also there to lie both body and soul forever unless it had pleased the Lord in mercy to take us out of his claws. As for our bodies, they are as much transformed as this doth come unto, and more too, when as they become dust and ashes and the meat of worms as well as the bodies of any beast doth. Last of all, as touching the transformation of Nebuchadnezzar, neither the words of the text nor the interpreters of the same do so agree with your opinion but that there is of that matter great diversity of opinions amongst them. Very plain it is by the text and by the assent of all interpreters that I have read that his human sense and understanding was for that time taken from him, and that he fell upon

---

207 A principle in logic, stating that when a strong claim has been demonstrated it also demonstrates any weaker claims following from the stronger.

208 In full, '*pronaque cum spectent animalia cetera terram, os homini sublime dedit caelumque videre iussit et erectos ad sidera tollere vultus*'; 'Where other animals walk on all fours and look to the ground, man was given a towering head and commanded to stand erect, with his face uplifted to gaze on the stars of heaven.' Ovid, *Metamorphoses*, translated by David Raeburn (London: Penguin, 2004); 1.84–6. Scot's English verse translation is provided in the excerpt above.

the grass as the oxen did, [fol. 83v] which should argue that he had not now a man's body if your assertion a little before be infallible, for you said man's body must be fed with bread and not with hay. And hereto it may be said that man's body, especially of kings living before in all delicacy, could not for so long time live under the open air in all kind of weather, and that without clothes or better diet, but that he must needs perish. Also, if he had been in the shape of a man it is probable that the beasts of the wilderness would have fallen upon him and destroyed him. It is also probable that his people and princes if he had been in man's shape would have succoured him and brought him to his palace though he could not of himself return, his senses being taken from him. These I suppose be as good probabilities to prove that Nebuchadnezzar was transformed into a beast as you used to prove that the foresaid young man was not transformed into an ass, but I set not down these reasons to rely upon them, for seeing the matter is made so doubtful by the diversities of opinions I had rather suspend my opinion than to be resolute therein, the matter especially being such as concerneth not our salvation. Wherefore I would rather stand with you upon the transformations of Lot's wife into a pillar of salt, of rods into serpents and of serpents into rods, of water into blood and wine, which are certain by the scriptures to be verily and truly done, than I would stand upon this transformation of Nebuchadnezzar. And yet in him you must confess a transformation far against nature and God's ordinance in his creation if it were no more but that his hairs were grown like unto eagle's feathers and his nails like unto the claws of birds, and that his human sense and understanding was quite taken from him. But in the end you say if he were transformed it was done by God (and not by devil or witch) and if it lieth in God to bring to pass such a mighty work and miracle at his pleasure, I ask why it lieth not in God then to bring such a thing to pass by a witch or a devil if it please him? Again, if this be true, then is it very false which before you said, to wit that God should be contrary to himself and against his own ordinance if he should so transform a man. Yea, you plainly said it might not be done if God would give leave to man to do it, when as I take it you fall into apparent contrariety.

[fol. 84r] Reason 77

> For the maintenance of witches transportations, they object the words of the Gospell, where the divell is said to take up Christ, and to set him on a pinnacle of the temple, and on a mountaine, &c. Which if he had doone in maner and forme as they suppose, it followeth not therefore that witches could doo the like; nor yet that the divell would doo it for them at their pleasure; for they know not their thoughts, neither can otherwise communicate

with them. But I answer, that if it were so grosselie to be understood, as they imagine it, yet should it make nothing to their purpose. For I hope they will not saie, that Christ had made anie ointments, or entred into anie league with the divell, and by vertue thereof was transported from out of the wildernes, unto the top of the temple of Jerusalem; or that the divell could have maisteries over his bodie, whose soule he could never laie hold upon; especiallie when he might (with a becke of his finger) have called unto him, and have had the assistance of manie legions of angels. Neither (as I thinke) will they presume to make Christ partaker of the divels purpose and sinne in that behalfe. If they saie; This was an action wrought by the speciall providence of God, and by his appointment, that the scripture might be fulfilled: then what gaine our witchmongers by this place? First, for that they maie not produce a particular example to prove so generall an argument. And againe, if it were by Gods speciall providence and appointment; then why should it not be doone by the hand of God, as it was in the storie of *Job*? Or if it were Gods speciall purpose and pleasure, that there should be so extraordinarie a matter brought to passe by the hand of the divell; could not God have given to the wicked angell extraordinarie power, and cloathed him with extraordinarie shape; whereby he might be made an instrument able to accomplish that matter, as he did to his angell that carried *Abacuck* to *Daniell*, and to them that he sent to destroie *Sodome*? But you shall understand, that this was doone in a vision, and not in veritie of action. So as they have a verie cold pull of this place, which is the speciall peece of scripture alledged of them for their transportations.

Heare therefore what *Calvine* saith in his commentarie upon that place, in these words; The question is, whether Christ were carried aloft indeed, or whether it were but in a vision? Manie affirme verie obstinatlie, that his bodie was trulie and reallie as they saie taken up: bicause they thinke it too great an indignitie for Christ to be made subject to sathans illusions. But this objection is easilie washed awaie. For it is no absurditie to grant all this to be wrought through Gods permission, or Christes voluntarie subjection: so long as we yeeld not to thinke that he suffered these temptations inwardlie, that is to saie, in mind or soule. And that which is afterwards set downe by the Evangelist, where the divell shewed him all the kingdoms of the world, and the glorie of the same, and that to be doone (as it is said in *Luke*) in the twinkling of an eie, dooth more agree with a vision than with a reall action. So farre are the verie words of *Calvine* ... He that will saie, that these words; to wit, that Christ was taken up, &c: can hardlie be applied to a vision, let him turne to the prophesie of *Ezechiell*, and see the selfe-same words used in a vision: saving that where Christ is said to be taken up by the divell, *Ezechiell* is taken up, and lifted up, and carried by the spirit of God, and yet in a vision. (Scot, 5.7)

The story of Christ's transportation is not alleged by any as I think to prove that witches do or can do the like by their own power, but to prove that transportations may be done by devil or witches if it please God to give them the like leave which here he gave to the devil, and that therefore it is not absolutely unpossible to be done as you affirm. Of witches' ointments and other their extern actions, charms, and ceremonies, enough hath been said before to your 4 Reason and 61 Reason. That the devil did this without any league made between Christ and him doth make much against you, as proving that there is no such necessity in the league as you before affirmed, who would have all their doings to depend upon their league. For the devil's mastery over Christ's body, it cannot be denied but that the devil and his ministers had some mastery over his body given unto them, for how else could they have beaten, scourged, buffeted him and in the end put him to death if they had had no mastery over his body, and how else could Christ have said unto Pilate (confessing Pilate's power over him), 'thou could have no power at all against me except it were given thee from above' &c.[209] Item, though Christ were no partaker of the devil's purpose yet was he a partaker in some sort of the devil's actions and speeches, vz. in guiding and diverting them to the purpose of his heavenly father, and this is by the text most plain, because it is there said that he was led by the spirit (to wit, the holy ghost) to be tempted of the devil. Therefore had God a part in this temptation as well as the devil. Item, this particular example is not produced to prove a general but to disprove a general by you affirmed, who generally deny that any such thing can be done by devil or witch, and in this case a particular is of very good force. Item, to your question why it should not be done by the hand of God as in the story of Job, it is in the h{?} of that story showed that Job was punished by the hand of the devil. But who shall prescribe any means unto God, or tie him to do things always after one sort? And this shall also serve for answer to your next question. Finally, to your conclusion where you say this transportation was by vision and not in verity of action, the text is manifest to the contrary, and few or none of the interpreters do say as you say; no, not Mr Calvin, for as touching the transporting of Christ first to the temple he giveth no censure at all in the words by you alleged or in any words of his upon that place, but only showeth the vanity of one reason which some (even the papists) do bring to prove those transformations to be corporal. And when he speaketh of the other transportation of Christ [fol. 84v] to the mountain (where all the kingdoms of the world were there showed unto him by the devil in the twingling of an eye) he sayeth that the same doth more agree to a vision but

---

209 John 19:11.

yet he doth in that also suspend his opinion, as by his words immediately following the same is most manifest, for thus he sayeth of that matter: *In re tamen dubia, et quam absquae periculo nescire licet, malo judiciam suspendere, quam contentiosis praebere litigandi ansam.*[210] Here you may see that Mr Calvin maketh the matter so uncertain and doubtful as he is contented to suspend his judgement therein. And besides yourself I know none that is so resolute as you are in this case, but I could allege very many resolute to the contrary of your opinion herein. As for your place of Ezekiel it can prove nothing to the purpose, no more than if I should on the contrary part say that Habakkuk and Philip were corporally transported, *ergo* this of Christ was also corporal.[211]

Reason 78

> *Calvine* saith; We derogate much from Gods glorie and omnipotencie, when we saie he dooth but give sathan leave to [afflict Job]: which is (saith he) to mocke Gods justice; and so fond an assertion, that if asses could speake, they would speake more wiselie than so. For a temporall judge saith not to the hangman; I give thee leave to hang this offender, but commandeth him to doo it. But the mainteiners of witches omnipotencie, saie; Doo you not see how reallie and palpablie the divell tempted and plagued *Job*? I answer first, that there is no corporall or visible divell named nor seene in any part of that circumstance; secondlie, that it was the hand of God that did it; thirdlie, that as there is no communitie betweene the person of a witch, and the person of a divell, so was there not any conference or practise betwixt them in this case. (Scot, 5.8)

This matter of Job is answered before sufficiently to your 63 Reas. And for Mr Calvin's words here alleged they are nothing at all to your purpose but

---

210 'the matter is not certain, and there is no harm in admitting ignorance. Hence I prefer to leave it with judgment suspended, rather than give a loophole for contentious disputation.' Calvin, *A Harmony of the Gospels: Matthew, Mark and Luke*, vol. 1, translated by A. W. Morrison (Grand Rapids, MI: William B. Eerdmans, 1972), p. 140.

211 Habakkuk, the Old Testament prophet, was transported by an angel in the story of Bel and the Dragon, related in the 14th chapter of Daniel, which was regarded as apocryphal in the early modern English Church: 'Then the Angel toke him by the crowne of the head, and bare him by the heare of the head, and through a mightie winde set him in Babylon vpon the denne' (Daniel 14:36, included with the Apocrypha in the Geneva Bible). Philip the Evangelist (not to be confused with the apostle of the same name) is transported in Acts 8:39. After Philip baptises a eunuch, 'as sone as they were come vp out of the water, the Spirit of the Lord caught away Philippe, that ye Eunuche sawe him no more: so he went on his way rejoycing.'

only against them which (fearing to make God author of evil actions) dare not say that God hath any work or dealing in these actions but say that he doth only suffer and permit them, whereas the truth is no action is so wicked but that God hath some work and doing in it whilst he doth order, rule, and direct it and the worker of it as it seemeth good unto him.[212] And how God, the devil and man do join in actions hath been before showed in Reas. 3 *et* 65.

Reason 79

> ... the mainteiners of witches omnipotencie, saie; Doo you not see how reallie and palpablie the divell tempted and plagued Job? I answer first, that there is no corporall or visible divell named nor seene in any part of that circumstance; secondlie, that it was the hand of God that did it; thirdlie, that as there is no communitie betweene the person of a witch, and the person of a divell, so was there not any conference or practise betwixt them in this case.
>
> And as touching the communication betwixt God and the divell, behold what *Calvine* saith, writing or rather preaching of purpose upon that place, wherupon they thinke they have so great advantage; When sathan is said to appeere before God, it is not doone in some place certeine, but the scripture speaketh so to applie it selfe to our rudenes. Certeinlie the divell in this and such like cases is an instrument to worke Gods will, and not his owne[.] (Scot, 5.8)

To the first point hereof I have answered in your said 65 Reason, to the second point I say it is to us unknown whether there were any communication or practice between the devil and a witch in this matter, but if there were none then it doth not follow that there was not or cannot be some at some other times between them. The two points remaining in this reason may be granted you without prejudice to your adversaries for they prove nothing that is in question, except that you grant the devil to be God's instrument in punishing Job (which also all men say) and therefore was he the executioner of those punishments, which before you would not acknowledge but imputed the execution thereof only to God.

---

212 Calvin's views on this matter were available in print in English translation by the time the treatise was written; see the *Sermons of Maister Iohn Calvin, vpon the booke of Iob*, translated by Arthur Golding (London, 1580), where Calvin states that both the devil and 'wicked men' are actively directed to do harm by God (p. 34).

Reason 80

> And wheras by our witchmongers opinions and arguments, the witch procureth the divell, and the divell asketh leave of God to plague whom the witch is disposed: there is not (as I have said) any such corporall communication betweene the divell and a witch, as witchmongers imagine. Neither is God mooved at all at sathans sute, who hath no such favour or grace with him, as to obteine any thing at his hands. (Scot, 5.8)

What corporal communication is between witches and the devil I suppose no man can tell but they which are of their sort, and therefore I leave it as an uncertain matter. But that God sometime granteth the request of Satan, though he do it not to gratify him thereby or of favour, is by sundry examples manifest, as in this of Job, in the lying spirit that went to Ahab's false prophets, and in them which went into the herd of swine.

[fol. 85r] Reason 81

> But what sorts of witches so ever *M. Mal.* or *Bodin* saie there are; *Moses* spake onlie of foure kinds of impious couseners or witches (whereof our witchmongers old women which danse with the fairies, &c; are none.) The first were *Praestigiatores Pharaonis*, which (as all divines, both Hebrues and others conclude) were but couseners and jugglers, deceiving the kings eies with illusions and sleights; and making false things to appeare as true: which nevertheles our witches cannot doo. The second is *Mecasapha*, which is she that destroieth with poison. The third are such as use sundrie kinds of divinations, and hereunto perteine these words, *Kasam, Onen, Ob, Idoni*. The fourth is *Habar*, to wit: when magicians, or rather such, as would be reputed cunning therein, mumble certeine secret words, wherin is thought to be great efficacie. (Scot, 5.9)

It were no hard matter to prove that Moses did speak of more than 4 sorts of such impious persons. But it shall not be needful to stand upon that point, for admit he spake of no more, yet might there be more in his time, and if there were no more in his time yet might there be more of that sort since, as well as there be now and have been since his time many sorts of idolatries, heresies, and other impieties which were not in his time.[213] But hereof you may see more said to your 1 and 2 Reas. And further I say that this word *chasaph* is taken of the learned in such a large sense (howsoever you restrain

---

213 Author's note: 'here might I also have noted that the Rabyns [i.e. rabbis] do not agree (as y[ou] sayd they do with you in the interp[re]tacion of thes words ther dyssent ys shewed by wyer[us] in the place here coted de p[re]stig daemo li 2 ca 1'. See note 215 below.

the same upon the opinion of Masseus) that it comprehendeth all sorts of cozeners and magical practices whatsoever.[214] For thus doth Wierus (whose learning you much commend) write of that word or of the word *mechassephim* derived of the same: *Ego vero si meum iudicium requiris putarii illud vocabulum latè patere atquae ad quamvis magicam artem spectare: et in hac sententia video etiam esse vulgus Haebreorum.*[215] This then being true, Moses in this word did not include 4 sorts of cozeners but 400 sorts if there were so many. And as for this word *venefica*, that the same doth only signify poisoners you can never prove by the scriptures nor by the common use of the word in any author.[216] And Wierus himself, though in the said place he go about to appropriate special words to distinct sorts of cozeners as you call them, yet doth he confess that the words *magi, malefeci, incantatores, prestigiatores, venifici* do in the scriptures (by common acceptation) denote or signify those whom we call *lamias* or *sagas*.[217] And sure I am all translations that I have seen do so use and understand the said words, wherefore if you will restrain the word *venefica* only to a poisoner you must do it by better authority than can be alleged to the contrary thereof.

---

214 In the printed version of the *Discoverie*, the word *chasaph* is discussed at length in 6.1. 'Masseus' is the Catholic priest and humanist Andreas Masius (1514–73), described by Scot as 'the most famous Hebrician in the world' (5.9). In addition to his expertise in Hebrew, Masius published a dictionary and grammar of Syriac in 1571: see Robert J. Wilkinson, *Orientalism, Aramaic, and Kabbalah in the Catholic Reformation* (Leiden: Brill, 2007), pp. 77–94.

215 This quotation is from Johannes Weyer's *De Praestigiis Daemonum* (Basel, 1568) 2.1 (p. 127). Translation from George Mora (ed.) *Witches, Doctors and Devils in the Renaissance* (Binghampton: Medieval & Renaissance Texts and Studies, 1991): 'If you wish my opinion as well, I should think that the word has broad application and that it refers to every sort of magical art, and I see that the majority of the Hebrews are also of this opinion' (p. 94).

Author's note: 'Heare also might I have shewed y[ou] that all dyvines do not think of the things done by pharaos sorcerers as you affyrme for St August dothe thinke they dyd in deede & not in shewe only doo thoes miracles as y[ou] may se li 3 de trinitate ca 9. and in his 2 & 7 epistle.' Immediately below follows another note: 'and w[ith] Aug the very text semeth to agre for yt sayth they dyd the same w[hich] Moses did & not yt they made a shewe therof'.

216 The word 'venefica' is discussed at length in the printed version of Scot (6.4).

217 Weyer writes that 'When a question is raised or a discussion begun about the activities of witches, men soon offer the testimony of scriptural passages containing the term "magician," or "evil-doer," or "enchanter," or "poisoner," or even "juggler" (as some translate). They then affirm that these terms denote, without distinction of meaning, the women who are commonly called "witches" or "wise women."' He goes on to dispute this view; Mora (ed.), *Witches, Doctors and Devils in the Renaissance*, p. 93.

Reason 82

... let us examine the description of a notable witch called *Simon Magus*, made by S. *Luke*; There was (saith he) in the citie of *Samaria*, a certeine man called *Simon*, which used witchcraft, and bewitched the people of *Samaria*, saieng that he himself was some great man. I demand, in what other thing here do we see anie witchcraft, than that he abused the people, making them beleeve he could worke miracles, whereas in truth he could doo no such thing; as manifestlie may appeare in the 13. and 19. verses of the same chapter: where he wondered at the miracles wrought by the apostles, and would have purchased with monie the power of the Holy-ghost to worke wonders [...] let us all abandon such witches and couseners, as with *Simon Magus* set themselves in the place of God, boasting that they can doo miracles, expound dreames, foretell things to come, raise the dead, &c: which are the workes of the Holy-ghost, who onlie searcheth the heart and reines, and onelie worketh great wonders, which are now staied and accomplished in Christ, in whome who so stedfastlie beleeveth shall not need to be by such meanes resolved or confirmed in his doctrine and gospell. And as for the unfaithfull, they shall have none other miracle shewed unto them, but the signe of *Jonas* the prophet. (Scot, 6.1)

That Simon Magus did no miracles nor could do is an assertion against all authority of writers and against the scriptures if the text itself or the circumstances thereof be considered, for it is said he bewitched the whole city or people of Samaria and that he used witchcraft and did in such sort bewitch them all [**fol. 85v**] with his sorceries that they gave heed unto him from the least unto the greatest, saying that he was the great power of God, and this he did for a long time.[218] Now if it be considered what a great city Samaria was, what a number of people it contained of all sorts in it, is it credibly to be thought that all without exception, as well the learned and wise as the simple and unlearned, as well the chief and greatest as the meanest and least, should or could ascribe unto Simon Magus such great power and give such heed unto him for a long time together if they had not been brought thereunto by some strange and extraordinary miracles done by him, and would the text say that he used witchcraft and did bewitch them with his sorceries if there had been no such thing and if all this came to pass because he had bewitched them? But you think he could do no miracles because he did wonder at the miracles done by the apostles, and would have given them money to have power of them to do miracles. This is in effect no more than if a cunning artificer should meet with another that had more cunning than himself and

---

218 Acts 8:9–11.

should wonder at the other man's cunning, supposing before that none had been so cunning as himself and being desirous to attain to that further cunning which he saw in the other man, would offer him money to teach him the same. To be brief, the wondering of Simon Magus at the apostles' miracles and his offering of money unto them can argue no more but that he could not do those miracles which they did, and therefore he did not absolutely require power to do miracles but only to do that one miracle of giving the holy ghost by the imposition of hands which he saw in the apostles. So that as you may not say that the cunning artificer hath no cunning because he would have bought some cunning more than he had of a more cunning man, no more may you say that Simon could do no miracles at all because he would have learned one or two miracles at the apostles' hands. [fol. 86r] As for the saying of Christ to the scribes and Pharisees wherein he sayeth no sign should be given them but the sign of the prophet Jonah, if hereof you would gather the ceasing of all signs and miracles you do much mistake the matter, for certain it is that both Christ himself and also his apostles did after this was spoken do many signs and miracles in the presence of that cursed and adulterous generation.[219] Wherefore you must understand the meaning of Christ in this place to be that he would not at their request and for their sakes show any other sign than that of Jonah, or that he would not show any such sign as they would appoint. Again, this saying of Christ is only to be understood of good signs such as he would do or cause to be done by his apostles and other holy men and not of the wicked signs of Satan and his ministers, and therefore howsoever you take this saying, it cannot serve at all to prove the ceasing of wicked signs and miracles. But of this matter enough is said before to your 44 Reason.

Reason 83

> The greatest and most common objection is, that if there were not some, which could worke such miraculous or supernaturall feats, by themselves, or by their divels, it should not have beene said; Let none be found among you, that maketh his sonne or his daughter to go through the fier, or that useth witchcraft, or is a regarder of times, or a marker of the flieng of fowles, or a sorcerer, or a charmer, or that counselleth with spirits, or a soothsaier, or that asketh counsell of the dead, or (as some translate it) that raiseth the dead. But as there is no one place in the scripture that saith they can worke miracles, so it shalbe easie to proove, that these were all couseners, everie one abusing the people in his severall kind; and are accurssed of God. Not that they can doo all such things indeed, as there is expressed; but for

219 The reference to the sign of Jonah is in Matthew 12:39–41.

> that they take upon them to be the mightie power of God, and to doo that which is the onelie worke of him, seducing the people, and blaspheming the name of God, who will not give his glorie to anie creature, being himselfe the king of glorie and omnipotencie [...] And to proove that these sooth-saiers and witches are but lieng mates and couseners; note these words pronounced by God himselfe, even in the selfe same place to the children of Israell: Although the Gentiles suffered themselves to be abused, so as they gave eare to these sorcerers, &c: he would not suffer them so, but would raise them a prophet, who should speake the truth. (Scot, 6.2)

When in your 81 Reas. you said Moses made no mention of our old witches, it was hereof to be gathered that if he had made mention of them you would then have yielded that there had been such as they are thought to be. But now in denying that there were such witches, enchanters, and cozeners as Moses doth mention, it seemeth all one whether he had spoken or not spoken of our witches. For if he had spoken of them in as plain words as you would wish, yet would not you believe there had been or could be such, as plainly may appear by your denial of the others, of which your denial I do not a little marvel sith the whole course of the text is so apparently against you, which in sundry places sayeth that there were such as had spirits and did ask counsel of spirits and work with spirits.²²⁰ And is it to be thought that God would give commandments of things which never were nor never could be?²²¹ Did he lack words to express his meaning that he could not in proper speech show the manners and practices of cozeners and deceivers, but that he must show the same by such words and things as never were nor could be? But admit that were [fol. 86v] as you say, yet here have you confessed and needs must that God's curse and the punishment of death is due to such deceivers and cozeners for abusing and deceiving the people in taking upon them to do those things which you say indeed they cannot do. Wherefore you should not have pleaded so much as you do for the excusing of our witches from the punishment of death, sith all the world doth see and know that they do likewise deceive and abuse the people in taking upon them to do those things by sorcery and witchcraft which you think they cannot do:

---

220 Author's note: 'deutro 18 4 Regu[m] 9 1 cro 10'; Deuteronomy 18:11, 1 Chronicles 10:13. The Geneva text of 2 Kings 9 does not contain a specific reference to working with spirits, but it does mention Jezebel and her 'witchcraftes' (verse 22).

221 Author's note: 'Mr Calvin saythe *Certe si nullae esse[n]t inca[n]tationes frustra lege dei p[ro]hibitae ac damnatae essent* in psal 58', a reference to Calvin's commentary on Psalm 58: 'Had there been no enchantments practised, where was the necessity of their being forbidden and condemned under the Law?'; Calvin, *Commentaries on the Book of Psalms*, vol. 2 of 5, translated by James Anderson (Edinburgh: Calvin Translation Society, 1846) p. 372.

like sin, according to the rule of scripture and equity, must have like punishment. As touching reasons here used for proof of your purpose, they may be soon answered. For first I find not said in the text which you allege, that the gentiles suffered themselves to be abused, but this only: that they gave ear or did hearken to such persons and practices as are there forbidden.[222] But what if {it} had been said that they suffered themselves to be abused by them? Do you not think that men are greatly abused whenas by sorceries and witchcraft &c they are kept or drawn from the ever living God and their salvation to the trust and confidence of such wicked things, though the said wicked things should be indeed done? Would the verity of those wicked actions make it be thought that they which trust in them rather than in God are not thereby abused? I trow not. Is it not said in sundry places of the scripture that the people were deceived and abused by the false doctrine of false prophets, and is this said only because the said false prophets did but make a show of false doctrine, and preached none indeed? If not, then may it be said that the people are abused as well when false things are indeed done or taught as when there is but a show or promise made of the same. Your second reason is that none can raise up the dead, and yet is this forbidden, whereof you gather that all the rest forbidden is as impossible as this; *sed non sequitur*.[223] This is an argument from a particular to a universal or a *secundum quid ad simpliciter*, the invalidity of which kind of argument is showed sufficiently before to your 29 Reas.[224] But here I must put you in remembrance the text speaketh not of raising the dead but of asking counsel of the dead, which may be done without raising the dead if a man would be so foolish to ask counsel where none is to be [fol. 87r] had.[225] Howbeit I say with the scriptures and with all divines, old and new, that although the dead cannot indeed be raised up by the devil and his ministers, yet is there more in their attempts that way than a plain cozening, for they can sometime make a show of the dead man raised up in such sort that a man would think he were the very man whom they promised to raise, whereof the story of the supposed raising of dead Samuel may give sufficient testimony to other, though to you (which are herein of a contrary opinion to all others) it be of no force. Now to make a man appear to the eyes and outward senses

---

222 Deuteronomy 18.14: 'For these nations which thou shalt possesse, hearken vnto those that regarde the times, and vnto sorcerers: as for thee, the Lord thy God hath not suffred thee so.'
223 'but it does not follow'.
224 See note 57 to reason 29 above.
225 The distinction made here between raising the dead and asking counsel of the dead appears to have been taken into account in the printed *Discoverie*; see the excerpt quoted above.

of men in speech, in proportion and favour and in apparel all one to him that was dead cannot be done by cozening but must needs be done by some strange and miraculous practice with the devil, and therefore is it said in the said story that the woman of Endor which in appearance raised Samuel according to the foresaid circumstances did work with a spirit or counsel with a spirit. So then though here were a deceit and abuse, yet was it not without a plain practice of sorcery or witchcraft, and therefore was not the practice of such things only pretended but indeed done, as it was also by Pharaoh's sorceries, as before I have noted out of St August and by the text.[226] To the which you may add also the devil's plaguing of Job indeed and not in show only. As for your authorities of St August and the rest here alleged they prove nothing to your purpose; yea, I dare undertake by these authorities to overthrow the most of your assertions throughout your whole book if you would stand to that trial.[227]

Reason 84

> ... as they must confesse, that none in these daies can doo as *Moses* did: so it may be answered, that none in these daies can doo as *Jannes* and *Jambres* did: who, if they had beene false prophets, as they were jugglers, had yet beene more privileged to exceed our old women or conjurors, in the accomplishing of miracles, or in prophesieng, &c.[228] (Scot, 13.21)

As touching ceasing of miracles enough is answered to your 44 Reas. Neither is this a good reason that because none can now do as Moses did, therefore none can now do as Jannes and Jambres did. We see by the scriptures that it hath pleased God as well for the trial of his elect as for the punishment of the reprobate and for other respects also to leave unto Satan and his pernicious ministers power to do wicked miracles, and that most specially towards the end of the world, because his time is but short he shall therefore have the more wrath.[229] But as touching Jannes and Jambres, it is not certain whether they were the sorcerers of Egypt which encountered with Moses by miracles or whether they were other that resisted him some other way.

226 Author's note: 'these aucthoryties do not inp[ro]ve [i.e. disprove] ye power of sorcerers but rep[ro]ve yer wyckednes & thoes that seake unto them shewinge how detestable and Iniurious to god that ys'.
227 See Scot, 6.2; these lengthy passages are omitted from the excerpt above.
228 Jannes and Jambres are names that were conventionally ascribed to the magicians in Exodus 7:10–12, although they are not named in the biblical text itself, as the author points out.
229 Author's note: 'Apoca 12.'; Revelation 12:12.

[fol. 87v] Reason 85

Saule ... goeth to certeine of his servants, that sawe in what taking he was, and asked them for a woman that had a familiar spirit, and they told him by and by that there dwelt one at *Endor*. By the waie you shall understand, that both *Saule* and his servants ment such a one as could by hir spirit raise up *Samuell*, or any other that was dead and buried. Wherein you see they were deceived, though it were true, that she tooke upon hir so to doo. To what use then served hir familiar spirit, which you conceive she had, bicause *Saules* servants said so? Surelie, as they were deceived and abused in part, so doubtlesse were they in the rest [...] But now forsooth *Saule* covereth himselfe with a net; and bicause he would not be knowne, he put on other garments. But to bring that matter to passe, he must have beene cut shorter by the head and shoulders, for by so much he was higher than any of the people. And therfore whatsoever face the craftie quene did set upon it, she knew him well enough [...] By these and manie other circumstances it may bee gathered, that she dissembled, in saieng she knew him not, and consequentlie counterfaited, and made a foole of him in all the rest. (Scot, 7.11)

When *Saule* had told hir, that he would have *Samuel* brought up to him, she departed from his presence into hir closet, where doubtles she had hir familiar; to wit, some lewd craftie preest, and made *Saule* stand at the doore like a foole (as it were with his finger in a hole) to heare the cousening answers, but not to see the cousening handling thereof[.] (Scot, 7.12)

... it is the divels condition, to allure the people unto wickednes, and not in this sort to admonish, warne, and rebuke them for evill ... If it bee said, that it was at Gods speciall commandement and will, that *Samuel* or the divell should be raised, to propound this admonition, to the profit of all posteritie: I answer, that then he would rather have doone it by some of his living prophets, and that sathan had not beene so fit an instrument for that purpose[.] [...] Howbeit, concerning the veritie of this prophesie there be many disputable questions: first, whether the battell were fought the next daie; secondlie, whether all his sonnes were killed with him; item, whether they went to heaven or hell togither, as being with *Samuel*, they must be in heaven, and being with sathan, they must be in hell. But although everie part of this prophesie were false, as that all his sonnes were not slaine (*Ishbosheth* living and reigning in Israel two yeares after *Saules* death) and that the battell was not on the morrow, and that wicked *Saule*, after that he had killed himselfe, was not with good *Samuel*; yet this witch did give a shrewd gesse to the sequele. Which whether it were true or false, perteins not to my purpose; and therfore I will omit it. But as touching the opinion of them that saie it was the divell, bicause that such things came to passe; I would faine knowe of them where they learne that divels foreknow things to come. If they saie he gesseth onelie upon probabilities, the witch may also doo the like. But here I may not forget the decrees, which conclude, that *Samuel* appeared not unto *Saule*; but that the historiographer set foorth *Saules* mind and *Samuels* estate, and certeine things which were said & scene, omitting whether they were true or false: and further, that it were a great offense for a man to beleeve the bare words of the storie. (Scot, 7.13)

The reasons which move you in this matter to vary as {you} d{o} from all other men are of small force as I think, and will now in order as they stand endeavour to show you. First, as there is no reason to believe the pythonist had a familiar spirit because Saul's servants said it, so do I not think that any man doth only ground thereupon. At the least they need not so do, for the words of the holy ghost are that Saul did ask counsel of a familiar spirit which he did not unless this pythonist had such a spirit or did in Saul's behalf counsel with such a one. Yea, and this fact of Saul is there set down as the principal cause why he was rejected of God and slain.[230] Secondly, the dissembling of this woman with Saul in pretending not to know him is uncertain, and very like it is that he did so disguise himself as she did not know him, and hereof (I mean of his disguising) the text doth make some mention, saying that he changed himself and did put on other raiment, which he did no doubt to be unknown, and therefore if he had not seen that he might have been thereby unknown he neither would nor needed to have changed himself.[231] Besides, the text sayeth he came in the night time which did also help this his purpose. And it may be that this woman did never see Saul before, being on{e} of that sort whom he persecuted with death and banishment. As for Saul's stature it might easily have escaped her knowledge in the dark night and somewhat also it might be cloaked by stooping and sitting down before the woman came unto him: and it may be that this woman had never heard so much of his stature as the scripture reporteth, neither can you by that scripture gather that he was higher by the shoulders than any other man of the people of God generally and without exception, for his stature in that place is only compared to all the people that were then present when he was by Samuel presented unto them for their king. But admit now that this woman did in this point dissemble with Saul; yet is that no reason for you to conclude that she did so likewise

---

230 Author's note: '1 cronicoru[m] 10'; 1 Chronicles 10:13: 'So Saul dyed for his transgression, that he committed against the Lord, *euen* against the worde of the Lord, which he kept not, and in that he soght and asked counsel of a familiar spirit'.
231 1 Samuel 28:8. Scot appears to have taken this point into account in the printed *Discoverie*, judging by the excerpt above.

in all the rest, as I have before showed and proved in answering your like reasons Reas. 29. You cannot deny but she dealt truly with Saul when she told him how he persecuted the sorcerers, and likewise when she told him by and by after that he was Saul, therefore you might as well say she spake and dealt truly in all the rest. [fol. 88r] Thirdly, you say Saul did see nothing but stood without. This proveth nothing if it were so, but it seemeth by the text and by the best interpreters thereof that he did see a wicked spirit in the show of Samuel when he inclined his face to the ground and bowed himself. For why else did he use that gesture? Besides it is by the text apparent that there was talk and communication between him and the woman's Samuel, which Samuel if he had been but some cozening priest could never have counterfeited the voice of Samuel in such sort as Saul should think it to be the voice of Samuel, with whom he was so well acquainted in his lifetime, and especially that it could be so well and so exactly counterfeited upon the sudden, Saul's coming and purpose being before utterly unknown to the witch or sorceress. Fourthly, it agreeth not, you say, with the devil's nature and manner to reprove men for their wickedness but rather to allow them in it. That I confess to be very true so long as the devil is to win them to wickedness, or feareth by threapning and reproving them for sin to drive them from him. But when he hath gotten men where he would have them and thinketh himself sure of them, then his manner is (as infinite examples may teach us) to urge and aggravate their sins and the just judgements of God against sin by all possible ways and means, that so he may bring them to a most desperate horror and vexation of conscience as now he did by Saul, and doth the like by all desperate caitiffs. Fifthly, that the devil is no fit instrument for God to use in propounding such a profitable admonition to all posterity, I answer that he is as fit for this purpose as he was to confess unto all posterities that Christ Jesus was the son of God, and I think it to be a great declaration of God's omnipotent power over devils and their wicked ministers that he can use them, even maugre[232] their hearts to the setting forth of his glory and to the testifying of his truth no less than he can use his chosen servants that are most willing to be at his beck and commandment. Do you think it was anything at all to God's dishonour that he used Saul, a child of Satan, to be king over his people and a prophet also, that he used Balaam to bless his people, or Judas to be his apostle and so the preacher of his holy gospel and a worker of his divine miracles? If you allow of these to be fit instruments for God to use there is no reason why you should disallow of another.

---

232 OED: 'To defy, oppose; to get the better of, master'. The earliest recorded use of 'maugre' as a verb in the OED is in 1597 in Beard's *Theatre of God's Judgement*; this predates it.

[fol. 88v] Sixthly, for the disputable questions that you propound, they are not material to your purpose whether they did in all points fall out according to the words uttered by the pretenced Samuel yea or no, for who will look for such truth or honesty at the devil's hands, as if he should speak nothing but the truth? It were of your side more strong if there were no lie at all in those words, for so should they the less appear to be the words of a lying spirit or devil. Howbeit, it seemeth by the circumstance of the text and by the opinion of the best of writers thereupon that every one of these things which you bring in question did fall out according to the words of the said Samuel. As for the remaining of Ishbosheth alive, it proveth in deed very well that all the sons of Saul were not slain with him, but what needed that proof sith there be no words which say that he and all his sons should be slain with him?[233] Seventhly, you ask where men learn that devils do foreknow things to come, and I answer: that may you learn very well to your satisfaction of St August, whose opinion in that matter you could not but see even in the same papal decrees whereof you speak here. In the eighth and last place, for the authority here by you alleged touching the mind of the historiographers upon this story of Samuel is not indeed any papal decree (as you term it) but the very words of St August in his 18 book *De Civitate Dei* ca 18, book of questions upon the old and new testament ca 27.[234] And for your more full and better satisfaction in this matter how devils may foreknow things to come, I refer you to Mr Martyr writing upon this story of Saul in his commentary upon 1 Sam ca 28, where he doth at large show many and sundry ways by the which the devils do and may foreknow things to come. Now to your 8th and last point, vz. the papal *decretalias* of St August. You do here wrest his words far otherwise then he meant, as the words themselves will show {if} you considered one part of them with another, for where you apply them generally to the whole story St August doth speak them but in respect of some particular point of the same, as when he sayeth the writer of the history doth omit to show whether the things which he wratt were true or false he doth not [fol. 89r] mean this generally (as you take it) of the whole story, but only to answer thereby the objection of those which urge the letter of the history

---

233 1 Samuel 28:19 does imply that Saul and at least some of his sons will die, when the apparition of Samuel says 'tomorowe shalt thou and thy sonnes be with me'. Three of Saul's four sons are killed with him soon afterwards (1 Samuel 31:6).

234 The second reference provided by the author is to question 27 of pseudo-Augustine's *Quaestiones Veteris et Novi Testamenti*. The author criticises Scot for misattributing what he believes to be Augustine's words to a papal decree, but is himself incorrect about the authorship of these passages: see the 'Sources' section of the introduction above.

for proof that true Samuel appeared to Saul. And hereof also doth he only mean in the other words (where he sayeth it were a great offence to believe the bare words of the story). For that he meaneth not this or the other generally of the whole story but only of this one point, vz. that it were a great offence to believe the bare words of the story which say it was Samuel that appeared, may full well appear unto you first by these words in that decree, vz. *Quomodo enim fieri poterat ut arte magica attraheretur vir a nativitate sanctus et operibus vitae iustus* &c.[235] These words do render plainly the cause and reason why he said immediately before that which is here by you alleged, vz. *indignum omnino facinus esse si secudum verba historie commodetur assensus*,[236] for as soon as these words were spoken the other, vz. *Quomodo enim fieri poterat* &c are by and by added to show as I say the cause or reason why he counted it a heinous fault to believe the bare words of the story. And yet more plainly doth St August in this very decree express his meaning to be as I have said, saying afterward after this manner: *sed si quis propter Historiam ea quae verbis expressa sunt putet non praetermittenda ne ratio historiae inanis sit, recte facit quidem, si tamen istud minime ad veri rationem rapiat sed ad visum et intellectum Saul.*[237] Lo, here you see the mind of St August was so far from drawing men from believing the bare words of the story generally that he commendeth the believing of the same, so as it be not in this one point wrested to the truth of Samuel's appearing unto Saul, but be understood of such an appearing of Samuel only as seemed to be true unto the sight and understanding of Saul who, being a reprobate, could not have a good understanding, as it is there said in the words following.[238] And that this also was the meaning of St August in his other words of this decree by you here alleged doth no less plainly appear if you mark what followeth the same his words. For as soon as he had said the words by you alleged, vz. *Historicus enim mentem Saulis et statum Samuelis describit et ea quae*

---

235 'How could it happen that a man hallowed in his birth and upright in the actions of his life was drawn up by the art of magic?' – translation from Mora (ed.), *Witches, Doctors and Devils in the Renaissance*, p. 130.
236 Scot's version of these words, reprinted in the excerpt above, is in English: 'it were a great offense for a man to beleeve the bare words of the storie'.
237 'But if anyone should feel, in view of the story, that the things literally described should not be neglected, lest the meaning of the story be lost, he will be correct – provided that he applies this principle not to a reckoning of the truth, but to what was seen and understood [by Saul]' – translation adapted from Mora (ed.), *Witches, Doctors and Devils in the Renaissance*, p. 131.
238 The 'words following' are, in the version of *nec mirum* presented in the *Decretum*, '*Neque enim reprobus factus, bonum poterat intellectum habere*', and are translated by the author above.

dicta et visa sunt exprimens praetermittens si vera sint an falsa[239] he by and by addeth and goeth on saying [**fol. 89v**] *Quae ait: audiens in quo habitu esset excitatus, intellexit inquit hunc Samuelem esse: quod intellexit retulit {et} quia non bene intellexit contra scripturam alium adoravit quam deum et putans Samuelem adoravit diabolum.*[240] This I suppose is plain enough to show that the words by you alleged out of this decree are only to be understood of that one particular point whereof I have now spoken and {not} generally of all the history. For if it should be said in a general sense that it were a heinous offence to believe the bare words of this history, then would it follow that it were a great offence to believe that Saul came to the pythonist or that he or she did or spake any of the things that are mentioned in the same history. But here by the way I would have you to note that there be in this decree (if you will allow the authority thereof) some things which make directly against you in some of your former assertions, as first where you said it was some cozening priest only with whom this woman had conference. This decree sayeth it was the devil which, to the end he might cause an error wherein he might be glorified, did show himself adorned under the habit and name of a just man. Also where you say Saul did see nothing but stood without, this decree sayeth that the appearing of Samuel is in that story set out as the same appeared to the sight and understand{ing} of Saul, which argueth that he saw somewhat. Again, where you deny that there was any working of the woman with the devil in this matter, or any magical practice done by her, this decree confesseth both the one and the other against you.

Reason 86

> Christs coming was not so fruteles and prejudiciall in this point unto us, as to take awaie his spirit of prophesie and divination from out of the mouth of his elect people, and good prophets, giving no answers of anie thing to come by them, nor by *Urim* nor *Thumim*, as he was woont, &c.[241] And yet to leave the divell in the mouth of a witch, or an idoll to prophesie or worke

---

239 Scot, 7.13 (see excerpt quoted above): 'the historiographer set foorth Saules mind and Samuels estate, and certeine things which were said & scene, omitting whether they were true or false'.

240 'What in fact does he say? "Hearing in what form he was raised, he understood" (says the historian) "that this was Samuel." The writer has reported what Saul understood; and because he did not understand correctly, he worshipped another than God, in defiance of Scripture. Thinking him to be Samuel, he adored the devil' – Mora (ed.), *Witches, Doctors and Devils in the Renaissance*, p. 131.

241 The words *Urim* and *Thummim* refer to items used in divination in the Old Testament; see Exodus 28:30, 1 Samuel 14:41.

miracles, &c: to the hinderance of his glorious gospell, to the discountenance of his church, and to the furtherance of infidelitie and false religion, whereas the working of miracles was the onelie, or at least the most speciall meanes that mooved men to beleeve in Christ (Scot, 7.15)

... we ordinarilie read in the scriptures, that it is the Lord that worketh great wonders. Yea *David* saith, that among the dead (as in this case of *Samuel*) God himselfe sheweth no wonders. I find also that God will not give his glorie and power to a creature. *Nichodemus* being a Pharisie could saie, that no man could do such miracles as Christ did, except God were with him, according to the saieng of the prophet to those gods and idols, which tooke on them the power of God; Doo either good or ill if you can, &c. So as the prophet knew and taught thereby, that none but God could worke miracles ... S. *Augustine*, among other reasons, whereby he prooveth the ceasing of miracles, saith; Now blind flesh dooth not open the eies of the blind by the miracle of God, but the eies of our hart are opened by the word of God.
[...]
The miraculous healing of the sicke, by annointing, spoken of by S. *James*, is objected by manie, speciallie by the papists, for the maintenance of their sacrament of extreame unction: which is apishlie and vainelie used in the Romish church, as though that miraculous gift had continuance till this daie: wherein you shall see what *Calvine* speaketh in his institutions. The grace of healing (saith he) spoken of by S. *James*, is vanished awaie, as also the other miracles, which the Lord would have shewed onelie for a time, that he might make the new preaching of the gospell mervellous for ever. (Scot 8.1)

You can never prove that any did ever truly believe in Chr{ist} by the only means of his miracles, and that miracles were not the only means whereby Christ did win men to faith is showed sufficiently in my answer to your 17 Reas. And for the ceasing of miracles what is to be thought I refer you again as before I have done to my answer of your 44 Reas. As for your authorities here brought and other reasons to prove your purpose, they may be easily taken away. As first where you say it is not to be thought that it should lie in devils or witches to d{o} miracles, they being to the hindrance of the gospel and to the furtherance of infidelity, you might as well say that we may not think it lieth in the devil to stir up or procure any sin or wickedness, especially so many and so horrible sins as are committed sith the same do more directly tend to the dishonour of God and his holy gospel and to the furtherance of men's damnation than any miracles do or can do. For no miracle is of [fol. 90r] itself damnable to the beholders of it, but all sin is damnable of itself to the committers of it. But you ought to understand that God worketh all things for the best unto those that love him, and therefore can neither devil nor witch hinder the gospel or further infidelity by miracle or by any other means to the hurt of God's elect children or to the dishonour of God how much soever they mean and endeavour the same. But all the hurt they can do lighteth upon themselves and the reprobate sort, who justly deserve to be illuded by Satan through his wicked signs and miracles and by all other his sleights and subtleties because they would not believe the truth, which the apostle plainly declareth in one of his epistles to the Thessalonians, saying that the coming of the son of perdition should be by the working of Satan with all power and signs and lying wonders and in all deceivableness of unrighteousness among them that perish, because they regarded not the love of the truth that they might be saved, and therefore God shall send them strong delusion that they should believe lies, that all they might be damned which believed not the truth but had pleasure in unrighteousness.[242] As touching this saying of the psalmist, God showeth no wonders amongst the dead, I answer first that this is spoken of God's working of miracles and not of Satan's miracles, which are the miracles now in question between us.[243] Secondly, we speak of miracles not done amongst the dead but amongst the living. And thirdly, it is far from the scope of the prophet to draw that saying to prove thereby the ceasing of miracles, for you know very well the chief time of doing miracles was to come when it was spoken, Christ being then and long after unborn. As for the meaning of the prophet in that saying, it was no other but that he, being in extreme anguish and trouble by sickness, persecution, and trouble, and thereby brought to the very point of death, and yet not feeling the present help and favour of God in the same his distress, doth after a pathetical manner cry and call upon God to help him, and doth after a sort expostulate with him for deferring his help so long from him, saying amongst other his pathetical words used in this psalm, wilt you show a miracle to the dead or shall the dead rise up and praise thee, as if he should say unto God, 'if you help me not out of hand I shall die, and then all occasion of help and opportunity to relieve my restless estate will be taken away, except it should be thy will to do a miracle upon me being dead, and from death to raise me up that I might praise thee.' This shall you find to be the very sense and meaning of the prophet in these words if you consider the whole context of the psalm or the judgements of the best interpreters of the same. But in what sense so [fol. 90v] ever you take these said words, they can by no means serve your turn for the respects before touched. To which also may be added that the

---

242 Author's note: '2 thess 2'; 2 Thessalonians 2:9–12.
243 Author's note: 'Psal 88'; Psalm 88.10: 'Wilt thou shewe a miracle to ye dead? or shal the dead rise & praise thee?'

prophet doth not in these words affirm that God doth not show wonders among the dead as you set the words down, but he only asketh a question of God whether he would show a miracle upon the dead. Yea and if he had spoken affirmatively as you make him to speak, yet might you not understand the same in such a general sense as you do, for you know that God did a miracle among the dead when upon Christ's death and passion many of the dead did rise out of their graves and went into Jerusalem, and the very last and one of the great{est} of all miracles shall be showed upon the dead when as in the last day the dead shall be raised up by the great and mighty power of God. To the saying of God by Isaiah which you allege, where it is said that God will not give his glory to a creature, if this be to be understood as you take it then are the prophets and apostles hereby excepted from all power of doing miracles as well as devils or witches, for creatures are they as well as the other.[244] Yea if you take this saying generally without exception, how may any of us look for any good thing and especially for our salvation in the kingdom of God? For whatsoever is good or heavenly is in some sense a part of God's glory, yea the good works which men by the grace of God do work are a part of his glory, and are to be done that he may be glorified by them. Wherefore you must not take these words in such a general sense as you do, but you must acknowledge the glory of God to be of two sorts, whereof the one sort is never imparted to any creature, as his divine nature and essence none can be partakers of, neither can any be a partaker with him in giving us life, sanctification, redemption, or in partaking the invocation, honour, and worship that is due to his holy name with many other the like things. The other sort of God's glory is such as he may and doth communicate to his creatures in such sort as they may through his grace, power, and permission be partakers in the same with him, as for example whereas it is a part of God's glory to be merciful, loving, holy &c, it is the will of God that we should be endued with this part of his glory, for we are commanded to be merciful as our heavenly father is merciful, to love one another as he loves us, to be holy because he is holy, and of this sort of God's glory is also the power to do miracles, to preach his word, and to minister his sacraments as Christ did. For this [fol. 91r] kind of glory God hath not so reserved to himself but that he hath imparted his power therein unto men to do the like, and so for many other matters of his glory hath he also done. But now, to come to the proper sense of the words by you here alleged, the meaning thereof is that God will not give his glory to any creature in any such sort as the same should be diminished or impaired thereby, neither can that be. For howsoever men or devils do abuse the grace and power of God to all

---

244 Isaiah 42:8, quoted in Scot 6.2 and 7.11.

abominable sin and wickedness, yet God doth so guide and direct their doings as he turneth them to his great glory in spite of all his adversaries. As touching the saying of Nicodemus and this of the prophet Isaiah, 'do either good or evil', there can be nothing gathered of them (for the matter we talk of) but only this: that no man can of his own strength, virtue, and power do any miracles.[245] Howbeit the saying of Nicodemus is more against you than with you, for he doth not say that no man can do any miracles except God were with him or that (as you expound it) except some excellency or divinity were in him, but he sayeth no man can do such miracles as Christ did except &c.[246] *Ergo* for all other miracles that were not such as Christ did, he doth not deny but seemeth rather to confess that they may be done though God were not with the doers of them. As touching the foresaid exposition by you ascribed to Villerius, you do not deliver the same as he setteth it down, for he sayeth not 'except some excellency or divinity were in him' but he sayeth 'except a divine excellency doth appear to be', between which words there is great difference insomuch that Villerius in that place noteth that if Nicodemus had well known Christ he would not have only said God were with Christ but also that he was in him.[247] Whereby you may perceive that Villerius doth not accompt the appearing of divinity in Christ and the being of it in him to be all one, as indeed it is not, for that may appear to be in a man which is farthest from him indeed, as we may see by hypocrites who appear very honest and godly when as they are so far from it that *Simulata Sanctitas*[248] is justly accompted to be *duplex iniquitas*.[249] Now as touching the saying of St August here

---

245 Isaiah 41:23: 'Shewe the things that are to come hereafter, that we may know that you are gods: yea, do good or do euil, that we may declare it, and beholde it together.'
246 Scot, 8.1 (see excerpt quoted above): 'Nichodemus being a Pharisie could saie, that no man could do such miracles as Christ did, except God were with him' – the author's criticism here suggests that Scot revised this part of his text before the *Discoverie* was printed.
247 'Villerius' was Pierre Loiseleur de Villiers (1530–90) a Reformed minister from Lille who was at one time in exile in London. He does not seem to be mentioned in the printed *Discoverie*, and Scot does not include his name in his list of 'forren authors used in this Booke'. His annotation to John 3:2 is included in some early modern bibles. The following translation of the text and annotation is from the 1615 editon of Whittingham's translation of Beza's Latin New Testament: 'no man could doe these miracles that thou doest, except God were with him' (John 3:2); annotation: 'But he in whom some part of the excellencie of God appeareth. And if Nicodemus had known Christ aright, he would not onely have said that God was with him, but in him, as Paul doeth, 2 Cor. 1.19.'
248 'pretended holiness'.
249 'a double iniquity'.

alleged for the proof that miracles be ceased and determined,[250] [fol. 91v] you know very well that it was not St Augustine's purpose in that place to prove the ceasing of miracles, but rather hereby to persuade the people not to hang upon a desire of corporal miracles nor to dislike of their time because they saw not such miracles, as though it were a less happy time than that was wherein those corporal miracles flourished which, that he might the rather persuade, he told them that by how much the soul was better than the body, by so much were the miracles which were in their time wrought in the soul and mind to the conversion and amendment of the same better than the corporal miracles that were done in times before to the help and benefit of the bodily members.[251] This I say is the scope and effect of St August in the words by you alleged, wherein though he do *obiter*[252] and not of purpose confess the ceasing of extern and corporal miracles, yet it is confessed only of good miracles and not of wicked. Neither can he so be taken as though he meant that all good miracles were then utterly ceased, for he doth in other places of his works plainly show the contrary, as in the 22 book *De Civitate Dei* ca 8 you may most specially see where he maketh mention of sundry corporal miracles do{ne} in his time, and some of them in his presence.[253] The same you may also see in the 9 book of his *Confessions* ca 7, and in the history of his own life written by Possidius a bishop of his time and his very familiar acquaintance. You shall find it recorded ca 29 of the same life that certain great miracles were done by St August himself, of some of the which the historiographer was an eye witness as he there sayeth.[254] Last of all, as touching the saying of Mr Calvin contained in the 19 ca of his Insti. Sect 18, he doth not there

---

250 OED: 'Terminated, ended.'
251 Luther made this point in a sermon of 1535; see D. P. Walker, 'The Cessation of Miracles', in *Hermeticism and the Renaissance*, edited by Ingrid Merkel and Allen G. Debus (Cranbury: Associated University Presses, 1988), pp. 111–24 (pp. 111–12).
252 'in passing'.
253 Augustine, *City of God*, 22.8: 'as for miracles, there are some wrought even now in His name'; 'The miracle that was done at Milan when I was there, might well become famous' (p. 366).
254 Augustine's *Confessions*, translated by E. B. Pusey (London: J. M. Dent, 1966) mentions the cure of people 'vexed by unclean spirits' and the restoration of sight to a blind man in Milan (pp. 187–8). Possidius was a friend and biographer of St Augustine. In chapter 29 of his *Life of Augustine*, translated by Herbert T. Weisskotten (Princeton, NJ: Princeton University Press, 1919), Possidius writes that 'I know also that both while he was presbyter and bishop, when asked to pray for certain demoniacs, he entreated God in prayer with many tears and the demons departed from the men. In like manner when he was sick and confined to his bed there came a certain man with

speak of the vanishing away of all miracles generally but only of those miracles which it pleased the lord to have done for the time of Christ and his apostles, whereby he might for ever make the new preaching of the gospel to be wondered at. For if he had meant generally of all miracles without exception then would he not have said, as he there doth, that *Caeterum evanuit gratia illa curationum quemadmodum et reliqua miracula quae ad tempus edi dominus voluit quo* &c[255] but he would have [fol. 92r] spoken without any such restraint or exception. Howbeit if you think he meant more generally of the vanishing away of miracles than I understand, yet can you not stretch his meaning any further than to good miracles tending to the confirmation of the gospel, and therefore this place doth nothing at all serve you to prove thereby the ceasing of devilish and wicked miracles, which as you said a little before tend to the defacing of the gospel. But in truth, in what author soever you read that miracles are ceased you must not understand the same in such a general sort, neither of good nor of evil miracles, as though the meaning of the author were that all miracles are wholly and utterly ceased (for that is not true, as I have showed you a little before by St August, and more in my answer to your 44 Reas.) but the meaning is that they are ceased in comparison of the time present to the time of Christ and his apostles, for that now miracles be neither so common and ordinary as then they were, neither yet so public and universally known to the world as they were in the said time of Christ and his apostles. Hereunto may the words of St August persuade you, saying thus of this matter: *nec miracula illa in nostra tempora durare permissa sunt ne anima semper visibilia quereret, et eorum consuetudine frigesceret genuus humanum, quorum novitate flagravit: verum est quidem: non enim nunc usque cum manus imponitur baptisatis sic accipiunt spiritum sanctum ut loquantur linguis omnium gentium, aut nunc usque ad umbram transeuntium predicatorum Christi sanantur infirmi, et si quae talia tunc facta sunt quae postea cessase manifestum est. Sed non sic accipiendum est quod dixi ut nunc in Christi nomine miracula fieri nulla*

> a sick relative and asked him to lay his hand upon him that he might be healed. But Augustine answered that if he had any power in such things he would surely have applied it to himself first of all; to which the stranger replied that he had had a vision and that in his dream these words had been addressed to him: "Go to the bishop Augustine that he may lay his hand upon him, and he shall be whole." Now when Augustine heard this he did not delay to do it and immediately God caused the sick man to depart from him healed' (p. 117).
>
> 255 'But that gift of healing, like the rest of the miracles, which the Lord willed to be brought forth for a time [etc]' (Calvin, *Institutes of the Christian Religion*, vol. 2, p. 1467).

credantur. Nam ego ipse quando istum librum scripsi, ad Mediolanensium corpora martirum in eadem civita caecum illuminatum fuisse iam noveram, et alia nonnulla qualia tam multa istis etiam temporibus fiunt, ut nec omnia cognoscere, nec ea quae cognoscimus enumerare possimus.[256] Hereof may you read more in many other places of St August and namely in his 22 book *De Civitate Dei* ca 8.[257]

Reason 87

That witches, nor the woman of *Endor*, nor yet hir familiar or divell can tell what is to come, may plainelie appeare by the words of the prophet, who saith; Shew what things are to come, and we will saie you are gods indeed. According to that which *Salomon* saith; Who can tell a man what shall happen him under the sunne? Marrie that can I (saith the witch of *Endor* to *Saule*.) But I will rather beleeve *Paule* and *Peter*, which saie, that prophesie is the gift of God, and no worldlie thing [...] And therefore I saie that gift of prophesie, wherewith God in times past endued his people, is also ceased, and counterfeits and couseners are come in their places, according to this saieng of *Peter*; There were false prophets among the people, even as there shalbe false teachers among you, &c. And thinke not that so notable a gift should be taken from the beloved and elect people of God, and committed to mother *Bungie*, and such like of hir profession.[258] The words of the prophet *Zacharie* are plaine, touching the ceasing both of the good and bad prophet, to wit: I will cause the prophets and uncleane spirits to depart out of the land, and when anie shall yet prophesie, his parents shall saie to

---

256 Author's note: 'Retractionu[m] ca 13': 'Likewise, this statement of mine is indeed true: "These miracles were not allowed to last until our times lest the soul ever seek visible things and the human race grow cold because of familiarity with those things whose novelty enkindled it." For not even now, when a hand is laid on the baptised, do they receive the Holy Spirit in such a way that they speak with the tongues of all nations; nor are the sick now healed by the passing shadow of the preachers of Christ. But what I said is not to be so interpreted that no miracles are believed to be performed in the name of Christ at the present time. For, when I wrote that book, I myself had recently learned that a blind man had been restored to sight in Milan near the bodies of the martyrs in that very city, and I knew about some others, so numerous even in these times, that we cannot know about all of them nor enumerate those we know.' Augustine, *The Retractions*, translated by M. Inez Bogan (Washington, DC: Catholic University of America Press, 1968), p. 55. See also Walker, 'The Cessation of Miracles', pp. 119–20.

257 As the treatise author previously indicated, Augustine describes the miracle in Milan in this section of the *City of God*; 22.8.

258 Mother Bungie, a reputed witch from Rochester who inspired a play by John Lyly, is mentioned several times in the printed *Discoverie*.

him; Thou shalt not live, for thou speakest lies in the name of the Lord: and his parents shall thrust him through when he prophesieth, &c. No, no: the foretelling of things to come, is the onelie worke of God, who disposeth all things sweetlie, of whose counsell there hath never yet beene anie man ... Also *Phavorinus* saith, that if these cold prophets or oraclers tell thee prosperitie, and deceive thee, thou art made a miser through vaine expectation: if they tell thee of adversitie, &c: and lie, thou art made a miser through vaine feare. (Scot, 8.2)

What I have answered touching miracles and the ceasing of them may be answered for prophecies the ceasing of them: to wit, that as there are **[fol. 92v]** miracles two sorts, good and evil, so are there also of prophecies and prophets. And as the ceasing of miracles is not to be understood absolutely and without exception, as though all miracles were wholly and utterly taken away, no more must we understand the ceasing of prophecies to be absolute and without exception. But because you allege here divers particular authorities {to} prove the ceasing of prophecies I will also particularly answer unto them. And first, to your authority of Isaiah ca 41 you must not stand to the bare text with{out} admitting some interpretation of the same, for then will it follow that either the true prophets of God did not show what things were to come, or else if they did that they were gods.[259] If hereunto you shall answer (as I know you must) that these prophets received the power of prophecy from God, I might also answer the like for false prophets, for all power as well of the wicked as of the godly is from God insomuch that the devil himself ha{th} no power but the same is of God. But I will rather answer as all the godly learned interpreters of this place answer, vz. that God in requiring here the showing of things to come of false gods or devils doth not mean the foreshowing of some particular thing or things that are near at hand, the foreshowing whereof may be done many and sundry ways by devils as you may see at large in the places whither I have for that purpose referred you in the 85 Reason, as also you may see the same in St August *De Divinatione Daemonum* and in his 2 book *De Doctrina Christiana* ca 22 et 23. But the meaning here is that to prove themselves to be gods they should in such sort know and foreshow things to come as God doth, who by his prescience knoweth and can foreshow most certainly all things without exception, for that they are to him present no less before they come to pass than they are when they do come to pass, though the coming of them be never so long to be deferred. And to this exposition agreeth most pla{inly}that which is in the text annexed to this saying, vz. do good or do evil that we may declare it. This is also another argument (as the other was) whereby God requireth the

---

259 See the excerpt to reason 86 above.

gods of the gentiles or Babylonians to prove themselves to be gods. Now no man is so ignorant but he will confess that both devils and all mankind doth either good or evil, wherefore both the one sort and the other must needs go for gods, unless we will take the meaning of these words to be of doing good or evil in such sort as God doth and can do it, who doth it when and as often and in what sort [fol. 93r] it pleaseth him, no creature or power being able to resist or interrupt him: in which sort it is neither in man or devil to do either good or evil, and therefore are they no gods. By doing evil in this place is not meant that *malum* which is *peccatum* but that which is *paena peccati*[260] as in the prophet Amos, where it is said *non est malum in civitate quod non fecit dominus.*[261]

2ly, to the saying of Solomon here alleged there is no other answer to be made than I have now made to the foresaid saying of Isaiah.

3ly, to Paul and Peter saying that prophecy is the gift of God and no worldly thing, I would have you here first to understand that Peter and Paul speak not in these places both alike of the gift of prophecy, for Peter speaketh of the gift thereof as it was in good and holy men only, saying prophecy came not in old time by the will of man, but holy men of God spake as they were moved by the holy ghost. But St Paul as I take it speaketh in the foresaid place more generally of this gift, vz. as it was or might be as well in evil men as in good, and therefore he there exhorteth them that have the gift of prophecy to use it according to the proportion of faith, which exhortation should not have needed if the same gift had not been bestowed upon some that might abuse it to an evil end and purpose. Again, St Peter in the foresaid place speaketh of that gift of prophecy whereby the holy men of God did foreshow things to come, but the learned interpreters of this place of Paul take by the gift of prophecy in this place not to be meant the gift of foreshowing things to come but rather the gift of teaching, exhorting, and comforting, whereof the same apostle speaketh in another place, saying he which doth prophesy speaketh edification, exhortation, and consolation. And again: 'ye may all prophesy one by one that all may learn and all receive consolation'.[262] But to the matter, you say that inasmuch as the gift of prophecy is now taken from the godly, it is not like that it is given to Mother Bungey, to the which I answer that this gift is not by you proved to be taken from the godly, and therefore you conclude upon a thing not granted; no, nor possible to be proved if you mean of a general taking away of that gift, for the histories of all times and ages will yield many examples

---

260 'evil/harm'; 'sin'; 'punishment for sin'.
261 The passage quoted is Amos 3:6: 'shal there be euil in a citie, and the Lord hathe not done it?'
262 Author's note: 'Corinth 14'; 1 Corinthians 14:3, 14:31.

in this point against you. And the saying of the scripture in sundry places of the false prophets that shall rise towards the end of the world do nothing make with you. Besides, forasmuch as this gift is of itself no certain sign of God's grace or favour nor doth sanctify and further to salvation those that are endued with the same, but hath been at all times [fol. 93v] bestowed as well upon the reprobate as upon the elect, I see no cause why it may not be in a reprobate to prophesy things that were not in the elect to do the same. When God would not suffer any true prophet to speak or prophesy to Saul he suffered the devil to do it and many reprobates shall say in the last days 'lord, have we not prophesied in thy name?' &c which I note to show that the gift of prophecy is no inseparable accident to the godly.[263] And if I should here demand which of the godly were in the time of Balaam, that reprobate so notably endued with the gift of prophecy as he was, I think it could hardly be answered. It might seem as unlike that God should bestow kingdoms and the government of his people upon wicked men whenas he suffereth the godly to live in most vile estate and condition as it is that wicked men should have a gift to prophesy when good men have it not. Yea, and why should we think that God bestoweth many times more wisdom, more learning, more strength {&c} upon the reprobate than he doth upon his children, if we may not think so for the gift of prophecy as well as for these things? If you should reckon up all the gifts and blessings of God bestowed upon mankind (which make not to sanctification and salvation) I do suppose you should find the same in a more large and ample measure to be for the more part[264] bestowed upon the wicked than upon the godly. Therefore I do conclude that prophecy (being no such gift as whereby men may be sanctified or saved) may well be found in a witch or devils mouth when it is not in the mouth of a godly man or woman.

 4ly, to the saying of the prophet Zechariah here alleged, I say it is not generally to be extended to all times and to all nations but to the people of God of that time, vz. the Jews, to their posterity, and to their land, and yet not so generally to them and to their land as there should never be any false prophets or unclean spirits amongst th{em} which you may easily see even by the words going immediately before, being a part of the verse by you alleged, for these be there the prophet's words: 'And in that day sayeth the lord of hosts I will cut out the names of the idols out of the land and they shall no more be remembered, and I will cause the prophets and the unclean spirits to depart out of the land' &c. Here you see that as the lord promiseth to rid the land of prophets and unclean spirits, so doth he promise (and that

---

263 Author's notes: '1 sam 28', 'math 7'; Matthew 7:22: 'Manie wil say to me in that day, Lord, Lord, haue we not by thy Name prophecied?'
264 An older variant of the phrase 'for the most part'.

much more vehemently) to rid the land of idols, for of idols he promiseth such a riddance and cutting off as that not so much as the names of them should not be any more [fol. 94r] remembered. Therefore what you can of this place gather for the utter abolishing of prophecy, the same may be much more gathered for the utter abolishing of idols and the remembrance of them. Wherefore if idols or the remembrance of them do yet remain in the world (as you know they do in most, yea in all nations of the world) then cannot this place serve you to prove thereby a general ceasing of prophecy as you would have it, unless you will say (as I am sure you will not) that some part of this verse is true and some false. So then you see that this text pertaineth to the people of that time and to their posterity as containing one of these blessings which God promised unto them upon their repentance and reconciliation with God, which blessing was not longer to have continuance than they should remain in their repentance and true service of his majesty. And again, it is certain that this was meant only of the wicked prophets, even such as their own parents should thrust through when they prophesied and therefore could in no wise be applied (as by you it is) to the ceasing as well of good prophets as of bad.

5ly, touching the saying of St Chrysostom here alleged, I find in the place by you quoted these words, vz. *praedictio futurarum immortalis dei dumtaxat opus est*,[265] but that which you have further added vz. 'who disposeth all things sweetly, of whose counsel there hath never yet been any man' I do not find in that place.[266] For answer to the words of Chrysostom I cannot better answer than I have done at the first to the words of Isaiah 41, for those very words of the prophet doth Chrysostom (not past 7 lines before his words by you alleged) use to prove that God only foreshoweth things to come, whereby it is plain that he speaketh of such a foreshowing of things to come as the prophet meant of in that place, and what the prophet meant is before showed.[267] Now where you add that no man hath ever yet been of God's counsel it is not generally true, for how then could Paul have said to the ministers of Ephesus that he had opened to them the whole counsel of God, or how could it be true which God himself hath

---

265 In the printed *Discoverie* this is given in English: 'No, no: the foretelling of things to come, is the onelie worke of God' (see excerpt quoted above). Scot provides a reference to Chrysostom's 18th Homily on John.
266 Scot uses precisely these words after the passage from Chrysostom (see excerpt quoted above). Scot's marginal note in the printed version of the *Discoverie* refers to 'Pet. Blest, Epist. 49'. This reference is to Peter of Blois (or Petrus Blessense), a twelfth-century theologian whose epistles were widely read at the time. Pierre Kapitaniak has identified Weyer as Scot's direct source for both of these references (*La Sorcellerie Démystifiée*, p. 260, footnote 40).
267 See above.

said by his prophet Amos, vz. surely the lord God will do nothing but he revealeth his secret unto his servants the prophets?[268] Wherefore thus must your words be understood: that no man is of God's counsel unless it please God to reveal it unto him, which many times and in many things he doth, and therefore many times and in many things may men prophesy, and devils too, for unto them also doth God sometime reveal his counsel, as we may see in the story of Job and of the lying spirit that was sent unto Ahab's false prophet. [fol. 94v] Last of all, touching that notable saying of Favorinus with the which you conclude, it serveth nothing to prove the ceas{ing} of prophecies but only to reprove the believing of the{m for} some respects there touched wherein he useth a dilemma or bicorn proposition as logicians term it.

Reason 88

> Touching oracles, which for the most part were idols of silver, gold, wood, stones, &c: within whose bodies some saie uncleane spirites hid themselves, and gave answers: as some others saie, that exhalations rising out of the ground, inspire their minds, whereby their priests gave out oracles; so as spirits and winds rose up out of that soile, and indued those men with the gift of prophesie of things to come, though in truth they were all devises to cousen the people, and for the profit of preests, who received the idols answers over night, and delivered them backe to the idolaters the next morning: you shall understand, that although it had beene so as it is supposed; yet by the reasons and proofes before rehearsed, they should now cease: and whatsoever hath affinitie with such miraculous actions, as witchcraft, conjuration, &c: is knocked on the head, and nailed on the crosse with Christ, who hath broken the power of divels, and satisfied Gods justice, who also hath troden them under his feete, & subdued them, &c. At whose comming the prophet *Zacharie* saith, that the Lord will cut the names of idols out of the land, and they shall be no more remembered; and he will then cause the prophets and uncleane spirits to depart out of the land. It is also written; I will cut off thine inchanters out of thine hand, and thou shalt have no more soothsaiers ... And if ever these prophesies came to take effect, it must be upon the coming of Christ, whereat you see the divels were troubled and fainted, when they met him, saieng, or rather exclaming upon him on this wise; *Fili Dei cur venisti nos cruciare ante tempus?* O thou sonne of God, whie commest thou to molest us (or confound us) before our time appointed? [...] And of this defection and ceasing of oracles writeth *Cicero* long before, and that to have happened also before his time. (Scot, 8.3)

268 Author's notes: 'acts 20', 'Amos 3'; Acts 20:27, Amos 3:7.

As you for this matter of oracles do refer yourself to your proofs before used for the ceasing of prophecies and miracles, so I likewise refer myself to my answers before made unto the same. But where you add that the oracles were but mere cozenings and no such thing was supposed, in that all the learned and all the wise that lived in those times are quite against you, confessing that devils did in very deed give oracles out of those temples and idols where oracles were heard, {and} therefore your private opinion to the contrary may not stand for authority.

2ly, that oracles are by the cro{ss} of Christ so knocked on the head and trodden under that they can never be used, I see no proof why it should so be thought. Truth it is that Christ hath {with} his cross so trodden the power of Satan under his feet to all the faithful that he now understandeth he cannot work their damnation as before he hoped to do, for there is now no condemnation to them that are in Christ Jesus. Howbeit as the faithful are not so fully purged from all their sins by his blood but that there do remain in us and shall do whilst we are in this life some dregs and strength thereof, so Satan {is} not as yet so fully knocked on the head or trod{den} underfoot but that he hath yet some power and strength to play his devilish parts, and to walk up and down like a roaring lion in such sort as we have need of the whole armour of God to withstand his assaults and fiery darts.[269] And as for the wicked and reprobate he doth and still shall no less reign {and} triumph over them than ever he did, for they are his children, his servants, and slaves. For your place of Zechariah it is answered in your 88 Reason.[270] For that of Micah here alleged, it must receive the same answer to that of Zechariah, saving that there the lord of favour promised to cut off their idols, but here of displeasure he promiseth to cut off their enchanters and soothsayers, thereby to let the Jews understand that he would not in the day of his wrath {when} he threapned leave them so much as their said enchanters and soothsayers to flee unto for help, counsel, or comfort as they were wont to do. So doth the lord also in that chapter say that he will cut off their horses, their chariots, their idols, their cities and strongholds, and [**fol. 95r**] groves; wherefore this place of the prophet may serve as well to prove that there be no horses, chariots, or idols in the world as it may serve to prove that there be no enchanters and soothsayers.[271] Where by the way you add upon the devil's words unto Christ, saying *fili dei cur venisti nos cruciari ante tempus* that Christ did in deed prevent the time, this seemeth not to agree with this saying of St

---

269 Author's note: 'Ephe 6'; Ephesians 6:11, 13, 16. 1 Peter 5:8 states that 'your aduersarie the deuil as a roaring lyon walketh about, seking whome he may deuoure'.
270 The relevant response is in fact reason 87.
271 Author's note: 'mycheas 5'; Micah 5:12, quoted by Scot in the excerpt above.

Paul: *At postquam venit plenum tempus emisit deus filium suum factum ex muliere* &c.[272] Neither doth it agree with Villerius' note made thereupon, which is thus: *plenum dicitur tempus cuius omnia spatia sunt peracta: itaque nec citius nec tardius venire debuit Christus*.[273] I use not here this note of Villerius for want of other authority but because I see you to make good accompt of him, for that you used a note of his upon the 3 of John in a place before handled.[274] Touching the human authorities here by you alleged, as they tend all to one end, so shall they all have one answer, and this is that you understand them too largely and too generally in applying their sayings to a full and final cutting off of all oracles, as most specially for Cicero, and how can his sayings be understood of any such cutting off of oracles in that time if they were cut off by Christ's coming? And as for your authors that were since Christ's time, I could (if it were worthwhile to stand upon) prove by every one of them that oracles have been given out of idols since the time of Christ, though not so commonly as they were before. But what shall I need to stand upon this proof? For sith you make no other accompt of these oracles but that they were no devils that spake them but cozening priests and such like, I see no reason why they should now cease more than at any time before, we having (as no doubt we have) as cozening merchants in this time as ever the world had at any time, if not here in England (*quod absit*)[275] yet in other countries.

Reason 89

This is soon answered, for the prophesying done by devils and witches (whereof our controversy is) is not of that kind of prophesying which is proper to God, as before I have showed to your 87 Reas. Again, if it were no way in human power any way to prophesy, yet why should we not believe they may receive power therein from God, knowing that Balaam, Saul, and other reprobates have {?}[276]

---

272 Author's note: 'Galat 4'; Galatians 4.4: 'But when the fulnes of time was come, God sent forthe his Sonne made of a woman.'
273 Villerius' Latin note to Galatians 4.4 was included in Theodore Beza's Latin New Testament (London, 1576) and in William Whittingham's English translation of that work (London, 1583): 'The time is sayde to bee full, when all partes of it are past and ended, and therefore Christ coulde not haue come eyther sooner or later.'
274 See reason 86 above.
275 'heaven forbid'.
276 Author's note: 'even by power fro[m] god'.

[fol. 95v] Reason 90

> As for casting out of divels (which was another kind of miracles usuall with Christ) witches and conjurors are said to be as good thereat as ever he was: and yet, if you will beleeve Christs words, it cannot be so. For he saith; Everie kingdome divided against it selfe, shall be brought to naught, &c. If sathan cast out sathan, he is divided, &c: and his kingdome shall not endure, &c. (Scot, 9.7)

I do not know it to be affirmed of any that a witch doth cast out devils by devils or by any other means. But if so be when one witch doth unwitch that which another hath witched be a casting out of Satan by Satan (as in some sort I do think it to be) yet this is not by any division or falling out of one devil with another (which Christ meant should be a decay to Satan's kingdom) but it is by a willing conspiracy and consent amongst themselves to draw men thereby from trusting to God and from seeking help at his hands, to a trust in witches and in their devilish and detestable practices, as too often by experience we see it come to pass even as the devils would wish it: more recourse being made to witches in time of sickness and other distress than unto God or to such godly means as he hath appointed.

Reason 91

> Concerning the charming of serpents and snakes, mine adversaries (as I have said) thinke they have great advantage by the words of *David* in the fiftie eight psalme; and by *Jeremie*, chapter eight, expounding the one prophet by *Virgil*, the other by *Ovid*. For the words of *David* are these; Their poison is like the poison of a serpent, and like a deafe adder, that stoppeth his eare, and heareth not the voice of the charmer, charme he never so cunninglie. The words of *Virgil* are these, *Frigidus in pratis cantando rumpitur anguis*. As he might saie, *David* thou liest; for the cold natured snake is by the charmes of the inchanters broken all to peeces in the field where he lieth. Then commeth *Ovid*, and he taketh his countriemans part, saieng in the name and person of a witch; *Vipereas rumpo verbis & carmine fauces*; that is, I with my words and charmes can breake in sunder the vipers jawes. (Scot, 12.15)

And I think this place of the psalmist maketh very much both to prove that there be charmers and enchan{ters} and also that their charms and enchantments be of some force. For first if there had been no charms or no charmers which use to charm and enchant then had it been (as Mr Calvin here sayeth) a childish and an absurd thing which is here spoken, for so should the prophet take a similitude of nothing.[277] Yea in {that} very place he sayeth that which I have in another place before noted, vz. *Certe si nulla essent incantationes frustra lege dei prohibitae ac damnatae essent.*[278] Now for the force of charms and enchantings I say, if in them there had been no force, to what end need the asp or adder to stop her ears to avoid the force of the same, which our text sayeth she doth? St August writing upon this text showeth the manner how she doth it, saying that she, refusing {to} hear those voices of the enchanter or charmer by the which she perceiveth herself to be forced, doth clap the one of her ears close to the ground and with her tail fast stoppeth the other ear and so avoiding those voices (as much as is possible for her to do) she doth not go out of her hole or cave at the enchantment.[279] Hereby as also by the text it plainly appeareth that if the adder or asp did [fol. 96r] not stop her ears she should be subject to the force of the charmer's voice. And therefore hath she no such privilege not to be charmed more than other things have, whereof you make in your book a question, asking why we should think her to be more privileged herein than all other things are, which question might easily be answered if she had that privilege, as she hath not.[280] For why might not

---

277 Calvin is in this instance a little more ambivalent than the author suggests: 'But is there such a thing, it may be asked, as enchantment? If there were not, it might seem absurd and childish to draw a comparison from it, unless we suppose David to speak in mere accommodation to mistaken, though generally received opinion. He would certainly seem, however, to insinuate that serpents can be fascinated by enchantment; and I can see no harm in granting it ... I do not mean to say that there is an actual method or art by which fascination can be effected. It was doubtless done by a mere sleight of Satan, whom God has suffered to practise his delusions upon unbelieving and ignorant men' (*Commentaries on the Book of Psalms*, pp. 372–3).

278 'Had there been no enchantments practised, where was the necessity of their being forbidden and condemned under the Law?' (*Commentaries on the Book of Psalms*, p. 372). See reason 83 above.

Author's note: 'hereto agreeth Mr Martir sayinge of this matter *Leges aute[m] no[n] feru[n]tur nisi de rebus quae exista[n]t et solea[n]t evenire* [laws are only made on matters which exist and usually happen] & as touching this text of the psal he saythe thus *no[n] laudat david hijs verbis excantatione[m] sed haud dubie ostendit esse vim quanda[m] excanta[n]di.* in 1 sam 28.' [David does not by these words praise enchanting, but without any doubt he shows that there is a certain power in the act of enchanting.] Both passages are from Vermigli's *In duos Libros Samuelis Prophetae* (Zurich, 1575), p. 166r. The translations from Vermigli are mine.

279 A paraphrase of St Augustine; see his *Expositions on the Book of Psalms*, edited by A. Cleveland Coxe (Grand Rapids, MI: Wm B. Eerdmans, repr. 1983), Psalm 58 (sec. 6), p. 232.

280 See reason 97, and the accompanying excerpt from Scot, below.

God engraft in the nature of an asp or adder some privilege in this behalf proper to herself as well as he hath in stones, herbs, fowls, &c engrafted such special privileges and virtues as are not common to any other things? As touching the contrariety of our text to the poets fabling, saying *frigidus in pratis cantando rumpitur anguis*[281] I see no contrariety at all herein, for the prophet speaketh of an asp or adder and the poet speaketh of a snake, between which two things there is great difference, as you may first note by their genders, the one being of the feminine gender only, the other both masculine and feminine. Besides snakes are with us very frequent and common, but the asp or adder here spoken of (as Pliny doth describe him) is only in Africa, and is a kind of serpent of a far other property than our snakes are, for (as he doth write) her sting is incurable except it be taken away by that water only wherewith a stone is washed which they of Africa take out of the sepulchre of an ancient king. And further, if the male or female happen to be killed the survivor followeth the slayer continually until he have stung the party and so revenged his fellow's death.[282] But whether this be true or no, sure it is that *aspis* and *anguis* do differ much, neither shall you as I think ever find these two words confounded in any author as words that are *aequepollentia*[283] as you make them to be. And thus much of this matter have I said for the truth's sake and not to defend the poet who may lie if he list by authority, as you know another of that sort affirmeth, saying *pictoribus atque poetis quidlibet audendi semper fuit aequa potestas*.[284]

Reason 92

But as herein we are not to imitate the papists, so in such things, as are the peculiar actions of God, we ought not to take upon us to counterfet,

---

281 'The cold snake is burst by incantation in the meadows'; the quotation is from Virgil's 8th Eclogue. See Scot, 12.1; Scot's verse translation (credited to Abraham Fleming) is 'The coldish snake in medowes greene, With charmes is burst in peeces cleene.'

282 The asp is referred to frequently in Pliny's *Natural History*, 10 vols, translated by H. Rackham (Cambridge, MA: Harvard University Press, 1949). Pliny tells the story about the desire for revenge of bereaved asps in 8.35. While various cures for the asp's bite are suggested, including vinegar (23.27), 'bugs' (29.17), and drinking one's own urine (29.18), I have been unable to find the author's more exciting cure in the Loeb edition of Pliny.

283 equivalent, synonymous.

284 This claim is in many translations ascribed to a speaker other than Horace; '"Artists and poets", you say, "have always enjoyed / An equal right in daring whatever they liked."' Horace, *The Art of Poetry*, translated by Michael Oakley, in *Collected Works* (London: J. M. Dent & Sons, 1961), ll. 9–10. (Horace accepts, but also immediately qualifies, this claim.)

> or resemble him, which with his word created all things. For we, neither all the conjurors, Cabalists, papists, soothsaiers, inchanters, witches, nor charmers in the world, neither anie other humane or yet diabolicall cunning can adde anie such strength to Gods workmanship, as to make anie thing anew, or else to exchange one thing into another. New qualities may be added by humane art, but no new substance can be made or created by man. And seeing that art faileth herein, doubtles neither the illusions of divels, nor the cunning of witches, can bring anie such thing truelie to passe. (Scot, 12.2)

I confess with you that it lieth not in any creature to make anything anew absolutely or in truth. But to our apparance[285] the devil and his ministers may well seem to make things anew, for they know better than we those things which are *semina et initia rerum*[286] and then may they get together and compound the one with the other with such celerity and expedition as they may seem to our eyes and senses (not being able to comprehend the reason of their doings which they do both so quickly and so closely) that they were in deed the creators of those things which they present newly unto us. For your better satisfaction in which matter (because it is too long here to be debated) [fol. 96v] I refer you to the 3 booke of St August *De Trinitate* {ca} 7 *et* 8 and to his 18 book *De Civitate Dei* ca 18 and to Gratian *causa* 26 *quest* 5 *nec mirum* in all which places you shall find this matter plainly and at large discussed.[287]

Reason 93

> What is not to be brought to passe by these incantations, if that be true which is attributed to witches? & yet they are women that never went to schoole in their lives, nor had any teachers: and therefore without art or learning; poore, and therefore not able to make any provision of metal or stones, &c: whereby to bring to passe strange matters, by naturall magicke; old and stiffe, and therefore not nimble handed to deceive your eie with legierdemaine[.] (Scot, 12.3)

Whatsoever witches want by poverty, stiffness or lack of learning it is easily supplied by their good {master} the devil who being able (when it pleaseth God not to restrain him) to move and stir up th{ings} insensible and without

---

285 OED: 'appearance'.
286 'the seeds and beginnings of things'.
287 The references are to Augustine's works *On the Trinity* and *City of God*, and to the canon *nec mirum* in Gratian's *Decretum* (see the section on sources in the introduction).

life contrary to kind and to all possibility of nature is much more able to move and stir up old witches to do more than we would think or look for at their hands; you know the old proverb, they must needs run whom the devil doth drive.

Reason 94

This reason being all one with your 63 Reas towards the end thereof is to have no other answer than {is} there made and therefore I do refer you thither for answer hereof.

Reason 95

> If they could kill men, children, or cattell, they would spare none; but would destroy and kill whole countries and housholds. If they could transfer corne (as is affirmed) from their neighbors field into their owne, none of them would be poore, none other should be rich. If they could transforme themselves and others (as it is most constantlie affirmed) oh what a number of apes and owles should there be of us! If *Incubus* could beget *Merlins* among us, we should have a jollie manie of cold prophets. (Scot, 12.3)

That it is not in the power of devils and witches {at} their pleasures and when they list to do these things {but} only when it pleaseth God to give them leave and liberty hath been sufficiently showed in {?} my answers before made to your 3.10.18 Reas. and in other places also. We must think of the devil's power in these things as we do of his power in drawing men to sin and wickedness, wherein we see he can do {much} with mankind and as much as he would wish to do with s{ome} men, yet can he not herein prevail when and with whom he listeth, for then would he draw all men utterly to forsake God and to be damned. Even so I say though he can at some times and upon some men perform by witches such things as you here speak of, yet can he not do the same where, when, and to whom it pleaseth him.

Reason 96

> I confesse, the customes and lawes almost of all nations doo declare, that all these miraculous works, before by me cited, and many other things more woonderfull, were attributed to the power of witches. The which lawes, with the executions and judicials thereupon, and the witches confessions, have beguiled almost the whole world. What absurdities concerning witchcraft, are written in the law of the twelve tables, which was the highest and most ancient law of the *Romans*? (Scot, 12.4)

That the law makers of the 12 tables were abused in the case here mentioned you only say, but do not prove the same. Mr Martyr in the place before quoted is plainly of opinion that they would never have made this law if there had been no such thing, and therefore speaking of this law doth allege it for a proof of the devil's power in doing such things, and says of it *Leges autem non feruntur nisi de rebus quae existant et soleant evenire*.[288] And St August, nothing differing from Mr Martyr's opinion, doth allege this law of the 12 tables as a most evident argument of the hurts to mankind by magical arts and practices as you may see in the place here quoted.[289] And let this suffice for this mat{ter}.

[fol. 97r] Reason 97

> But here it will be objected, that bicause it is said (in the places by me alledged) that snakes or vipers cannot be charmed; *Ergo* other things may: To answer this argument, I would aske the witchmonger this question, to wit; Whether it be expedient, that to satisfie his follie, the Holie-ghost must of necessitie make mention of everie particular thing that he imagineth may be bewitched? I would also aske of him, what privilege a snake hath more than other creatures, that he onelie may not, and all other creatures may be bewitched? (Scot, 12.15)

Touching this matter of snakes, vipers, and adders which your questions here used, of that matter enough is said before to your 91 Reas, saving that your first question here used may be well returned as an answer unto you, when you ask why that Christ nor Moses never spake of the devils league, of their hagging,[290] of their riding in the air, of transferring corn, of hurting children and cattle with their charms, of bewitching butter and cheese, and of their transubstantiations &c, of all the which you speak in your 2 Reas.[291]

---

288 This is the passage from Vermigli quoted in the author's marginal note on fol. 95v above: 'Laws are only made on matters which exist and usually happen'.

289 Author's note: 'de civitate dei li 8 ca 19'; *City of God* 8.19: 'In that these diabolical arts were reported to have power to remove whole harvests of corn and fruits whither they pleased, was not this (as Tully says) recorded in the twelve tables of Rome's ancient laws, and a punishment proclaimed for all such as used it?' (p. 242).

290 OED: 'To torment or terrify as a hag; to trouble as the nightmare.' The earliest recorded use in the OED is 1598.

291 The author's response to reason 2 has not survived, but reason 2 itself appears to have survived in Scot's epistle to the readers: 'Christ himselfe in his gospell never mentioned the name of a witch. And that neither he, nor Moses ever spake anie one word of the witches bargaine with the divell, their hagging, their riding in the aire, their transferring of corne or grasse from one feeld to another, their hurting of children or cattell with words or charmes, their bewitching of butter, cheese, ale, &c: nor yet their transubstantiation'.

Reason 98

> Surelie *Nero* prooved all these magicall arts to be vaine and fabulous lies, and nothing but cousenage and knaverie. He was a notable prince, having gifts of nature enow to have conceived such matters, treasure enough to have emploied in the search thereof, he made no conscience therein, he had singular conferences thereabout; he offered, and would have given halfe his kingdome to have learned those things, which he heard might be wrought by magicians; he procured all the cunning magicians in the world to come to *Rome*, he searched for bookes also, and all other things necessarie for a magician; and never could find anie thing in it, but cousenage and legierdemaine. (Scot, 15.32)

Touching the example and sentence of Nero here alleged, I may answer that the makers of the 12 tables were of the wisest men in the world, both Athenians and Romans, and unto that law the greatest reverence and dignity was given above all other laws: if therefore you will not allow their judgements and authorities for transferring of corn, as you do not but say they were abused so to think, I may then reject with more reason the trial and opinion of Nero and think he was abused so to pronounce and think as he did of this matter. But I will rather answer to this as Master Martyr doth, who sayeth thus: *Cur autem in Neronis et Juliani gratiam (diaboli) nihil facere voluerint Deus solus scit non enim vult diabolum posse plus quam ipse patiatur, et velit. Vis enim daemonum et potestas operandi pendet a solo deo, non minus quam scientia.*[292]

Reason 99

> It is marvell that anie man can be so much abused, as to suppose that sathan may be commanded, compelled, or tied by the power of man: as though the divell would yeeld to man, beyond nature; that will not yeeld to God his creator, according to the rules of nature. (Scot, 15.32)

---

292 Author's note: 'in 1 sam ca 28'; *In duos Libros Samuelis Prophetae* (Zurich, 1575), p. 165v. The quotation comes from a discussion of ancient opinion on magic, in the course of which Vermigli notes Nero's opinion that magic is ineffective (as Scot does), before concluding with the passage quoted above: 'But why (the devils), being in the grace of Nero and Julian, didn't want to do anything, God alone can tell; he does not want the devil to be more powerful than he would suffer or want him to be. For the Devil's force and power to act depends solely on God, not less so than does art [*scientia*]'. The word *diaboli* [(the devils)] is a clarifying interjection added by the author of the treatise; it is used (also in the plural) by Vermigli in the previous sentence. Vermigli suggests that the devils responsible for magic refused, for reasons unknown, to perform for Nero during his investigations into magic.

That the devil doth rather yield to man than unto God is no marvel at all, for the yielding which God will have at the devil's hands is required and obtained against his will and in such things as are most to the destruction of his tyranny and kingdom, but the yielding which is required of him by man (especially such wicked men and women as we speak of) is such a kind of yielding and employed in such things as he most of all delighteth to have done and do best serve to the maintenance of his devilish kingdom and tyranny over men: so that he should be a stark fool if he would not yield for such an advantage. After this sort was yielding to crosses, holy water, masses, censings, conjurings of the papists that he might the more confirm them to cleave to those abominations.

Reason 100

> Here I may not omit to tell you how *Cor. Agrippa* bewraieth, detecteth, and defaceth this art of conjuration, who in his youth travelled into the bottome of all these magicall sciences, and was not onelie a great conjuror and practicer thereof, but also wrote cunninglie *De occulta philosophia*. Howbeit, afterwards in his wiser age, he recanteth his opinions, and lamenteth his follies in that behalfe, and discovereth the impietie and vanities of magicians, and inchanters, which boast they can doo miracles: which action is now ceased (saith he) and assigneth them a place with *Jannes* and *Jambres*, affirming that this art teacheth nothing but vaine toies for a shew. *Carolus Gallus* also saith; I have tried oftentimes, by the witches and conjurors themselves, that their arts (especiallie those which doo consist of charmes, impossibilities, conjurations, and witchcrafts whereof they were woont to boast) to be meere foolishnes, doting lies, and dreames. (Scot, 15.32)

> And the more throughlie to satisfie you herein, I thought good in this place to insert a letter, upon occasion sent unto me, by one which at this present time lieth as a prisoner condemned for this verie matter in the kings bench, and reprived by hir majesties mercie, through the good mediation of a most noble and vertuous personage, whose honorable and godlie disposition at this time I will forbeare to commend as I ought. The person truelie that wrote this letter seemeth unto me a good bodie, well reformed, and penitent, not expecting anie gaines at my hands, but rather fearing to speake that which he knoweth further in this matter, least displeasure might ensue and follow. (Scot, 15.42)

As Agrippa, Gallus, and Elks pronounce of magical arts and practices in like sort as Nero did, so do I in like sort answer thereunto as before I did to Nero, saving for Agrippa this more may be said: that he generally complaineth of the vanity of all arts and sciences. And for Elks, sith he remaineth a pri{soner} for those or other as lewd doings I would not con{sider} him wise if he would say otherwise than he doth.[293]

[fol. 97v] Reason 101

> I assure you, that even all sorts of writers heerein (for the most part) the very doctors of the church to the schoolemen, protestants and papists, learned and unlearned, poets and historiographers, Jewes, Christians, or Gentiles agree in these impossible and ridiculous matters. Yea and these writers, out of whome I gather most absurdities, are of the best credit and authority of all writers in this matter. The reason is, bicause it was never throughlie looked into; but everie fable credited; and the word (Witch) named so often in scripture. (Scot, 2.10)

I am sorry to see you so much leaning to your own opinion in this place as to pronounce so hard a sentence generally of all the writers of this matter, sith many of these writers are most learned and godly men and have written hereof as godly and as learnedly as lieth {in} man to do. If you should publish your book with this assertion, that alone would procure you much dislike and discredit amongst the best and learnedest sort, howsoever they should like of you in other things. And therefore as y{our} friend I wish you to qualify this sentence or rath{er} clean to suppress it, thinking that your private opinion cannot prejudice or hurt them so much as it may you{r}self and the cause you have in hand. For what will men thi{nk} of this, your general condemning of all writers in this matter, but that they are all generally against you and that you cannot otherwise answer their reasons than by th{ese} means?

Reason 102

> ... the assaults of sathan are spirituall, and not temporall: in which respect Paule wisheth us not to provide a corselet of Steele to defend us from his clawes; but biddeth us put on the whole armour of God, that we may be able to stand against the invasions of the divell. For we wrestle not against flesh and bloud; but against principalities, powers, and spirituall wickednesse. And therefore he adviseth us to be sober and watch: for the divell goeth about like

---

293 The first two persons named are the humanist Heinrich Agrippa (1486–1535), reputed to be a magician, and Carolus Gallus (1530–1616), a Dutch Reformed minister. Thomas Elks (or Elkes) was arrested for his magical activities in late 1580. Scot reproduces a letter received from 'T. E. Maister of art' following the passage from 15.42 quoted above, but does not actually name Elks in the printed version of the *Discoverie*; see the discussion in the introduction above.

> a roring lion, seeking whome he may devoure. He meaneth not with carnall teeth: for it followeth thus, Whome resist the stedfastlie in faith. And againe he saith, That which is spirituall onelie discerneth spirituall things: for no carnall man can discerne the things of the spirit. Why then should we thinke that a divell, which is a spirit, can be knowne, or made tame and familiar unto a naturall man; or contrarie to nature, can be by a witch made corporall, being by God ordeined to a spirituall proportion? (Scot, 17.12)

That Satan doth not only spiritually assault us in our minds and consciences but also temporally in our bod{ies} and temporal goods the example of Job, of Christ himself tempt{ed}, and of all those that are recorded in the scriptures of {the} new testament (besides infinite examples in histo{ries} since that time) to have been possessed of Satan bodily, and by him to have been many and sundry ways vexed in their bodies, are as I think sufficient to persuade you. But here and also after you allege reasons to the contrary, to the which I will answer in order as I find the places. And first for your sayings of Paul and Peter here alleged that we should put on the armour of God because we do not wrestle against flesh and blood &c and that we should by faith resist the devil, I see not what you can of these sayings conclude for your purpose, unless you will say we have only need of the armour of God and of faith when we are spiritually assaulted and not when we are assaulted temporally in the hurt of our bodies and goods. But I think if Job had not had upon him the armour of God and a true and strong faith when he was in his body and goods assaulted of Satan, he had never been able to bear those assaults with such godly patience as he did, and daily experience teacheth us that except we have the armour of God and faith when our bodies are vexed with some great hurt or sickness, and our goods consumed by some extraordinary means, we do soon{er} rage and murmur against God than with patience take this bodily and temporal cross upon us. Where{of} we may consider that whether our assaults be temporal or spiritual, God's armour and faith are still necessary **[fol. 98r]** for us. As touching your second place of Paul, 1 corinth 2, you do not allege his words as they are there set down, for his words are *At spiritualis dijudicat quidem omnia*[294] and again *Animalis homo non est autem capax eorum quae sunt spiritus dei* &c.[295] Now how any of these words may be applied to your purpose I see not, for Paul doth here make a plain antithesis between a man not yet regenerate by the spirit of God and him that is regenerate by the same spirit and endued with it, showing that the one, by the want of God's

---

294 I Corinthians 2:15: 'But he that is spiritual, discerneth all things'.
295 Part of I Corinthians 2:14: 'But the natural man perceiueth not the things of the Spirit of God'.

spirit, remaineth ignorant of the mysteries of God pertaining to salvation and revealed in the gospel, whereas the other, being endued with that spirit, doth know and is able to judge of the same mysteries in all things so far as is needful to his salvation. This shall you find to be the very sense and meaning of the apostle in this place, if you will mark the whole context of that chapter or accept the interpretations of the godly writers upon the same, so that you wrest these places far out of square to draw them to your purpose in the matter we have here in hand. If they might be wrested to that matter they would make {ve}ry much against you, for if a spiritual man, that is to say a man endued with the spirit of God can discern all things, then might it be said that he can discern spirits and devils also. But in truth you are to blame to apply that which is here spoken of the spirit of God only to the spirit of a devil or to a devil, as by your conclusion you do.

Reason 103

> I denie not therefore that there are spirits and divels, of such substance as it hath pleased GOD to create them. But in what place soever it be found or read in the scriptures, a spirit or divell is to be understood spirtuallie, and is neither a corporall nor a visible thing.
> [...]
> There were seven divels cast out of *Marie Magdalen*. Which is not so grosselie understood by the learned, as that there were in hir just seven corporall divels, such as I described before elsewhere; but that by the number of seven divels, a great multitude, and an uncerteine number of vices is signified: which figure is usuall in divers places of the scripture. And this interpretation is more agreeable with Gods word, than the papisticall paraphrase, which is; that Christ, under the name of the seven divels, recounteth the seven deadlie sinnes onelie. Others allow neither of these expositions; bicause they suppose that the efficacie of Christs miracle should this waie be confounded: as though it were not as difficult a matter, with a touch to make a good Christian of a vicious person; as with a word to cure the ague, or any other disease of a sicke bodie. I thinke not but any of both these cures may be wrought by meanes, in processe of time, without miracle; the one by the preacher, the other by the physician. But I saie that Christs worke in both was apparentlie miraculous: for with power and authoritie, even with a touch of his finger, and a word of his mouth, he made the blind to see, the halt to go, the lepers cleane, the deafe to heare, the dead to rise againe, and the poore to receive the Gospell, out of whom (I saie) he cast divels, and miraculouslie conformed them to become good Christians, which before were dissolute livers; to whome he said, Go your waies and sinne no more.
> (Scot, 17.13)

No man as I think calleth it in question whether the devil be a spirit or a corporal thing, and therefore if it should be granted you that this word spirit or devil doth in all places of the scripture signify and is to be understood spiritually (which may be denied) it would not make at all with you. For the question is not of the devil's nature but of his assaults and afflictions, which are and may be not only spiritual but also temporal, though the devil himself be a spirit. You are therefore to prove that it is not in a spirit temporally to hurt or assault a man, which if you could prove then would it follow also that God, being a spirit, could not plague and punish our bodies or cattle no more than the devil can. But now to come to your examples, and first for the 7 devils cast out of Mary Magdalen, which as you say were a multitude of vices and no corporal devils, and thus to understand it you think it no derogation to Christ's miracles because it is no less miraculous with a touch to make a good Christian than to heal any disease of the body. And this you confirm by the example of the adulterous woman to whom [fol. 98v] Christ said go thy way and sin no more.[296] To this I first answer if they were indeed devils which Christ did cast out of Mary Magdalen (as I think it will be so proved), then do you derogate very much from this miracle forasmuch as there is in this act a miracle done not only to her soul but also to her body, which bodily miracle you deny and so do derogate from the miracle the one part thereof, which I do take to be no less offence than to derogate from the word of God any part thereof. As touching your confirmation by the example of the said adulterous woman I think it not pertinent to prove your purpose thereby, for his dealing with her was never reputed a miracle either the one way or the other, but for that he came not to exercise here any temporal jurisdiction (his kingdom not being of this world), he left the crime of her adultery undecided (as he left the cause of the two brethren striving for their inheritance, being requested to determine the same) and for his bidding her go her way and sin no more, it proveth not that he made her a good Christian but is rather a lesson teaching her how to become such a one.[297] Besides there is some question of this history touching this woman whether it be canonical, as you may see in Mr Beza his testament of the largest volume upon that place.[298] But now let us examine whether the devils said to be cast out of Mary Magdalen were only sins and not devils indeed. I say devils indeed inste{ad} of your words 'corporal devils' because I think you mean as I

---

296 Luke 8:1–3, John 8:1–11.
297 The 'two brethren' are from Luke 12:13–14. Calvin's commentary on this passage from John makes the same comparison.
298 As many modern editions of the Bible note, the earliest manuscripts do not contain this episode; see Barton, *A History of the Bible*, pp. 293–5.

speak, unless you understand those to be corporal devils which do occupy a corporal body either truly or in apparence assumed unto them, in which sense I refuse not to use the word corporal, but not otherwise. Yet am I not ignorant that some of the learned (and amongst them St Augustine) have held that all spirits (God only excepted) have naturally certain bodies allotted unto them of a thin and airy substance, of which matter I will not now stand to entreat of.[299] But to our matter I say that Christ did cast out of the said Mary, as out of many other, not only sins but also very and true devils indeed. [fol. 99r][300] The reasons moving me thus to say are these. First, I think you cannot throughout the scriptures show me where sins are called devils. Secondly, I think you will not deny but that the holy ghost in speaking of the 7 devils cast out of Mary Magdalen did thereby mean to demonstrate unto us some rare and special things done unto her in that action which was not common to others. But if her devils signify nothing but a multitude of sins, then was there nothing done to her in the casting out of her devils which is not done to all the faithful and regenerate children of God. For if the prophet David confessed his sins to be more in number than the hairs of his head, what other faithful man is th [...] can be said to be without a multitude of sins [...] how many soever the sins of the faithful are th [...] purged and washed away by the blood of Christ [...] out of all faithful persons hath Christ cast o [...] devils as well as out of Mary Magdalen [...] be as you interpret her devils there was no specia [...] done to her in that action as before I said. A [...] shall by devils understand sins then ma [...] gather that Christ's Apostles did as well [...] from sins as Christ did, for he gave the [...] over unclean spirits, or devils to cast [...] divers persons.[301] As touching the number of 7 [...] know that number to be diversely used in the [...] will not stand upon it, neither shall [...] needful to stand upon the signification [...] in this place for that there be other places [...] scriptures which do so plainly prove that very devils [...] bodily possess men as that cannot be shifted off[302] by any exposition

---

299 For a discussion of the competing views of spirits as either embodied or entirely incorporeal, see Pudney, *Scepticism and Belief in Witchcraft Drama, 1538–1681*, pp. 247–52.
300 The edge of this page is damaged by a tear, creating gaps in the text which are represented here by [...]. The writing on the verso seems to have been added after the page was torn, as there are no such gaps.
301 Author's note: 'math 10'; Matthew 10:1: 'And he called his twelue disciples vnto him, and gaue them power against vncleane spirits, to cast them out, and to heale euerie sickenes, & euerie disease.'
302 OED: 'To evade, turn aside (an argument); to evade fulfilment of (a duty, a promise).'

which shall interpret those devils to be sins or lunacy or other diseases as you in the rest of your examples here alleged would have it, being thereunto moved by very slender reasons or rather slender conjectures.

Reason 104[303]

> As touching those that are said in the Gospell to be possessed of spirits, it seemeth in manie places that it is indifferent, or all one, to saie; He is possessed with a divell; or, He is lunatike or phrentike: which disease in these daies is said to proceed of melancholie. But if everie one that now is lunatike, be possessed with a reall divell; then might it be thought, that divels are to be thrust out of men by medicines. But who saith in these times with the woman of *Canaan*; My daughter is vexed with a divell, except it be presupposed, that she meant hir daughter was troubled with some disease? ... Some are of opinion, that the said woman of *Chanaan* ment indeed that hir daughter was troubled with some disease; bicause it is written in sted of that the divell was cast out, that hir daughter was made whole, even the selfesame houre. According to that which is said in the 12. of *Matthew*; There was brought unto Christ one possessed of a divell, which was both blind and dumbe, and he healed him: so as, he that was blind and dumbe both spake and sawe. But it was the man, and not the divell, that was healed, and made to speake and see. Whereby (I saie) it is gathered, that such as were diseased, as well as they that were lunatike, were said sometimes to be possessed of divels. (Scot, 17.14)

As first you say to be 'lunatic' and 'possessed with devils' is many times taken for one and the self same thing, for proof whereof you quote the 4 of Mathew, in which chapter I see nothing making with you but very plain words making against you. For there it is said they brought unto Christ them that were possessed with devils, and those that were lunatic, and those that had the palsy, and he healed them.[304] [fol. 99v] Here you see a plain distinction to be made between the possessing with devils and lunacy, as there is between the same and palsy and the other diseases there spoken of, and here you also see the word 'healing' applied as well to the casting out of devils as to all other diseases and sicknesses. But admit that these words 'possessed with devils' and 'lunacy' were many times confounded in the scriptures as you say they are. This cannot serve your turn unless you can prove they are so confounded not only many times but also at all times, for

---

303 Author's note: 'note that heare cometh in the 104 Reas.'; the author indicates that he is now responding to reason 104, which does not have a separate heading in the manuscript, but has been given one here.
304 Matthew 4:24.

if there were but one only place in the scriptures where to be possessed with devils doth not signify either sins, or lunacy, or some disease, that alone were sufficient to overturn and take away all that is here alleged for your purpose. Touching your example of the woman's daughter of Canaan, you use divers reasons or conjectures why it should be thought that she was not vexed with a devil indeed but rather with some disease signified by those words. Your first reason is that except it should be so interpreted as you say none can in these days say with the woman of Canaan 'my daughter is vexed with a devil', and what will you conclude if this be granted unto you? I for my part can conclude no better thereof than to say God be thanked if he have in these days not suffered the devil to use such bodily vexation and tyranny upon our children as he suffered him in those days to use upon this woman's daughter and upon many others. Your second reason is the opinion of those which think as you say, being thereunto moved because it is not written that the devil was cast out of her daughter but that she was made whole. Here you do well to suppress the names of those which are of the said opinion, for I dare assure myself that (yourself excepted) you are not able to nominate one man learned and of sound religion that is of that opinion. As touching this word 'healing', I have before showed that the same is generally and indifferently applied as well to casting out of devils as to healing of diseases, and if you think it no absurdity to say that a man bodily vexed and possessed with a devil is in his body diseased and vexed (as I suppose it were a great absurdity to say or think the contrary), how then is {it} not aptly said of such a one when the devil is cast out that he is healed? For what else doth this word 'healing' import but that he is delivered and made sound from the grief and vexation wherewith he was troubled and vexed? But I marvel why you should thus grate[305] in this matter upon this example and the next following of the blind and dumb man for the [fol. 100r] signification of this word 'healing' when as you may find the same two stories expressed by other of the Evangelists in such a plain manner of speech (if this were not plain enough) as no man can doubt but that the healing of the said parties was no other thing but the casting of their devil out of them with whom they were possessed and vexed. For first, as touching the healing of the woman of Canaan's daughter mentioned by St Mathew, it is in St Mark reported thus, vz: after this woman had said unto Christ, 'truth lord yet indeed the whelps eat under the table of the children's crumbs', then said he unto her for this saying, 'go thy way the devil is gone out of thy daughter' and when she was come home to her house she found the devil departed and her daughter lying on the bed.[306] Here sir

---

305 OED: 'To "harp" or dwell querulously *upon* a subject.'
306 Author's note: 'marc 7'; Mark 7:28–30.

may you plainly see by the interpretation of the holy ghost what was the healing which St Mathew spake of as touching this woman's daughter, and as touching the other example it is recorded as well by St Mathew himself as by St Mark and St Luke, that as soon as Christ had healed this dumb and blind man possessed (as the text sayeth) with a devil, the scribes and Pharisees hearing thereof said that he did cast out devils by Beelzebub, the chief or prince of the devils, whereby it is plain that he did not heal this man otherwise than by casting out the devil from him which before did possess him in such sort as he thereby became both blind and dumb. And therefore whereas St Mathew sayeth he healed him, St Luke writing the same story sayeth 'and he was casting out a devil and it was dumb and when the devil was cast out the dumb spake'.[307] Furthermore in the histories of the New Testament mention is made of devils coming out of graves, of their speaking and crying out, of their going out of men into swine and their carrying of the same swine with violence into the sea, of their falling down before Christ, of his charging them not to utter him, of their fierceness towards those that passed by the way where they were, of their tearing them whom they possessed, of casting them sometime in the fire, sometime in the water, of their making some deaf, some blind, some dumb, some crooked, of their breaking in sunder chains and fetters, of their confessing of Christ [fol. 100v] to be the son of God and of his apostles to be the servants of the high God &c, all the which things with many other the like in the scriptures cannot be understood to be nothing else but sins, lunacy, or sicknesses as you would have it, but must needs be understood to be devils indeed, as both the text sayeth and all the godly learned in all times and ages have taken it.

Reason 105

> The nature therfore and substance of divels and spirits, bicause in the scripture it is not so set down, as we may certeinlie know the same: we ought to content and frame our selves faithfullie to beleeve the words and sense there delivered unto us by the high spirit, which is the Holie-ghost, who is Lord of all spirits; alwaies considering, that evermore spirits are spoken of in scripture, as of things spirituall; though for the helpe of our capacities they are there sometimes more grosselie and corporallie expressed, either in parables or by metaphors, than indeed they are. (Scot, 17.16)

Your bare assertion saying that the letter of the scripture making mention of devils in any corporal or real manner must be otherwise understood than the letter soundeth may not stand for any authority sith especially you alone are of that opinion against all other that ever I have read. Yea,

---

307 Luke 11:14.

the whole course and consent of the scripture is herein plainly against you, as by the matter mentioned in the Reas going before may appear. I would therefore you would in this point do according to your own rule here prescribed, vz. that you would faithfully believe the word and the true sense of the same, which surely you do not in this point unless you only have the true sense of the word concerning the same. As for the nature and substance of devils, it is so far forth plainly set down in the scriptures as is needful for us to know, and further to search thereof is no piety but curiosity. And if you will have nothing to be spoken of in the scriptures concerning spirits but that which is spiritual, I marvel how you will have us to understand the visible apparence of God's angels, their eating, drinking, and lodging with men, their killing and destroying of men and cities with such like corporal and real actions of the which there is store in the scriptures.

Reason 106

> As for example (and to omit the historie of Job which elsewhere I handle) it is written; The Lord said, Who shall entise *Ahab*, that he maie fall at *Ramoth Gilead*, &c? Then came foorth a spirit, and stood before the Lord, and said; I will entise him. And the Lord said, Wherewith? And he said; I will go and be a lieng spirit in the mouth of all his prophets. Then he said; Go foorth, thou shalt prevaile, &c. This storie is here set foorth in this wise, to beare with our capacities, and speciallie with the capacitie of that age, that could not otherwise conceive of spirituall things, than by such corporall demonstrations. And yet here is to be noted, that one spirit, and not manie or diverse, did possesse all the false prophets at once. Even as in another place, manie thousand divels are said to possesse one man: and yet it is also said even in the selfe same place, that the same man was possessed onelie with one divell.[308] (Scot, 17.16)

Your allegation of the spirit which became a lying spirit in the mouth of Ahab's false prophets doth prove that only which no man ever denied; to wit, that it was done by some spiritual means. But what is this to prove that all other actions of the devil be of the same sort? This is again a reason *a secundum quid ad simpliciter*[309] and therefore very unfit to [**fol. 101r**] prove your purpose, as hath been before in sundry places declared. And where you say it is to be noted that not many or divers spirits but one only did possess all the false prophets at once, as in another place many thousands of devils are said to possess one man when as yet it is said in the self-same place that the self-same man was only possessed with one devil &c, I do not

---

308 Scot provides marginal references to 1 Kings 18, Luke 8, and Mark 5.
309 See note 57 to reason 29 above.

see how you could well couple these two examples together to confirm the truth of the one by the other. For first they are very unlike in that wherein you do first liken them together, for of the spirit which did possess the false prophets it was never said that his name was *legio* because they were many or thousands, as it is said of the other devil that possessed the man. Again, inasmuch as it is plain by this example that thousands of devils were called but one devil, it might hereof be gathered by great probability against you that though there was no mention but only of one spirit that did possess the false prophets, yet might there be thousands of them comprehended under the name of one as there was in this other place, but I will not urge that. Furthermore there was this dissimilitude between these two examples: that in the one the spirit did work a spiritual action in the mind of the false prophets, inclining the same to conceive the lie which after they uttered, but all that was mentioned in the other example was altogether corporal actions in the bodies of the possessed, both men and swine, so that (as I said before) I see no cause in any one point why these two examples being so divers should be matched the one with the other as if they were like and agreeable. But there is in the latter example a kind of contradiction, in that it is said at one time that thousands of devils possessed this man and at another time that he was only possessed with one devil, of which contradiction you gather that there was indeed but one devil, and yet I see no reason but you might well gather that there were thousands of devils for that the one is affirmed by as good authority as [fol. 101v] the other. And except we hold the one to be true as well as the other, we must make the holy ghost a liar in the one of them, which to avoid, the true sense of the places is to be sought out whereby they may be reconciled without any such reproach or blasphemy to the holy ghost, and not any one part of the story snatched and culled out to serve our purposes, the other part being thereby brought into a suspicion of falsehood. Where also by the way I would have you to consider that you do here add to the words of the text, when as you say it is said in the self-same place that the self-same man was only possessed with one devil, for you have not this word ('only') in all the text. But now let us consider how these places of the text importing some contradiction may be reconciled, whereupon the opinions of the learned are that when mention is made here but of a devil this is spoken either in respect of men's opinions and judgements who thought the thing here reported to be the work of one devil, being ignorant that many devils at once might possess a man, or else in respect either of the principality or of the power which one devil had in this action above the other that were joined with him. For that one devil is more mischievous than another and hath more superiority than another may appear in sundry places of the scriptures, as namely in the 12 of Mathew and the 11 of Luke, where the principality of one devil more than another is showed in that Beelzebub is there called the prince or chief of the devils. Where also that one devil is more mischievous and hurtful than another is showed, in that it is there said that the unclean spirit or devil being cast out of his house did after return thither again, taking with him seven other spirits or devils worse than himself.[310] Besides this a great number of devils may aptly be called by the name of one devil in respect of their unity, consent, and agreement in their devilish actions, the same being no less in them all if it is in one devil alone agreeing well with himself, even as in a contrary case all Christians being regenerate and made partakers of Christ Jesus by a true and lively faith are for their consent, fellowship, and agreement in that faith called by the apostle by the name of one new man.[311] For the which cause it is [fol. 102r] also said in the Acts that the multitude of them that believed were of one heart and one soul, whenas notwithstanding in other respects there were many hearts and many souls amongst them.[312] To be short, if you would not allow these interpretations in the matter we have in hand, yet can you not deny but the text doth more strongly serve to prove many devils than but one only. First, because there can be gathered of the text no other cause why Christ demanded the name of the devil but only to have it thereby appear to the standers by that there were many devils and not only one; that so the power and glory of his name might be the more apparent unto them in that his action. For a matter of far greater power and glory was it unto him to be able with a word to cast out a legion of devils than to cast out but one only devil, and therefore to affirm (as you do) that he did here cast out but one devil only is truly a great defacing or abridging of his power and glory. Secondly, inasmuch as the text doth plainly show that the devil first spoken of in the singular number was a legion of devils, why should any man doubt thereof, the latter speech being a very plain exposition of the former? But if you will say this later speech was uttered by the devil and not by the holy ghost and therefore we may doubt of the truth thereof, this objection will easily be taken away with that which after followeth in the text. For the text after sayeth that all the devils besought Jesus that they might be sent into the swine, and incontinently[313] Jesus gave them leave and they, the unclean spirits, went out and entered into the swine &c. And further it followeth in the text that the Gadarenites came to Jesus and saw him that had been possessed with the devil and had the legion, so that there can be no ambiguity but that there were many devils in the man here spoken of, though some time the text speaketh but singularly

---

310 Matthew 12:24, 43–5; Luke 11:15, 24–26.
311 Author's note: 'Ephes 2'; Ephesians 2:15.
312 Acts 4:32.
313 OED: 'Straightway, forthwith, at once, immediately, without delay'.

as it were of one devil, which might well be either for the respects aforesaid or else because one of those devils only did first speak unto Christ, saying 'what have I to do with thee' &c. Here also might I refer you to all the learned interpreters of this story that have from the first to our time written thereupon, assuring you and myself also that not one of them is herein of your opinion. Now after what sort your private opinion in this and in other matters mentioned in your book will be accepted against the opinions of all the learned of all ages you are wise enough to consider of the same, and I hope you will so consider of it as {your} [**fol. 102v**] adversaries shall have no cause to insult against you for attributing too much to yourself in such cases as derogate much from all other.

Reason 107

> Certeinlie the serpent was he that seduced *Eve*: now whether it were the divell, or a snake; let anie wise man (or rather let the word of God) judge. Doubtles the scripture in manie places expoundeth it to be the divell. And I have (I am sure) one wiseman on my side for the interpretation hereof, namelie *Salomon*; who saith. Through envie of the divell came death into the world: referring that to the divell, which *Moses* in the letter did to the serpent. But a better expositor hereof needeth not, than the text it selfe, even in the same place, where it is written; I will put enmitie betweene thee and the woman, and betweene thy seed and hir seed: he shall breake thy head, and thou shalt bruse his heele. What christian knoweth not, that in these words the mysterie of our redemption is comprised and promised? Wherein is not meant (as manie suppose) that the common seed of woman shall tread upon a snakes head, and so breake it in peeces, &c: but that speciall seed, which is Christ, should be borne of a woman, to the utter overthrow of sathan, and to the redemption of mankind, whose heele or flesh in his members the divell should bruse and assault, with continuall attempts, and carnall provocations, &c. (Scot, 17.29)

> This word Serpent in holie scripture is taken for the divell [...] where it is said, that the serpent was father of lies, author of death, and the worker of deceipt: methinks it is a ridiculous opinion to hold, that thereby a snake is meant; which must be, if the letter be preferred before the allegorie. Trulie *Calvines* opinion is to be liked and reverenced, and his example to be embraced and followed, in that he offereth to subscribe to them that hold, that the Holie-ghost in that place did of purpose use obscure figures, that the cleare light thereof might be deferred, till Christs comming. He saith also with like commendation (speaking hereof, and writing upon this place) that *Moses* doth accommodate and fitten for the understanding of the common people, in a rude and grosse stile, those

things which he there delivereth; forbearing once to rehearse the name of sathan.
[...]
I would learne what impietie, absurditie, or offense it is to hold, that *Moses*, under the person of the poisoning serpent or snake, describeth the divell that poisoned *Eve* with his deceiptfull words, and venomous assault. Whence commeth it else, that the divell is called so often, The viper, The serpent, &c: and that his children are called the generation of vipers; but upon this first description of the divell made by *Moses*? For I thinke none so grosse, as to suppose, that the wicked are the children of snakes, according to the letter[.] (Scot, 17.30)

The cursse rehearsed by God in that place, whereby witchmongers labour so busilie to proove that the divell entered into the bodie of a snake, and by consequence can take the bodie of anie other creature at his pleasure, &c: reacheth (I thinke) further into the divels matters, than we can comprehend, or is needfull for us to know, that understand not the waies of the divels creeping, and is farre unlikelie to extend to plague the generation of snakes: as though they had beene made with legs before that time, and through this cursse were deprived of that benefit. And yet, if the divell should have entred into the snake, in maner and forme as they suppose; I cannot see in what degree of sinne the poore snake should be so guiltie, as that God, who is the most righteous judge, might be offended with him. (Scot, 17.31)

Your denial that evil spirits or devils can take to themselves shapes or bodies proceedeth also from no other ground or authority but only your own private opinion, the same being not only in this point contrary to all divines of all times, but also contrary to infinite places and examples of the scriptures, of the which sufficient have been before alleged, as well in my answer to your 104 Reason as in other places. And as this your denial is only of your singular and private opinion, so is the same also which you do here allege for proof thereof, vz. that the serpent mentioned in the 3 of Gen was not indeed a serpent but the devil himself. If you can show me any credible and sound writer of this opinion with you, either of the old or of the new writers, I dare be bound to give you all the books I have, and yet had I rather give you an 100 £ than I would forgo them all. But sith you do here allege certain reasons to warrant your said assertion, I will in order as they stand answer them. First, therefore, where you do allege these words of God spoken to the serpent, 'I will put enmity between thee and the woman and between thy seed and her seed' &c.[314] This you say cannot be

---

314 Genesis 3:15.

spoken to any serpent indeed but must needs be spoken to the devil, forasmuch as by the seed of the woman is meant Christ Jesus born of the Virgin Mary who only hath broken Satan's head &c. To this I answer that you are much deceived to think that those words do only pertain to Christ and to Satan, for in truth they do also pertain to Eve and to the issue and posterity that should come of her and to the natural and true serpent having (besides the mystical and prophetical sense before spoken of) this literal sense, that whereas before there was love and familiarity between the serpent and the woman, there should for ever after this be a continual enmity and hatred between them and the seed or issue that should come of them, which how well it is performed common sense and experience may teach us, for what is there in the world that is more loathsome or hateful to mankind [fol. 103r] than serpents are? Or what is there in the world that serpents would more hurt and annoy with their stings and venom than mankind, if they could as easily hurt and annoy him as they can other things less able to resist or avoid them? For your better resolution touching this literal sense I refer you to the judgements of Mr Calvin and Mr Musculus upon this place, whom you shall find to allow of this literal sense and to show good reason why it should be allowed, which here I omit for brevity's sake.[315] But if you will needs understand the said words in no other than in the said mystical and prophetical sense, how yet can you understand the words before spoken of the serpent and to the serpent to be meant of the devil and not of a true serpent? The devil was never any of the beasts of the field, neither doth he go upon his belly and eat dust all the days of his life; therefore of him it could not be said that he was subtler or wiser then all the beasts of the field which God had made, neither could it be said to him that he should be cursed above all the cattle and above every beast of the field and that he should go upon his belly and eat dust all the days of

---

315 Wolfgang Musculus (1497–1563), Reformed theologian and author of a lengthy commentary on Genesis, *In Mosis Genesim plenissimi commentarii* (Basel, 1554). On Genesis 3:15, Musculus writes that 'the historical sense is not to be compromised ... The simple and proper meaning of words is to be retained, so that the woman is still Eve; the woman's seed is her offspring, the human race; it should be a genuine and natural serpent that misled the woman; the serpent's seed is its offspring as well.' Calvin writes of the same passage 'I therefore interpret seed to mean the woman's offspring in general.' John L. Thompson (ed.), *Reformation Commentary on Scripture: Genesis 1–11* (Downer's Grove, IL: InterVarsity Press, 2012), pp. 156, 158. The treatise author does not mention St Augustine, whose reading of this part of Genesis lays much more emphasis on the figurative sense: see his *On Genesis: A Refutation of the Manichees*, translated by Edmund Hill (New York: New City Press, 2002), II.26–8 (pp. 88–90).

his life. This therefore must be understood to be spoken of and to the serpent as the text sayeth it was, and yet I will not deny but it hath been of some, and may be for some good respects, allegorically applied to the devil as the other text following, vz. 'I will put enmity between' &c. But so to stick to the allegory as the literal sense shall be clean barred and denied, no good interpreter can or ever did allow thereof. And because you do attribute somewhat to Mr Calvin's judgement in this matter I am well contented to admit him for judge between us, for in truth he doth (no less than all other good interpreters do) understand the things here spoken of and to the serpent to be spoken and meant of a true and natural serpent, as you may see in his commentary upon this 3 ca of Gen. Throughout the same as often as he speaketh of this matter and amongst many of his sayings to this purpose he hath these words, vz. *Ita serpent{is}* [**fol. 103v**] *nomen non allegoricae (ut quidam inepte faciunt) sed in genuino sensu accipio.*[316] Wherefore I marvel much that you would in this part of your book allege Mr Calvin's words as touching this matter as if he had been of your mind when he is most plainly against you, pronouncing them to deal fondly or foolishly which take the name of the serpent altogether allegorically. I do add here this word ('altogether') for that I see Mr Calvin did so mean by his words after in the same chapter set down after this manner: *Quare hunc totum locum multi allegorice exponunt: et plausibiles sunt quae ab illis afferuntur argutiae, sed omnibus propius expensis facile animadvertent lectores sano iudicio praediti mixtum esse sermonem nam ita serpentem alloquitur deus ut clausula ad diabolum pertineat.*[317] Secondly, where you say here it was not the serpent that deceived Eve, therein referring yourself

---

316 'Thus, I take the name serpent, not allegorically, as some foolishly do, but in its genuine sense.' Thompson (ed.), *Reformation Commentary on Scripture: Genesis 1–11*, p. 117.

317 'Wherefore, many explain this whole passage allegorically, and plausible are the subtleties which they adduce for this purpose. But when all things are more accurately weighed, readers endued with sound judgment will easily perceive that the language is of a mixed character; for God so addresses the serpent that the last clause belongs to the devil.' Calvin, *Commentaries on the Book of Genesis*, vol. 1, translated by John King (Grand Rapids, MI: William B. Eerdmans, 1948), pp. 165–6. This translation interprets the word *totum* as an adjective applying to the noun 'passage', hence 'whole passage', whereas the author interprets it as an adverb describing how the passage is interpreted, hence 'altogether' allegorically. An early modern translation of Calvin's commentary on Genesis avoids the ambiguity by simply omitting the word *totum*: 'Wherefore many expound this place Allegorically: and the reasons whiche they bring ar plausible': *A Commentarie of John Caluine, vpon the First Booke of Moses called Genesis*, translated by Thomas Tymme (London, 1578), pp. 104–5.

to the judgement of wise men and of the word of God, reciting out of the same word certain authorities, as that Solomon sayeth death came into the world through the envy of the devil, as that also the serpent is called the father of lies, the author of death, and the worker of deceit. To all this I answer that both by the judgement of wise men and also by the express word of God it is certain that the serpent did deceive Eve. And first it was the judgement of Eve herself (who I suppose was in time of her best estate and innocency a most wise woman) that the serpent did deceive her, for little did she think of the devil's practice when she said unto God 'the serpent beguiled me', but she only thought of the very true and natural serpent which had commoned[318] with her, as may plainly appear by the words of God thereupon pronounced forthwith upon the serpent, saying unto him 'because you hast done this' (that is, because you hast beguiled the woman) 'you art cursed above all cattle' &c, the which words of almighty God do not only show that Eve imputed the beguiling of her to the serpent, but that God also himself doth the same, if it so be that he spake in these words to a true and natural serpent, as the opinion of all the learned is he did, the text also itself importing the same. And all this maketh nothing at all against your authorities, neither do they make at all against this, for most true it is that both [**fol. 104r**] the serpent and also the devil did deceive the woman: the one as the author, procurer, and deviser of the deceit, the other as the organ or instrument by whom it was put in practice and executed. You are not (I am sure) ignorant that there may be and are of one effect divers efficient causes; some principal, some secondary, some remote, some near, and some organical or instrumental, to every one of which causes one and the self same effect or thing done may be in several respects ascribed, and therefore you do against the rules of all logic and philosophy so to tie this effect of the woman's deceiving to one only cause, as you count it a ridiculous opinion to hold the effecting of the same by any other cause than that one. Here I speak according as I take the meaning of your words to be and not as your words are indeed set down, for your words are that it is a ridiculous opinion to hold that a snake is meant, and there I am of your mind, for seeing the text speaketh of a serpent and not of a snake I must needs accompt it ridiculous to think that a snake was meant. Thirdly, you allege Mr Calvin's words as though he spake on your side, whereas he is clean against you (as I have before declared) in taking the name of the serpent in his proper and natural sense. Yea even in this also he is against you: I mean as touching the deceiving of the woman, for that his opinion was that she was deceived by the serpent I

---

318 OED: 'To confer, converse, talk (with, together)'.

will now show you by his own words, which are as followeth: *Adde quod humanae ingratitudinis foeditas melius inde perspicitur, quod quum sibi dei manu in subiectionem cuncta animalia esse tradita Adam et Heva agnoscerent, ab uno tamen ex suis mancipijs abduci se passi sunt ad rebellandum Deo.*[319] Fourthly, whereas you ask what absurdity it were to think that Moses under the person of the serpent describeth the devil I think therein no absurdity at all, so as you did not so lean to the mystical sense as that you would deny the sense literal, when as there is no less truth in the one than in the other. And whereas you further [**fol. 104v**] ask whence it cometh else that the devil is called so often the viper, the fiery serpent &c, and that his children are called the generation of vipers but upon this first description made by Moses, I answer that I do not think or presently remember that the devil is often or so much as once called in the scriptures by the name of a viper or fiery serpent, but I do well remember he is often called by the name of a serpent, which name is given unto him (as all the godly learned interpreters do with one consent agree) because he did at the first tempting of mankind use and occupy the body of a true and natural serpent.[320] As for the place of Isaiah by you quoted to show that the said names are applied to the devil, it hath no such sense as you imagine it to have, but the sense thereof is briefly this.[321] The lord in that chapter reproveth the wickedness of his people in that they, being distressed by the Assyrians, did fly unto the king of Egypt for help and did send unto him their chief princes and noble men with riches and treasures to obtain succour at his hands: the vanity and wickedness of which fact is by the prophet greatly aggravated many and sundry ways, and amongst other

---

319 'The disgrace of human ingratitude is more clearly perceived from the fact that while Adam and Eve would have known that all animals were placed in subjection to them by the hand of God, they nonetheless allowed themselves to be led away by one of their own slaves into rebellion against God.' Thompson (ed.), *Reformation Commentary on Scripture: Genesis 1–11*, p. 117.

320 The 'dragon' in Revelation 12 (in both the King James and Geneva bibles) is called a 'fiery serpent' in some modern English translations. Isaiah 30:6 (see note below) and 14:29 mentions fiery serpents, but it is not at all clear that these are references to the devil.
  Author's notes: '2 corinth 11', 'Apoca 12 et 20'; 2 Corinthians 11.3, Revelation 12.9, 12.14, 12.15; 20.2.

321 Author's note: 'Esay 30 vers 6'; Isaiah 30:6: 'The burden of the beastes of the South, in a land of trouble and anguish, from whence shal come the yong and olde lyon, the viper and fyrie flying serpent against them that shal beare their riches vpo[n] the shoulders of the coltes, and their treasures vpon the bounches of the camels, to a people that can not profite.' There is a marginal reference to Isaiah 30:6 in the published version of Scot, but only the phrase 'fiery serpent' is actually quoted.

their follies in this enterprise committed, he putteth them in mind how noisome and dangerous a journey it was for their princes and messengers to pass into Egypt by that way which they went, for that in the same they should be afflicted and endangered with many and sundry sorts of cruel and hurtful beasts that had their being in that vast and great wilderness of Egypt through which they were to pass before they could come to the journey's end. Of which cruel and hurtful beasts he doth here reckon up unto them the young and old lion, the viper and the fiery flying serpent, saying that these should come out against the messengers that shall bear their riches and treasures upon colts and camels into Egypt, a land of trouble and anguish. So that the meaning of the holy ghost in this place is nothing less than, by the words of 'vipers' and 'fiery flying serpents' here mentioned, to signify the devil. And therefore for the better understanding of these words Mr Bullinger in his 86 homily upon this prophet referreth the reader to the books which [fol. 105r] entreat of natural things or causes, and namely to the natural history of Pliny which I suppose he would not have done if we had by these words to understand the devil, as you take them.[322] Now for that the devil's children are called the generation of vipers, it is not truly in any such respect as you set down but for some special property wherein the wicked do very aptly resemble the vipers, and therefore the ancient father Remigius writing hereupon sayeth thus: *Consuetudo scripturarum est ab imitatione operum nomina imponere secundum illud: pater tuus Amorreus, sic et isti (vz. saducei et pharasei) ab imitatione viperarum progeni{es} viperarum dicuntur.*[323] And St Chrysostom, to make this matter more plain, noteth certain points wherein the Sadducees and Pharisees (whom St John called a generation of vipers) did imitate and resemble vipers, saying thus: *Natura enim viperarum*

---

322 Heinrich Bullinger (1504–75), Reformed theologian and Zwingli's successor as head of the Zurich Church.
323 'The manner of scripture is to give names from the imitation of deeds, according to that of Ezekiel, Thy father was an Amorite; so these from following vipers are called generation of vipers'; quoted in Aquinas, *Catena Aurea: Commentary on the Four Gospels*, p. 99. The author adds a clarifying interpolation after 'these': 'viz. the Sadducees and Pharisees'. Judging by his description of Remigius as an 'ancient father', the author may have been thinking of Saint Remigius, Bishop of Reims (c. 437–533), but the Remigius quoted in the *Catena Aurea* was a ninth-century monk from Auxerre. The scriptural reference is to Matthew (and Luke) 3:7, where John the Baptist uses this phrase (the phrase occurs again in Matthew 12:34). The *Catena Aurea* contains both this extract from Remigius and the following extract from pseudo-Chrysostom: see Aquinas, *Catena Aurea in Quatuor Evangelia*, p. 37, and the discussion of sources in the introduction above.

talis est, cum momorderit hominem, statim currit ad aquam: si autem aquam non invenerit, moritur ideo et istos (vz saduceo et phariseos, Johannes) vocabat genimina viperarum, qui peccata mortifera committentes, currebant ad Baptismum, ut (quemadmodum viperae) per aquam periculum mortis evaderent. Item viperarum natura est, rumpere viscera matrum suarum, et sic nasci quoniam ergo Judaei assiduè persequentes prophetas, corr{u}perunt matrem suam synagogam, sicut ipsa lugens {dicit} in Canticis filij mei dimicarunt in me: ideo viper{arum} genimina nuncupantur. Item viperae a foris specios{ae} sunt, et quasi pictae, ab intus autem veneno ple{nae} sunt: ideo et hypochritas et phariseos viperarum geni mina appellat, quia hypochritae pulchritudinem sanctitatis ostendebant in vultum et venenum malitiae portabant in corde.[324] I set not down these sayings of Chrysostom as one purposing to justify all these comparisons or resemblances between vipers and wicked men to be apt and convenient (for it is not material to our controversy) but to show that his opinion was that when John Baptist resembled the wicked to vipers, he did not mean any other thing than the very true and natural vipers, and this also is the opinion of all the interpreters that I have ever read as touching that matter. Your opinion here ensuing, touching the curse God pronounced against the serpent, I shall {not} need in this place to meddle withal having {be}fore showed your error in the same by good {?} [fol. 105v] But whereas you do here last of all say that you cannot see how the poor snake could be guilty though the devil had entered into him (as is supposed) so as God the most

---

324 Author's note: '2 Expos in matheu[m] Ho. 3'. The reference is to pseudo-Chrysostom's *Opus Imperfectum in Matthaeum*. The Latin text, in the version edited by J. P. Migne (Paris, 1859) has been used to add the illegible sections shown in curly brackets. The author evidently believed, incorrectly, that the *Opus Imperfectum* was written by Chrysostom: see the sources section of the introduction above. Kellerman's translation of this passage is as follows: 'It is the nature of a viper to run immediately to water as soon as it has bitten anyone; if it does not find any water, it dies. So he called them also a brood of vipers who, while committing deadly sins, were running to baptism, in order to avoid the danger of death just as vipers do. Moreover, it is the nature of vipers to burst the belly of their mothers and to be born in this way. Therefore, because the Jews diligently persecuted the prophets and corrupted their mother, the synagogue, "My ... sons were angry with me," so they are called a brood of vipers. In addition, vipers are beautiful on the outside, almost as if they have been painted, but they are full of poison on the inside. So he was calling both the hypocrites and Pharisees a brood of vipers because the hypocrites showed a beauty of holiness on their face and yet carried the poison of malice in their heart' (p. 48). The scriptural passage quoted, as the Latin text above indicates [*dicit in Canticis*], is from the Song of Solomon (1:6), and like the preceding quotation contains a clarifying interjection added by the author.

righteous judge might be offended with him, if you cannot see this, how can you then see how this most righteous judge might punish the transgression of Adam and Eve, not only in themselves but also in all their posterity who offended no more than the serpent, no no{t} so much, because they were no parties in this transgression as the serpent was? How can you see how all the creatures of the world (those in the Ark only excepted) might be destroyed for the sins of sinful men and women, or how the houses, infants, and cattle of the Sodomites and Gomorreans might be destroyed, or how all the firstborn in Egypt or the Egyptian's horses and chariots might be destroyed? To be short, how can you see how our bodies (which are but organs and instruments of our minds as the serpent was to the devil) might be destroyed both here in this present world and also for ever in the world to come, if it were not of the lord's mercy that some shall be saved? If it would please you to peruse the histories of the scriptures you shall see it most often used of God the righteous judge, in detestation of sin and wickedness and for the more terrifying of sinners, to destroy not only the sinners themselves but even all things pertaining unto them, be they things that bear life or things insensible and without life. And seeing it seemeth by your alleging of Mr Calvin's words (in that you have read his commentaries upon this 3 chapter of Genesis) you might have seen by him in what respects it did please God to punish the serpent. For he doth there purposely handle this matter to answer and satisfy those that should suppose it to be an absurd thing that the brute beast should be punished for the fault and deceit of Satan. This shall you find in master Calvin writing upon these words of the text: *Et dixit Jehova ad serpentem*.[325]

Reason 108

> Did not the apostle *Thomas* thinke that Christ himselfe had beene a spirit; until Christ told him plainelie, that a spirit was no such creature, as had flesh and bones, the which (he said) *Thomas* might see to be in him? And for the further certifieng and satisfieng of his mind, he commended unto him his hands to be scene, and his sides to be felt. (Scot, 7.4)

---

[325] Gen 3:14: 'Then the Lord God said to the serpe[n]t'. Calvin's commentary on these words includes the following: 'If it seem absurd to any one that the punishment of another's fraud should be exacted from a brute animal, the solution is at hand. Since the serpent was created for human benefit, there was nothing improper in its being accursed from the moment that it was turned towards human destruction.' Thompson (ed.), *Reformation Commentary on Scripture: Genesis 1–11* (p. 155).

These words of our saviour Christ can in no wise be taken and understood in any such sense as though he did in them affirm that no manner of spirit can have or {at} the least seem to have flesh and bones.³²⁶ For then all that is written in the scriptures of the appearing {of} the good spirits or Angels of God unto men in the visible

[TEXT ENDS]

---

326 Luke 24.36–39: 'And as they spake these things, Iesus him self stode in the middes of them, and said vnto them, Peace *be* to you. But they were abashed & afraid, supposing that they had sene a spirit. Then he said vnto them, Why are ye troubled? and wherefore do doutes arise in your hearts? Beholde mine hands and my fete: for it is I my self: handle me, and se; for a spirit hathe not flesh & bones, as ye se me haue.' Scot conflates this passage with the version in John, which refers to doubting Thomas.

Bibliography

Manuscript sources

London, British Library, Add. MS 12506
London, British Library, Add. MS 45707
London, British Library, Add. MS 62135
London, British Library, Egerton MS 3777
London, British Library, Harley MS 2302
London, Lambeth Palace Library, MS 2004
London, Lambeth Palace Library, MS 2009
The National Archives, SP 12/176/1
The National Archives, SP 12/190/6

Printed works

Almond, Philip, 'King James I and the Burning of Reginald Scot's *The Discoverie of Witchcraft*: The Invention of a Tradition', *Notes and Queries* 56:2 (2009), 209–13.
—— *England's First Demonologist* (London: I. B. Tauris, 2011).
Anglo, Sydney, 'Reginald Scot's *Discoverie of Witchcraft*: Scepticism and Sadduceeism', in *The Damned Art*, edited by Sydney Anglo (London: Routledge & Kegan Paul, 1977), pp. 106–39.
Anon, *The fourth parte of Co[m]mentaries of the ciuill warres in Fraunce* (London, 1576).
Aquinas, Thomas, *Catena Aurea: Commentary on the Four Gospels*, translated by John Henry Newman (Oxford: John Henry Parker, 1841).
—— *Catena Aurea in Quatuor Evangelia*, in *Opera Omnia*, vol. 11 (New York: Musurgia, 1949).
Aristotle, *Nicomachean Ethics*, rev. ed., translated by Roger Crisp (Cambridge: Cambridge University Press, 2014).
Augustine of Hippo, *De Vera Religione*, in *Augustine: Earlier Writings*, edited by John S. H. Burleigh (Philadelphia, PA: The Westminster Press, 1953).
—— *De Civitate Dei*, edited by B. Dombart and A. Kalb (Turnhout: Brepols, 1955).
—— *Confessions*, translated by E. B. Pusey (London: J. M. Dent, 1966).
—— *The Way of Life of the Manicheans*, translated by Donald A. Gallagher and Idella J. Gallagher (Washington, DC: Catholic University of America Press, 1966).
—— *The Retractions*, translated by M. Inez Bogan (Washington, DC: Catholic University of America Press, 1968).

―― *City of God*, 2 vols, translated by John Healey (London: J. M. Dent, 1972).
―― *Expositions on the Book of Psalms*, edited by A. Cleveland Coxe (Grand Rapids, MI: Wm B. Eerdmans, repr. 1983).
―― *On Genesis: A Refutation of the Manichees*, translated by Edmund Hill (New York: New City Press, 2002).
pseudo-Augustine, *Quaestiones Veteris et Novi Testamenti*, edited by Alexander Souter (Vienna: F. Tempsky, 1908).
Baker, John, *The Oxford History of the Laws of England*, vol. 6 (Oxford: Oxford University Press, 2003).
Barton, John, *A History of the Bible* (New York: Penguin, 2019).
Baumann, Priscilla, 'The Deadliest Sin: Warnings against Avarice and Usury on Romanesque Capitals in Auvergne', *Church History* 59:1 (1990), 7–18.
Bernard, Richard, *A Guide to Grand-Jury Men* (London, 1627).
Beza, Theodore (trans.), *Iesv Christi D. N. Novvm Testamentvm* (London, 1576).
―― *The Newe Testament of our Lord Iesus Christ*, translated by William Whittingham (London, 1583).
Bilson, Thomas, *Certaine sermons touching the full redemption of mankind by the death and bloud of Christ* (London, 1599).
Bland, Mark, *A Guide to Early Printed Books and Manuscripts* (Chichester: Wiley-Blackwell, 2010).
Bodin, Jean, *De Magorum Daemonomania* (Basel, 1581), books.google.com.
―― *De la Démonomanie des Sorciers* (Antwerp, 1593), openlibrary.org.
―― *On the Demon-Mania of Witches*, translated by Randy A. Scott (Toronto: Centre for Reformation and Renaissance Studies, 1995).
Calvin, Jean, *Institutio totius christianae religionis*, 4th ed. (Geneva, 1550), e-rara.ch.
―― *Harmonia ex Evangelistis* (Geneva, 1555), e-rara.ch.
―― *Commentarii in Librum Psalmorum* (Geneva, 1557), books.google.com.
―― *Institutio christianae religionis*, 5th ed. (Geneva, 1559), archive.org.
―― *A Commentarie of John Caluine, vpon the First Booke of Moses called Genesis*, translated by Thomas Tymme (London, 1578).
―― *Sermons of Maister Iohn Caluin, vpon the booke of Iob*, translated by Arthur Golding (London, 1580).
―― *Commentary on a Harmony of the Evangelists, Matthew, Mark, and Luke*, 3 vols, translated by William Pringle (Edinburgh: Calvin Translation Society, 1845).
―― *Commentaries on the Book of Psalms*, 5 vols, translated by James Anderson (Edinburgh: Calvin Translation Society, 1846).
―― *Commentaries on the Book of Genesis*, 2 vols, translated by John King (Grand Rapids, MI: William B. Eerdmans, 1948).
―― *Institutes of the Christian Religion*, 2 vols, translated by Ford Lewis Battles (Philadelphia, PA: The Westminster Press, 1960).
―― *A Harmony of the Gospels: Matthew, Mark and Luke*, vol. 1, translated by A. W. Morrison (Grand Rapids, MI: William B. Eerdmans, 1972).
Carter, Christopher, 'The Family of Love and Its Enemies', *The Sixteenth Century Journal* 37:3 (2006), 651–72.
Chrysostom, *Homilies on the Gospel of St Matthew*, vol. 2, translated by George Prevost (Oxford: John Henry Parker, 1854).
pseudo-Chrysostom, *Opus Imperfectum in Matthaeum*, edited by J. P. Migne (Paris, 1859).

―― *Incomplete Commentary on Matthew*, translated by James A. Kellerman, edited by Thomas C. Oden (Downers Grove, IL: InterVarsity Press, 2010).
Cicero, Marcus Tullius, *De Officiis*, translated by Walter Miller (Cambridge, MA: Harvard University Press, 1913).
Clark, Peter, 'The Prophesying Movement in Kentish Towns during the 1570s', *Archaeologia Cantiana* 93 (1977), 81–90.
Clark, Stuart, *Thinking with Demons* (Oxford: Oxford University Press, 1997).
Cockburn, J. S. *A History of English Assizes* (Cambridge: Cambridge University Press, 1972).
―― (ed.), *Calendar of Assize Records: Kent, Elizabeth I* (London: HMSO, 1979).
Collinson, Patrick, *The Elizabethan Puritan Movement* (Oxford: Oxford University Press, 1967).
―― *Richard Bancroft and Elizabethan Anti-Puritanism* (Cambridge: Cambridge University Press, 2013).
Concordia Triglotta, edited by F. Bente (St Louis, MO: Concordia Publishing House, 1921), bookofconcord.org.
Coxe, Francis, *A Short Treatise Declaringe the Detestable Wickednesse of Magicall Sciences* (London, 1561).
St Cyprian, *On Jealousy and Envy*, translated by Ernest Wallis, in *Anti-Nicene Fathers*, vol. 5, edited by Alexander Roberts and James Donaldson, revised by A. Cleveland Coxe (Grand Rapids, MI: Wm B. Eerdman, 1978).
Daneau, Lambert, *A Dialogue of Witches* (London, 1575).
Darr, Orna Alyagon, *Marks of an Absolute Witch* (Farnham: Ashgate, 2011).
Davies, S. F., 'A Possible Stationers' Register Entry for Scot's *Discouerie of Witchcraft*', *Notes and Queries* 59:1 (2012), 41–3.
―― *Witchcraft and the Book Trade in Early Modern England* (unpublished PhD thesis, University of Sussex, 2012).
―― 'The Reception of Reginald Scot's *Discovery of Witchcraft*: Witchcraft, Magic, and Radical Religion', *Journal of the History of Ideas* 74:3 (July 2013), 381–401.
Daybell, James, *The Material Letter in Early Modern England: Manuscript Letters and the Culture and Practices of Letter-Writing, 1512–1635* (Basingstoke: Palgrave Macmillan, 2012).
Dixon, Leif, 'William Perkins, "Atheisme," and the Crises of England's Long Reformation', *Journal of British Studies* 50:4 (October 2011), 790–812.
Eckhardt, Joshua, *Manuscript Verse Collectors and the Politics of Anti-Courtly Love Poetry* (Oxford: Oxford University Press, 2009).
Elmer, Peter, *Witchcraft, Witch-Hunting, and Politics in Early Modern England* (Oxford: Oxford University Press, 2016).
Eskhult, Josef, 'Latin Bible Versions in the Age of Reformation and Post-Reformation', *Kyrkohistorisk årsskrift* 106:1 (2006), pp. 31–67.
Estes, Leland L., 'Reginald Scot and his *Discoverie of Witchcraft*: Religion and Science in the Opposition to the European Witch Craze', *Church History* 52:4 (1983), 444–56.
Ettenhuber, Katrin, 'The Preacher and Patristics', in *The Oxford Handbook of the Early Modern Sermon* (Oxford: Oxford University Press, 2011), pp. 34–53.
Eusebius of Caesarea, *Ecclesiasticall Historie*, in *Auncient Ecclesiasticall Histories*, translated by Meredith Hanmer (London, 1577).
Foxe, John, *Actes and Monuments* (London: 1563).

Gaskill, Malcolm, 'Witches and Witchcraft Prosecutions, 1560–1660', in Michael Zell (ed.), *Early Modern Kent, 1540–1640* (Woodbridge: Boydell & Brewer, 2000), pp. 245–78.
—— 'Witchcraft in Early Modern Kent: Stereotypes and the Background to Accusations', in *New Perspectives on Witchcraft, Magic, and Demonology*, vol. 3, edited by Brian Levack (New York: Routledge, 2001), pp. 173–203.
—— *Witchfinders* (London: John Murray, 2005).
Gaule, John, *Select Cases of Conscience Touching Witches and Witchcrafts* (London, 1646).
Gibson, Marion *Reading Witchcraft* (London: Routledge, 1999).
—— 'Understanding Witchcraft? Accusers' Stories in Print in Early Modern England', in *Languages of Witchcraft*, edited by Stuart Clark (Basingstoke: Macmillian, 2001), pp. 41–54.
—— (ed.), *Witchcraft and Society in England and America, 1550–1750* (Ithaca, NY: Cornell University Press, 2006).
Gifford, George, *A Discourse of the subtill Practises of Deuilles by Witches and Sorcerers* (London, 1587).
Goodcole, Henry, *The Wonderfull Discouerie of Elizabeth Sawyer, a Witch* (London, 1621).
Gordon, Bruce, 'Latin Bibles in the Early Modern Period', in *The New Cambridge History of the Bible* (Cambridge: Cambridge University Press, 2016), pp. 187–216.
Gyer, Nicholas, *The English Phlebotomy* (London, 1592).
Hall, John, *A Poesie in Forme of a Vision* (London, 1563).
Harsnett, Samuel, *A Declaration of Egregious Popish Impostures* (London, 1603).
Helmholz, R. H., *Roman Canon Law in Reformation England* (Cambridge: Cambridge University Press, 1990).
Henderson, J. R., 'On Reading the Rhetoric of the Renaissance Letter', in *Renaissance-Rhetorik*, edited by Heinrich F. Plett (Berlin: de Gruyter, 1993), pp. 143–62.
Holinshed, Raphael, *Chronicles*, vol. 6 (1587).
Holland, Henry, *A Treatise against Witchcraft* (London, 1590).
Hooker, Richard, *Of the Laws of Ecclesiastical Polity*, 2 vols (London: J. M. Dent, 1969).
Horace, *The Art of Poetry*, translated by Michael Oakley, in *Collected Works* (London: J. M. Dent & Sons, 1961).
Hyperius, Andreas, *Two Common Places Taken out of Andreas Hyperius, a Learned Diuine*, translated by R. V. (London, 1581).
Institoris, Heinrich and Jakob Sprenger, *The Hammer of Witches*, translated by Christopher S. Mackay (Cambridge: Cambridge University Press, 2009).
James, Thomas, *A treatise of the corruption of Scripture, councels, and fathers, by the prelats, pastors, and pillars of the Church of Rome* (London, 1612).
James VI of Scotland and I of England, *Daemonologie* (Edinburgh, 1597).
Jewell, Helen M., *Education in Early Modern England* (Basingstoke: Macmillan, 1998).
Jones, Karen and Michael Zell, '"The Divels Speciall Instruments": Women and Witchcraft before the "Great Witch Hunt"', *Social History* 30:1 (2005), 45–63.
Jones, Norman, 'Defining Superstitions: Treasonous Catholics and the Act against Witchcraft of 1563', in *State, Sovereigns and Society in Early Modern England*, edited by Charles Carlton (New York: St. Martin's Press, 1998), pp. 187–202.

Kapitaniak, Pierre, 'From Grindal to Whitgift: The Political Commitment of Reginald Scot', *Études Épistémè* 29 (2016), episteme.revues.org/1263.

Kempe, William, *The Education of Children in Learning* (London, 1588).

Kors, Alan and Edward Peters (eds), *Witchcraft in Europe, 400–1700: A Documentary History*, 2nd ed. (Philadelphia, PA: University of Pennsylvania Press, 2001).

Larner, Christina, *Witchcraft and Religion* (Oxford: Blackwell, 1984).

Lavater, Ludwig, *Of Ghostes and Spirites*, translated by Robert Harrison (London, 1572).

Levack, Brian P., *The Witch-hunt in Early Modern Europe*, 4th ed. (London: Routledge, 2016).

Love, Harold, *Scribal Publication in Seventeenth-Century England* (Oxford: Oxford University Press, 1993).

MacCulloch, Diarmaid, *Reformation: Europe's House Divided* (London: Penguin, 2004).

Macfarlane, Alan, 'A Tudor Anthropologist: George Gifford's *Discourse* and *Dialogue*', in *The Damned Art*, edited by Sidney Anglo (London: Routledge & Kegan Paul, 1977), pp. 140–55.

McGurk, J. J. N., 'Lieutenancy and Catholic Recusants in Elizabethan Kent', *Recusant History* 12:2 (1973), 157–70.

Marsh, Christopher W., *The Family of Love in English Society, 1550–1630* (Cambridge: Cambridge University Press, 1994).

Millar, Charlotte-Rose, *Witchcraft, the Devil, and Emotions in Early Modern England* (London: Routledge, 2017).

Montaigne, Michel de, 'Of Conscience', in *Essays*, vol. 2, translated by John Florio (London: Folio, 2006).

Muller, Richard A., *Post-Reformation Reformed Dogmatics*, vol. 2 (Grand Rapids: Baker, 2003), pp. 40–5.

North, Marcy L., 'Household Scribes and the Production of Literary Manuscripts in Early Modern England', *Journal of Early Modern Studies* 4 (2015), 133–57.

Notestein, Wallace, *A History of Witchcraft in England, 1558–1718* (Washington, DC: American Historical Association, 1911).

Oates, Rosamund, *Moderate Radical: Tobie Matthew and the English Reformation* (Oxford: Oxford University Press, 2018).

Ovid, *Metamorphoses*, translated by David Raeburn (London: Penguin, 2004).

Parry, Glyn, *The Arch-Conjuror of England* (New Haven: Yale University Press, 2011).

Pelling, Margaret and Frances White, *Physicians and Irregular Medical Practitioners in London 1550–1640 Database* (London, 2004), *British History Online* british-history.ac.uk/no-series/london-physicians/1550-1640.

Perkins, William, *Discourse of the Damned Art of Witchcraft So Farre Forth as It Is Reuealed in the Scriptures* (Cambridge, 1610).

Peters, Edward, *The Magician, The Witch, and the Law* (Philadelphia, PA: University of Pennsylvania Press, 1978).

Petroski, Henry, *The Pencil* (New York: Alfred A. Knopf, 1990).

Pharr, Clyde, 'The Interdiction of Magic in Roman Law', *Transactions and Proceedings of the American Philological Association* 63 (1932), 269–95.

Pliny, *Natural History*, 10 vols, translated by H. Rackham (Cambridge, MA: Harvard University Press, 1949).

Poeton, Edward, *The Winnowing of White Witchcraft*, edited by Simon F. Davies (Tempe, AZ: ACMRS, 2018).
Possidius, *Life of Augustine*, translated by Herbert T. Weisskotten (Princeton, NJ: Princeton University Press, 1919).
Pudney, Eric, *Scepticism and Belief in Witchcraft Drama, 1538–1681* (Lund: Lund University Press, 2019).
Purkiss, Diane, *The Witch in History* (London: Routledge, 1996).
Raciti, Gaetamo, 'L'Autore del *De spiritu et anima*', *Rivista di Filosofia Neo-Scolastica* 53 (1961), 385–401.
Rushton, Peter, 'Women, Witchcraft, and Slander in Early Modern England: Cases from the Church Courts of Durham, 1560–1675', *Northern History*, 18:1 (1982), 116–132.
Scot, Reginald, *A Perfite Platforme of a Hoppe Garden* (London, 1574).
—— *The Discoverie of Witchcraft*, edited by Brinsley Nicholson (London: Elliot Stock, 1886).
—— *La Sorcellerie Démystifiée*, translated by Pierre Kapitaniak (Grenoble: Jérôme Millon, 2015).
Scott, William, *The Model of Poesy*, edited by Gavin Alexander (Cambridge: Cambridge University Press, 2013).
Selden, John, *Table Talk* (London, 1689).
Shagan, Ethan, *The Rule of Moderation: Violence, Religion and the Politics of Restraint in Early Modern England* (Cambridge: Cambridge University Press, 2011).
Sharpe, James, *Instruments of Darkness: Witchcraft in England, 1550–1750* (London: Hamish Hamilton, 1996).
Shaw, Jane, *Miracles in Enlightenment England* (New Haven: Yale University Press, 2006).
Shrank, Cathy, '"These fewe scribbled rules": Representing Scribal Intimacy in Early Modern Print', *Huntington Library Quarterly* 67:2 (June 2004), 295–314.
Stephens, Walter, *Demon Lovers* (Chicago, IL: University of Chicago Press, 2001).
—— 'The Sceptical Tradition', in *The Oxford Handbook of Witchcraft in Early Modern Europe and Colonial America*, edited by Brian Levack (Oxford: Oxford University Press, 2013), pp. 101–21.
Sytsma, David, 'Thomas Aquinas and Reformed Biblical Interpretation: The Contribution of William Whitaker', in *Aquinas Among the Protestants*, edited by Manfred Svensson and David VanDrunen (Oxford: Wiley, 2018), pp. 49–74.
Theodoret, *Ecclesiastical History*, translated by Blomfield Jackson, in *Nicene and Post-Nicene Fathers*, Second Series, vol. 3, edited by Philip Schaff and Henry Wace. (Grand Rapids, MI: Wm B. Eerdman, 1953).
Thomas, Keith, *Religion and the Decline of Magic* (London: Penguin, 1991).
Trevett, Christine, *Montanism: Gender, Authority and the New Prophecy* (Cambridge: Cambridge University Press, 1996).
Trueman, Carl, 'Preachers and Renaissance and Medieval Commentary', in *The Oxford Handbook of the Early Modern Sermon* (Oxford: Oxford University Press, 2011), pp. 54–71.
Tyler, Philip, 'The Church Courts at York and Witchcraft Prosecutions 1567–1640', *Northern History*, 4:1 (1969), 84–110.
Vergil, Polydore, *De Inventoribus Rerum* (Lyon, 1546), bvh.univ-tours.fr/.

Vermigli, Peter Martyr, *In duos Libros Samuelis Prophetae* (Zurich, 1575), books. google.com.

W. W., *A true and iust recorde, of the information, examination and confession of all the witches, taken at S. Oses in the countie of Essex* (London, 1582).

Walker, D. P., 'The Cessation of Miracles', in *Hermeticism and the Renaissance*, edited by Ingrid Merkel and Allen G. Debus (Cranbury: Associated University Presses, 1988), pp. 111–24.

Walsham, Alexandra, *Providence in Early Modern England* (Oxford: Oxford University Press, 2001).

Weisheipl, James A., *Friar Thomas D'Aquino* (Oxford: Blackwell, 1974).

Weyer, Johannes, *De Praestigiis Daemonum* (Basel, 1568), archive.org.

—— *Witches, Doctors and Devils in the Renaissance*, edited by George Mora (Binghampton: Medieval & Renaissance Texts and Studies, 1991).

Wootton, David, 'Reginald Scot / Abraham Fleming / The Family of Love', in *Languages of Witchcraft*, edited by Stuart Clark (Basingstoke: Macmillan, 2001), pp. 119–38.

Woudhuysen, H. R., *Sir Philip Sidney and the Circulation of Manuscripts, 1558–1640* (Oxford: Oxford University Press, 1996).

Wright, Cyril E. and Ruth C. Wright, *The Diary of Humfrey Wanley*, 2 vols (London: The Bibliographical Society, 1966).

Index

Abraham 31, 90, 92
Agrippa, Heinrich Cornelius 48, 190
Ahab 107, 156, 180, 199
Alençon, Duke of 50
Almond, Philip 5n8, 57
Amalekite, the 93
angels 92, 152, 199, 211
   fallen/evil 44, 71, 135, 139n191
   see also devil, the
Anglo, Sidney 56, 59
animal transformation 47, 139–51
Anna the prophetess 77
Antichrist 38, 68, 69
apostasy 60, 134–5, 137–8
Aquinas, Thomas 63, 94n76, 208n323
Aristotle 13n27, 14, 114, 139n191
asps *see* snakes
Athanasius 107
Augustine of Hippo 31, 34, 44, 59–60,
   64, 71–2, 100n86, 101–2, 113,
   138, 140–2, 157n215, 162, 166–7,
   169, 172–6, 184, 186, 188, 195,
   204n315
   see also pseudo-Augustine

Basil of Caesarea 74
Benno of San Martino 60, 106n109
Bernard, Richard 5, 15, 39, 41–2
Bessus 98, 118–19
Beza, Theodore 60, 61, 172n247,
   182n273, 194
Bible, the
   books of
      Acts 28, 31, 68, 77, 82, 83, 89, 92,
         106, 113, 114, 125n166, 147,
         154, 158, 180, 201
      Amos 177
      Chronicles 125, 160, 164
      Colossians 79

Corinthians 87, 88, 89, 90, 91,
   105, 110, 113, 145, 177, 192,
   207
Deuteronomy 47, 55, 76, 104,
   117, 139, 160
Ephesians 87, 124, 125, 181, 201
Galatians 76, 181
Genesis 31, 33, 61, 80, 90, 92,
   106, 129, 135, 136, 137n189,
   139n191, 202–7, 210
Hebrews 79
Hosea 71
Isaiah 80, 116, 171, 176, 179,
   207
Jeremiah 62, 96n79, 106, 127,
   183
Job 30, 47, 58, 68–9, 78, 127–30,
   142, 149, 152–6, 162, 180, 192
John 73, 77, 79, 81, 136, 148,
   153, 172, 194, 211n326
1 John 79, 82, 95, 115
Kings 62, 66, 107, 111, 125, 136,
   147, 160, 199
Leviticus 111, 117–18
Luke 48, 70–1, 77, 90, 93n71,
   113, 152, 158, 194, 198,
   199n308, 200–1, 211n326
Maccabees 80
Matthew 63, 77–80, 87, 89, 94–5,
   101n92, 105–7, 109, 114–15,
   125, 149, 159, 178, 195–6, 201,
   208
Micah 181
Psalms 62, 160, 183–4
Revelation 38, 69, 75, 79, 88, 96,
   100, 149, 162, 207
Samuel 48, 52, 62, 83, 93, 110–11,
   130, 161–8
Thessalonians 147, 149, 170

Bible, the (*cont.*)
  books of (*cont.*)
    Timothy 74, 91, 149
    Wisdom of Solomon 61, 117–18
    Zechariah 178, 181
  interpretation of 14, 43, 47–8, 52–8, 135, 176, 192–8
  translations of 33, 60–2, 207n320
    Septuagint 62
    Vulgate 61–2
  see also Abraham; Ahab; Amalekite, the; Anna the prophetess; Caiaphas; Cain; David; Elijah; Elimas; Endor, witch of; Esau; Habakkuk; Herod; Ishbosheth; Jacob; John the Baptist; Judas; Lot; Magdalen, Mary; magi, the; Manasseh; Moab, king of; Moses, Nebuchadnezzar; Nicodemus; Pharaoh; Pilate, Pontius; Rachel; Samuel; Saul; Sceva, sons of; Shimei; Simon Magus; Virgin Mary, the
Bilson, Thomas 64
Bland, Mark 16n36
blasphemy 57, 100, 160, 200
Bodin, Jean 24, 34, 44, 50–1, 55, 69, 71, 78, 96, 99, 103n98, 130–1, 139–41, 144–5, 156
Brentius (Johannes Brenz) 44, 71–2, 104
Bullinger, Heinrich 60, 208
Burghley *see* Cecil, William
Burgundio of Pisa 63
Burr, George Lincoln 6, 8

Caiaphas 81
Cain 61, 79, 107, 116–17, 139n191
Calvin, Jean 31, 33, 47, 58–61, 94, 127–30, 137n189, 152–5, 160n221, 169, 173–4, 183–4, 194n297, 202, 204–6, 210
Canon *Episcopi* 35–6, 60, 132n176, 137
Castellio, Sebastian 61
Catholicism
  hostility to 38, 41n89, 51
  witchcraft, and 2, 34, 51
Cecil, William 20
Champe, Agnes 50
Chaucer, Geoffrey 135, 139
Chrysostom 60, 63, 94, 135, 139, 140–1, 179
  see also pseudo-Chrysostom

Cicero 14, 114, 180, 182
Circe 140, 145
Clark, Stuart 28
Coldwell, John 15–19, 21, 40, 42
conscience 23, 43, 98–9, 104, 116–19, 122, 144, 165, 192
Constantius 107
Cooper, Thomas 41
Coxe, Francis 4
cozeners/cozening 89, 157, 160–2, 165, 181–2
Cyprian 60, 107–8

Daneau, Lambert 4, 44, 66, 71–2, 90, 103n98, 130–1
D'Arcy, Brian 51
Darrell, John 39
David (biblical character) 69, 93, 113, 124, 129, 149, 169, 183, 184n277, 184n278, 195
Davie, Ade and Simon 121
Davies, S. F. 6, 8, 54–5
Daybell, James 13n28, 17n38, 20
demonic possession 33, 59, 78, 80, 89, 106, 149, 192, 195–201
devil, the
  bargains with 3, 4, 23, 28, 31, 34, 91–6, 105–12, 132, 155, 168, 189–90
  corporeal form 30–1, 80, 193–5, 198–9, 203
  powers of 30–1, 78–9, 83, 87–8, 128–9, 142, 148–51, 153, 161–2, 166, 169–70, 176, 178, 186–8
  sexual intercourse with 34, 135, 138
Dover harbour 18, 54

earthquakes 10, 101
Elijah 66, 107, 147
Elimas 82
Elizabeth I of England 2, 37, 41
Elks, Thomas 10–11, 190–1
Elmer, Peter 40
Endor, witch of 28, 48, 52–3, 83, 161–8, 175
envy 23, 107–8, 206
Epiphanius of Salamis 60, 81
Erasmus, Desiderius 61, 63–4
Esau 107
Estes, Leland L. 56–7
Eusebius of Caesarea 60, 81
exorcism 39, 48, 68n1, 183, 193–8, 201

Family of Love 40–1, 57
Fleming, Abraham 53, 60n121, 185n281
flight 35–6, 47, 51, 147, 151–4
Foxe, John 100n90

Gallus, Carolus (Karel de Haan) 48, 190
Gaule, John 23n50
Gibson, Marion 24
Gifford, George 5, 30–1, 39, 41–2
Goodcole, Henry 15, 39
Gratian 60, 132, 186
Gyer, Nicholas 18

Habakkuk 92, 154
Hall, John 4
handwriting 8, 19–22
Harsnett, Samuel 23n50, 36
Hatton, Christopher 41
hell/hellfire 105, 133, 145, 150, 163
Hemmingius (Niels Hemmingsen) 44, 72
Henry VIII of England 2, 38
heresy 3, 28, 36, 63, 81, 107
Herod 107
Herodias 107, 131
Holinshed, Raphael 10
Holland, Henry 4–5, 30–1, 41
Hooker, Richard 37n74, 38n77
Horace 185
Hyperius, Andreas 4, 44, 71–2, 135

idolatry 28, 135–6
incubus 134–5, 139, 187
Inquisition, the 91, 98, 104, 144, 146
Ishbosheth 163, 166

Jacob 92, 136
James VI of Scotland and I of England 5, 30
James, Thomas 62
Jannes and Jambres 47, 162, 190
Jews, the 73–4, 77, 80–1, 110–13, 178, 181
John the Baptist 77, 107, 208n323, 209
Judas 78, 117, 165

Kapitaniak, Pierre 53–4, 55n106, 57n114, 60n121
Kempe, William 13n27
Kennington (village in Kent) 19, 121

La Rochelle, siege of 10, 100
Larner, Christina 26
Lavater, Ludwig 118n154
law
  canon 35, 38, 60, 64, 104
  civil 2–3, 37, 84–5, 93, 97, 99, 104, 115, 133
  twelve tables, of the 104, 187–9
Lot/Lot's wife 92, 124, 148, 151
Love, Harold 12n26
Luther, Martin 63, 173n251

Magdalen, Mary 193–5
magi, the 77
Magnus, Albertus 73n10
Malleus Maleficarum 28, 34, 51, 69, 131, 139n191, 140n193, 145
Malling (village in Kent) 130–1
Manasseh 125
Manwood, Roger 15–18, 72n9
Mary I of England 40, 100
Masius, Andreas 156
Matthew, Tobie 15, 19, 21, 39
Maurus, Hrabanus 64
melancholy 23, 35, 47, 97, 105, 116–23, 132, 196
Millar, Charlotte-Rose 4n6, 35, 43n91
misogyny 26–8
Moab, king of 111
Montaigne, Michel de 118n154
Montanism 81
Moses 47, 72, 77, 86, 156–7, 160, 162, 188, 202–3, 207
'mother Dutton' 109–10
Musculus, Wolfgang 60, 204

natural magic 52–3, 70, 101, 148, 186
Nebuchadnezzar 70, 145, 147, 150–1
necromancy 4, 161
  see also Endor, witch of
Nero 33, 48, 189–90
Nicodemus 169, 172
Nider, Johannes 3, 91
Noel, Nathaniel 7–8
Notestein, Wallace 4, 6, 8, 45, 54

Ovid 14, 145, 150, 183

Pagnino, Santes 61
Parker, Matthew 19, 40
Parry, Glyn 6, 40
pencil 8
Perkins, William 17n40, 34, 36, 41

Index

Pharisees 71, 159, 169, 198, 208–9
philosophy 13n27, 14, 16, 33, 37, 52, 81, 96, 99–101, 114, 116, 119, 123, 125, 127, 206
physicians 14, 18, 73, 85, 102, 109, 116, 119, 122–3, 125, 138, 193
Pilate, Pontius 114, 153
Platina, Bartolomeo 60, 106n109
Pliny the Elder 185, 208
Plutarch 111, 118n154
Poeton, Edward 17n40
poison and poisoners 33, 75, 99, 102–4, 156–7, 183, 203
popes 38, 60, 61, 69, 88, 106, 131–2
Possidius 173
prophecy 37, 48, 81, 100, 176–80
  see also prophesyings
prophesyings 37
pseudo-Augustine 141n194, 166
pseudo-Chrysostom 63, 208–9
puritans 14, 19, 36–42, 63

Rachel (biblical character) 136
Redman, William 15–16, 18–20, 42
Reformation, the 3, 42, 62
  see also puritans
Remigius 63, 208
reprobates 38, 110, 124, 147, 150, 162, 167, 170, 178, 181, 182
Rogers, Richard 18–20, 22, 39

sacraments 90n63, 95, 143, 169, 171
Sadducees 5, 30, 208
Samuel (biblical character) 52, 110, 161–9
  see also Bible, books of the
Saul (biblical character) 52, 93, 162–8, 178, 182
Scepticism 30, 33
Sceva, sons of 68
Scot, Reginald
  A Perfite Platforme of a Hoppe Garden 59–60
  Discourse upon divels and spirits 46, 52, 64
  The Discoverie of Witchcraft
    compositor's errors in 45
    date of composition 54–5
    lost draft of 1–2, 11–13, 16–18, 45–6
    revisions to 55–6
    structure of 45–6, 53, 55n106

Scot, Thomas 15–16, 18–19, 41n89
Scott, William 58n119
Selden, John 35
Seneca 127
serpents see snakes
Severus, Sulpicius 135, 139
Shagan, Ethan 39
Shimei 129–30
Shrank, Cathy 17
Simon Magus 28, 47, 147, 157–8
Simons, Margaret 50, 54
sin 14, 23, 82, 84–5, 108, 112–13, 121, 124, 140, 147, 149, 165, 169, 172, 187, 210
snakes 33, 48, 80, 148, 184–5, 188, 202–7, 210
Spina, Bartolomeo 131–2, 142
Stella, Giovanni 60, 106n109
Stephens, Walter 33, 35, 36
Sytsma, David 63

Tertullian 60, 111, 135, 139
The fourth parte of Co[m]mentaries of the ciuill warres in Fraunce 10, 100n89
Theodoret of Cyrus 60, 107n114
thieves 86, 106, 116, 133
Thomas, Keith 23, 29
transformation, magical 34, 47, 120, 140–51, 153, 187
Tremellius, Immanuel 61
Trevett, Christine 81n37
Tyndale, William 37

Ulysses 140–1

ventriloquism 52
Vergil, Polydore 111
Vermigli, Peter Martyr 60, 93, 129n171, 166, 188–8
Villerius (Pierre Loiseleur de Villiers) 172, 182
Virgil 91
Virgin Mary, the 77, 204

'W. W.' 50–1, 54
Walker, D. P. 29
Wanley, Humfrey 7–8, 45
weather 44, 69–72, 123, 126–7
Westwell (village in Kent) 52
Weyer, Johannes 4, 51–4, 157, 179n266
Whitaker, William 33, 63
Whitgift, John 19, 36–7n73, 40, 42

wise men and women 26
witches and witchcraft trials
  1581 Rochester assizes 50
  author's experience of 14, 23–6, 93, 105, 183
  character of 26–8, 118, 138
  clergy's involvement in 14–15
  confessions 4, 15, 24, 35–6, 47, 88, 90–4, 97–9, 102, 104, 112, 118–25, 131–4, 187
  ointments 152–3
  St Osyth 3, 24, 51, 54
Wootton, David 57
Wyatt, George 58–9

EU authorised representative for GPSR:
Easy Access System Europe, Mustamäe tee 50,
10621 Tallinn, Estonia
gpsr.requests@easproject.com